BETWEEN WOODBUSH AND WOLKBERG

BETWEEN WOODBUSH AND WOLKBERG

Googoo Thompson's Story

Recorded and written up by Brigitte Wongtschowski

PROTEA BOOK HOUSE

Pretoria

2003

Between Woodbush and Wolkberg
B.E.H. Wongtschowski

Protea Book House
PO Box 35110, Menlo Park, 0102
protea@intekom.co.za

First edition, B.E.H. Wongtschowski, 1987
Second revised edition, B.E.H. Wongtschowski, 1990
Third revised edition, Protea Book House, 2003

Layout and cover design by Daniël du Plessis
Reproduction by PrePress Images, Pretoria
Printing by ABC Press, Cape Town

ISBN 1-86919-011-4

INTRODUCTION

During the past four years Mrs E.A. Thompson and I have been reliving nine decades of her full life, mostly spent in the Woodbush and Magoebaskloof area near Haenertsburg in the north-eastern Transvaal.

This story originated in my desire to learn more about the people who are buried in a small cemetery on Broedersdraai, next to our farm Koppie Alleen. Clifford Thompson referred me to his mother and expressed the hope that I would "find her approval" and start recording her memoirs.

As it happened I entered her quiet and restricted existence at the right time when Googoo (the anglicised version of the Sepedi word *Koko* for grandmother) was eager to leave to her children, grandchildren and great-grandchildren, an account of her life. She now spends most of her time listening to books on tape as her sight and her hearing are failing her.

Fortunately Googoo has a phenomenal memory for names and events although we struggled to establish a chronological sequence. A hatbox with letters and newspaper cuttings dating back to 1896 has been of immense help. One of the difficulties with memories is the way they will go leapfrogging up and down the years and I must apologise for possible lapses. We went over the same ground again and again while I asked innumerable questions and tried to verify historical facts. This led me to consult and delve into books I might otherwise not have read.

In many months of close contact we both grew very fond of each other. Once I got to know her I found a warm heart and a dynamic personality with strong likes and dislikes. The motto on the Thompson family crest, "I like a good fight," fits her well. Googoo's life did not change the country's history but her memories shed a warm light on a particular corner of the Transvaal which has become more beautiful because of her and her children's love of gardening. She has an untiring interest in the plants and animals around her.

I would like to express my gratitude to friends who helped with the manuscript and spent much time polishing my English. They are Mrs Joy Leyland, Dr Eric Leyland, Mr Alec Benjamin, Mrs Inez Rautenbach and Mrs Melanie Holland. The assistance of other people of the district and of members of the family is also much appreciated.

Regarding the illustrations I must mention Struan Robertson's professional work in reproducing prints from old existing photos. He also took the view from the Iron Crown to the Wolkberg, the Southon gravestone and the photo of the indigenous forest. Mr John Oxley supplied the photo of Morant's and Handcock's grave.

Most of the drawings were found in Googoo's sketchbook but the aloe, giraffe and cheese-mould were done by Sylvia Thompson and the map and dormouse by her husband, Louis W. Thompson. Numbers in the text refer to footnotes and figures in round brackets to notes at the end of the book. They are followed by three family trees, a bibliography and an index.

Lastly, I do realise that I have not created a work of literary merit but only collected a few old stories of human value. There will inevitably be some factual errors.

Brigitte Wongtschowski
Haenertsburg, in the year of its centenary, 1987

I believe a second edition of Googoo Thompson's Story has become desirable. Friends and relations drew my attention to some errors, and I wanted to add some more anecdotes and additional bits of information.

We had great fun receiving letters from old friends and distant members of the family. Even more rewarding was the appreciation of this simple biography by readers who enjoyed a glimpse of what life and people used to be, not so long ago.

One of the letters came from Harry Klein, author of *Land of the Silver Mist*, who thought it "a tribute to those wonderful old-timers of the Northern Transvaal who pioneered what was once the wilds of mountain and bush, the wonderful indigenous forests and the wide sweep of the Lowveld. It rekindles in my mind the names of the people I met long ago at Haenertsburg and around, the lives they lived, and the simplicity and happiness of a different form of life to that which we know today."

Brigitte Wongtschowski
Haenertsburg, March 1990

It has been twenty-six years since readers were first interested in Googoo Thompson's story. The second edition of 1990 was also received kindly. Since then, in 1996, the author has moved to Germany. Haenertsburg has grown and it is now 100 years since Edith Awdry Thompson came to the Woodbush with her pioneer parents. Visitors to this beautiful part of the country would like to know more about its history and the family decided on a new revised edition. This was agreed to by Brigitte Wongtschowski and new facts were added.

Brigitte Wongtschowski
Erfurt, Germany, 2003

Glimpses of the bygones and the "why gones" will always give us something to treasure. This book is a revised third edition of Brigitte Wongtschowski's recording of Googoo Thompson's spoken memories. The editor's insertions are in square brackets. Googoo was a remarkable woman and since the second edition of the book she died in 1991 at the age of 96. Whatever the edition, this book will always be a tribute to her.

Louis Changuion (Editor)
Haenertsburg, February 2003

CONTENTS

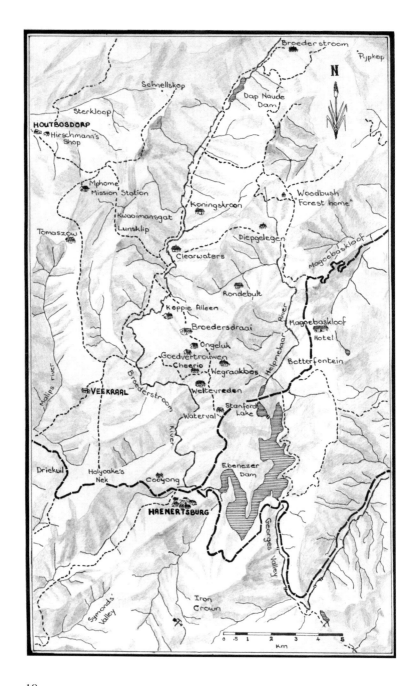

I   Parents and Grandparents

Nearly eighty-eight years have passed since we arrived in the Woodbush on 2 January 1903, on my eighth birthday. For my father it was the beginning of a settled, fruitful life after many years of wandering from job to job and place to place. For Mother it meant the making of a home for us under the most primitive living conditions. For me it started a new chapter of a happy childhood. Father had accepted the post of Government Forestry Officer for the Woodbush Forest Station near Haenertsburg, 58 km northeast of Pietersburg. Let me, however, start at the beginning.

My grandfather, John William Eastwood, grew up on a small estate in Yorkshire where he looked after his father's mill until he reached the age of 25. He then went to Hull as clerk in an accounting firm, ultimately making his way up and becoming manager of the Bradford Old Bank Limited. He retired in 1881 at the early age of 50 to Seaford in Sussex buying the Manor House and living off a retainer fee of 1000 guineas per annum for acting as an agent for some German banks in England. His wife, Emily Anne Bailey, had borne him seven children, four sons and three daughters. All her sons and one daughter, Daisy, eventually settled in South Africa.

Philip, who was the eldest, emigrated in 1879 and first entered the Cape Mounted Rifles. The second son, William, worked for Messrs Tyler and Bright in London. They were shipping insurance brokers and William acted as an accountant for them. The third brother, Alfred, born about 1865, was a trained engineer and joined A. Tylers and Company, a firm of hydraulic and sanitary engineers in Australia.

My father, Arthur,[1] born on 8 April 1867 in Bradford, Yorkshire, had always expressed a desire to "go to sea". Grandfather, not being in favour of this idea, took him on a visit to Liverpool harbour in an attempt to make him change his mind. An "old salt" on being told that the lad wanted to go to sea, replied after a long pause, "Wants to go to sea, does 'e! Cut 'is 'ead off!!" None of this deterred young Arthur, who at the age of 16 became a midshipman. In 1883 my father signed on as a crew member on the *South*

---

1   He was named Arthur Keble after the English clergyman John Keble, 1792–1866, who was one of the chief promoters of the Oxford movement.

Australian. Brother William, aged 22, had saved enough money to go on a trip around the world and embarked on the same ship as one of five passengers, three of whom were parsons and one a professor of music! The "Old South" as the ship was affectionately called, was a three-masted, fully-rigged sailing vessel commanded by a Tasmanian, Captain Sarrett, and used mainly on the wool-run back and forth between Adelaide and England. It was during such a journey that Father conceived the idea of becoming a pilot on the Hooghly River which enters the sea near Calcutta in India. He had served only six months of his apprenticeship when he met Philip in Seaford, both being on home leave, who asked what he was likely to earn once he had acquired his "ticket". This produced the reply "about 8 pounds a month". Horrified, Philip suggested that my father could earn a great deal more in South Africa. This was sufficient to lure him from the Hooghly River and he packed his camphor-wood sea-chest for the voyage to the South African Republic.

Father, according to his Rand Pioneer Certificate, arrived on the Reef in 1889. Here he found not only brother Philip, but also his brother William. The latter had emigrated to South Africa two years previously and Philip and William had set themselves up in business, trading as Eastwood Brothers & Le Roux, Financial Agents, Accountants, Insurance and Company Brokers! Such Jack-of-all-trade companies sprang to life almost overnight in the early days of Johannesburg. Apparently they had "touched" their father, John Eastwood, for the capital to start their operations. William described the situation in his unpublished reminiscences in the following words: "We tapped that solid old banker, my dear father, who had never bought a gold share in his life!" The sum involved was 500 pounds each, but a fair portion of this was dissipated in playing billiards, tennis and cricket as well as attending dances until the early hours of the morning.

Philip and William joined forces with a friend, Captain Maynard, and lived in rooms over the old Standard Bank. My father moved in with them for a short time and initially worked for a firm of auctioneers, Richard Currie's, which still functions today. There were, however, many occasions when business was slack. Father would mount the rostrum on the Market Square and, as he had nothing much to sell, he would start telling old sea yarns and in this way attract a crowd and manage to get rid of a few bits and pieces. As time passed he began to tire of this life and would often disappear for a couple of days' shooting. Prior to these departures he used to put up a notice "Closed on account of dust"! These trips into the bush were probably the origin of Father's love of the open spaces of the South African veldt.

After he left Currie's auctioneers he spent a year on an Orange Free State farm, owned by a butcher, who taught him not only the rudiments of agriculture, but also some of the finer points of butchery. This skill stood my father in good stead when he finally settled at his Woodbush Forest home. He would slaughter two pigs every winter, curing the bacon and ham and producing sausages.

In the interim his brother William was appointed secretary to the Sapphire Syndicate in Potchefstroom. Three or four years later he felt the urge to farm and purchased the farm Oakdene in the Pass Valley, the present-day Rosettenville. When brother William decided to go on a visit to England, he asked Arthur to keep an eye on the farm. Ostensibly the managing was done by a Mr Stanley who moved in with his wife and eight children. Amongst other misadventures Stanley managed to lose some bullocks en route to Johannesburg. Things went from bad to worse so that finally the hapless Mr Stanley got to the point where he threatened to cut his throat. My father was so disgusted with the whole situation that he said to Mrs Stanley, "For God's sake let him get on with it", and he offered her a sickle!

When William returned from England the brothers decided to run the farm together. Their first venture was to sow 100 acres of oats, mealies and manna. They lost this, their first crop, to locusts, but their cattle gave them plenty of milk and Dad used to do a daily milk delivery run.

It was round about this time that they received a message that Father Eastwood had died. As a result of the old man's death my father came into a little money, but the bulk of the estate was left in trust for Grandfather's widow. This legacy now enabled him to contemplate marriage and in due course he married my mother, Jane Emma Mary Bidwell. I have never been able to learn the circumstances of my parents' first meeting. It was probably in Johannesburg where Mother was employed as a governess to Mrs Fricker's[2] three children. Mrs Fricker was a sister of Mr A. Lennox Devenish, a land surveyor in the Northern Transvaal.

In view of my father's impending marriage, the brothers divided the farm Oakdene between them and Father built a house on his portion which he named Willowdene. Amusingly, just prior to his marriage he told his prospective father-in-law that he had a wonderful crop of pumpkins growing and as pumpkins commanded an excellent price he could afford to marry. He spoke too soon: a hailstorm battered all the pumpkins to pulp and Father was in dire straits. Nevertheless, Arthur Eastwood and Emma

---

2   Robert George Fricker, 1854–1914, mining engineer and manager of Consolidated Gold Fields of S.A. Ltd.

Bidwell got married, though in Johannesburg and not from the Bidwell family home in Uitenhage.

It would appear that under the circumstances Grandfather Bidwell did not approve of the match. This is understandable as Father was considered to be something of a character. Physically he was short, broad-chested and muscular, with slightly bow legs, presumably the result of shinning up masts during his seafaring days. He was a wanderer and the black sheep of the family, mainly because of his propensity for alcohol – a very common fault with early pioneers. Nonetheless he was considered to be very good with his hands and always made an excellent job of whatever he undertook. In addition he was a very good storyteller and painted lovely watercolours.

At some stage it became obvious to the brothers that farming alone was too precarious and they both had to take up additional occupations. To this end they built a cottage in Turffontein opposite the racecourse to be nearer to town. They started off by carting bricks, 40 000 of them, for the building of the Johannesburg Stock Exchange. William, being an accountant, was lucky enough to supplement his income by managing Turffontein Estates for about three years, until it was taken over by Consolidated Goldfields. Thereafter he became secretary and accountant to this company.

Uncle Bill, as I knew William, was introduced to my mother's sister, Edith, at my parents' home and not meeting any opposition from Grandfather Bidwell, they got married quietly one fine morning in 1895 in Uitenhage. Their honeymoon was spent on a boat from Port Elizabeth to Delagoa Bay. From there they returned by train to Johannesburg where they found the platform thronged with Boers: every Transvaal burgher had been given the opportunity between June and September 1895 to have a free ride to celebrate the opening of the line to Delagoa Bay! Bill and Edith also set up home in Turffontein. They built a house and, with my mother and father living next door, the two couples thoroughly enjoyed life. The Arthur Eastwoods must have been slightly encumbered though as, on 2 January 1895, I had made my entry into the world. I was named Audrey but this was spelt "Awdry" in memory of Bishop Awdry[3], a friend of Grandfather Eastwood.

My grandfather on the maternal side, Henry William Bidwell, was born in Norwich, England, in 1830. His home life became intolerable owing to a neglectful father and an unsympathetic stepmother. Thus, rather like a character from Charles Dickens's novels, at the tender age of nine he drifted off to London. There, lost, lonely and literally down to his last

3   William Awdry, 1842–1910, English bishop in Japan.

penny, he sought the help of a passing street-urchin newspaper vendor. He told the boy his sad story, saying that he was going to spend his last penny on a bun and wondered what he could then do for food. The reply from the young newspaper seller was that he could sell newspapers for *The Times*. Henry took this advice and the very next morning collected a stack of papers from *The Times'* office and thus started his first job. Later on he was fortunate enough to meet a wealthy benefactor, who seemed to realise that here was no ordinary street-urchin. He arranged for his housekeeper to give the lad a good breakfast regularly.

Gradually this unlikely friendship between the gentleman, Professor Frison, and the boy blossomed. Young Henry had already on his own initiative begun attending night classes which he paid for out of his meagre earnings. His benefactor offered to pay these fees, but Henry replied, "No thank you, Sir. I cannot accept anything for nothing." However, eventually the boy was won over and agreed to become a boarder at the famous Blue Coat School at Christ's Hospital on the strict understanding that when he earned again, every penny would be refunded. (1)

I am quoting here from a short write-up of Henry William Bidwell's life by W.S.J. Sellick in the book *Uitenhage – Past and Present*.

H. Bidwell later entered a printing establishment, where he took a keen interest in lithography. He made some discovery of importance in the production of fine work which put him on his feet. In 1862 he emigrated to South Africa as sub-editor of the Grahamstown Journal. *The following year he moved to Uitenhage and in 1864 founded the* Uitenhage Times. *The paper was sold to Mr Sellick in 1893 and it continued publication until 1971.*

Mr Bidwell represented the Uitenhage division in the House of Assembly in 1873, when he was appointed official shorthand writer to the Committees of the House, which post he retained for about 10 years, when he retired on pension. He was elected to the Town Council in 1882, and was a member of each of the boards of management of the various local public schools. He published several novels and poems and had few equals as a journalist in the Colony. In addition he established and for years conducted the first choral society of Uitenhage. (2)

Grandfather Bidwell was married to Mary White who was to bear him ten children, seven girls and three boys. He named his younger sons after two Cape statesmen who were their godfathers, William Porter and Gordon Sprigg. My mother was born in Grahamstown on 15 November 1863. She was always reluctant to reveal the year of her birth, as she was somewhat older than my father, a situation which tended to be frowned upon in Victorian days.

I met both my grandparents as a small child and remember them vividly. I would like to quote a letter which was read to me for the first time only the other day and which moved me deeply.

Uitenhage
4 August 1896

My darling little Audrey,

You are not old enough to read this letter, yet I feel that I must write to you, and if I put it off till you are old enough to read it, most likely I should be too old to write. I shall therefore ask your mother to keep the letter till you are able to read and understand it. I want you to know, when you grow older what a sweet, engaging child you were, and how your Grandfather and you loved each other. I dare say you have nearly forgotten me by this time, although only ten days ago you were making farewell calls with me, on your friends, Brown, Nicholl and the "Monkey". But I have not forgotten you, my darling. I miss your dear little feet trotting into my bedroom in the morning. I miss you when your old friends the cats "meauw", and I think they miss you too. I miss you when the Turtle Doves coo, for you imitated them so well. Then there is the old "Dwock" as you called the drake – he still walks up and down in front of my house; but you, who used to laugh at him so, are gone. I paid a visit to the Monkey on Saturday; I am sure he misses you and the fruit you used to take him.

Well, my Darling! If my prayers could be answered, you would always be as sweet, as innocent and as happy as you were while you were with us, and be as great a joy to your parents as you were to me. I have now three of your cousins with me. Your grandmother and I went to the Zwartkops to meet them last evening. As it was with you and me, so it was with us. We fell in love with each other at first sight, and I feel sure that I shall love them very much. But do not think, dear Audrey, that I shall love you any the less. The love of a Grandfather for his Granddaughters is of such a nature that he can love them all, no matter how many, without loving one of them any the less.

Your Grandmother, Aunt Tootsie and two of your cousins are now starting for Kamaëhs, to look at their new home. I hope they will be pleased with it and that some day I may see you on a visit to your cousins. Your mother will give you lots of kisses for me and teach you when you say your prayers to pray God to bless Grandma and Grandpa.

Mr and Mrs H.W. Bidwell with grandchildren at the old Mill House in Uitenhage, 1897. Awdry on grandfather's lap.

Awdry as a young girl feeding chickens at Clear Waters, about 1909.

A British blockhouse at Marabastad near Pietersburg. The soldiers must have taken
the signboard from the nearby hotel to illustrate the "luxury" of their abode.
(Thompson collection.)

The Anglo-Boer War, 1899–1902. Boers at the Pietersburg railway station
on their way to the front.
(Louis Changuion collection.)

Believe me my darling Audrey,
Your very affectionate Grandpa
Henry W. Bidwell.
Give my best regards to your father.

Apart from the visit referred to in this letter Mother and I must have stayed with my grandparents also at the beginning of 1898. I have in my possession a Certificate of Discharge which states that Father was employed as boatswain on the barque *Umvoti* on a short trip from East London to Lourenço Marques between 7 February and 13 April 1898. On the certificate his age is recorded as 31 years.

Later we spent an extended period in Uitenhage when Mother was recuperating from dengue[4] fever. She had contracted it in Delagoa Bay where we had joined Father although Grandpa had had serious misgivings about this venture [as confirmed in a letter he wrote to Emma]:

Uitenhage
15 September 1898

My dear Emma,
I am very glad Arthur continues to retrieve the past. I hope he will succeed in enabling himself to invite you to rejoin him with a pretty safe prospect of no more trouble overtaking you. Until he can do this it is far better you should wait and hope. I am not quite unselfish in saying this, for I feel I could never go through the distressing anxiety about you and Audrey again. In any case I hope you will not go to Delagoa Bay, for it is a most unhealthy place and I shall be glad to hear Arthur has left it for a more salubrious one. Neither he nor you need do anything in a hurry. So long as we are here there is a welcome home for you and Audrey.
Your affectionate father
Henry W. Bidwell.

Our little family's move to Moçambique had been typical of my father's attitude to life and the story goes more or less as follows: One day, whilst busy painting the roof of the Rand Club in Johannesburg, somebody from the ground called up to him, "Wouldn't you like to do a stevedoring job in Delagoa Bay?" Father never hesitated to try his hand at something new and immediately accepted the offer.

---

4   The name is derived from a Swahili word and the symptoms are lassitude, headaches, fever, painful joints and skin eruptions.

One of my earliest recollections of this period which made a lasting impression on me was when Father suggested that I join him in the sea for a bathe. Unfortunately, the first wave knocked me over and I have hated the sea ever since.

I must confess that I loved the sojourn in Uitenhage and I had a particular affection for my grandfather who was very fond of his grandchildren. I remember one day on a walk up Canon Hill when the cousins and I had run ahead he called us: "Oh, come and look at what I have found." We saw a small thorn bush with little sweets stuck all over it! I couldn't help loving him. He died in January 1899 and for a long time thereafter I included him in my prayers as follows: "Please God, let me die and go to Grandfather soon!" An old sepia photograph still exists of my grandparents and nine of their Heugh, Eastwood and Solomon grandchildren in front of the Old Mill House, Peter Heugh's family home. The two eldest Bidwell daughters, my aunts Flora and Cecilia, had married two brothers, William and Peter Heugh. Both these Heugh families lived in Uitenhage and while staying there I used to eagerly await my cousins' return from school or the local church. I myself did not attend Sunday School. In fact, I never received any formal schooling whatsoever. (3)

The Heugh girls always got one penny pocket money per week of which they spent halfpenny and saved the other for Christmas presents. I also had some spending money. There was a sweet-shop kept by a Mrs Brown who had a black mole on her nose and there you could get a candy or bull's eye, a peppermint with black and white stripes, for a farthing. She also sold a small celluloid doll, a "whizzyboy", in a little basket lined with blue cloth and I bought that for myself. Doris flew at me, "To think you could spend all that money on yourself. That's very selfish." I have never liked her since and have never been able to buy something for myself with a clear conscience.

I must turn now to my grandmother Bidwell, who I think, with the exception of my mother was the woman I most admired, respected and loved during these early days of mine. She was extremely kind, always compassionate and had a wonderful knowledge of life and nature which she was only too willing to impart to my eager ears.

Grandmother was always ready to extend a helping hand and I recall one such case in particular. Her son, William Porter Bidwell, whom we used to call "Little Uncle Bill", was training as a railway engineer at Zwartkops when he got friendly with a young man who, although a Port Elizabeth boy, had been born in Schleswig-Holstein, Germany. This lad, Carl Rose, had come to Natal with his mother after his father's death, and when his mother also died, grandmother took him in and he shared a room with "Little Uncle Bill". He virtually became one of the family and eventually married the fifth Bidwell daughter, Minnie Grace.

When Grandmother died I must have been about 14 years old. The only token of mourning I was permitted to wear was a black ribbon tied around my plait and this can clearly be seen in the accompanying photograph of myself with a feeding basin for chickens on my head.

But I must return to my father. He decided to terminate his employment at Delagoa Bay and join us at Uitenhage. Thereafter, true to his roving tradition, he managed his brother Philip's farms Uitkyk and Schaapplaats at Zebediela in the Northern Transvaal; both were mealie and cattle farms. At this time Uncle Philip was Acting Commissioner of Lands and he eventually sold the 28 000 acre farms to "Offie" Shepstone, who in turn sold them after the First World War to the Government. They used the land to resettle returned soldiers. Today, the entire area has been given over to citrus-growing and forms the Zebediela Citrus Estates.

As usual, my father's job proved to be short-lived. Whilst on a visit to Pietersburg he learned of the outbreak of the Boer War and promptly joined the Intelligence Corps on the British side.

He was first stationed in Nylstroom. It was during this period that my father, together with a Mr Clark and a Mr Gordon, a chemist in Pietersburg, was captured by the Boers. The three men escaped but unfortunately Mr Gordon could not keep up with the other two. Father and Mr Clark made their way to Potgietersrus where they found the British lines. At first they were treated as spies and marched blindfolded to the British camp. During their slow progress they fell into a large trench and in their disgust and frustration managed to tear off their blindfolds. Eventually their bona fides were established. (4)

After Pietersburg had been taken by the British on 8 April 1901, Father's duty was to ensure that the blockhouses between Pietersburg and Potgietersrus were adequately manned to protect the armoured trains travelling between Pietersburg and Pretoria. These railway lines were continually being blown up by the Boers and after the capture of their commandant, Barend Vorster, the British threatened the Boer commandos that they would tie their prisoner to the cowcatcher in front of the engines. This threat proved most effective!

One day, having seen a train safely on its southern run and expecting no others, Father felt free to take the week-end off and go by push trolley to visit his friend, Captain King of the Canadian Scouts, in Potgietersrus. A game of poker between the two men was abruptly stopped by the news

Major W.N. Bolton.
(Louis Changuion collection.)

Frank Eland.
(Louis Changuion collection.)

Harry (The Breaker) Morant.
(Louis Changuion collection.)

of the imminent arrival of an armoured train from Pietersburg, with Major W.N. Bolton,[5] Head of British Intelligence, aboard. My panic-stricken father hid under King's bed, only to hear Major Bolton declare, "I have a terrible job on hand. I need a stiff whisky. Poor old Tony Morant and Peter Handcock are prisoners on the train. They are to be court-martialled and probably shot." At that my father emerged from his hiding place, determined that, even if he were to be court-martialled as well, he must see Tony Morant for the last time. Fortunately, Major Bolton, whom in later years I knew as magistrate in Pietersburg, took no disciplinary action against Father; he had other problems.

Morant was known throughout the area as "Tony", but in fact his name was Harry Harbord Morant.[6] Soon Father was sharing cigarettes with the unfortunate Morant, whom he found handcuffed in a railway truck. Morant's cigarettes were contained in a beautiful leather case consisting of two halves that fitted together. It bore the family crest in tiny diamonds and emeralds, a gift from his mother before he sailed from England to settle in Australia. Somewhat pathetically he handed this over to my father and when Father wanted to put it back in his pocket, Tony said, "Have this as a keepsake in my memory."

Many years later, this cigarette case was spotted by my father's successor as forestry officer, Charles Lane-Poole, in our house in the Woodbush Forest. He advised Father not to leave it around in case it was stolen. Ironically, in a letter to my mother, written some years later from a new post he had taken up in Western Australia, Lane-Poole confessed that he himself had taken the cigarette case, which he considered "to be of great historical value".

At this stage I must recount Father's first meeting with Morant. This took place on an Australian cattle station outside Sydney. Father had been on a voyage to Sydney on the *Cutty Sark*, the famous sailing clipper built in 1869. During some leave of absence, while the ship was being patched up and re-caulked, he visited some friends of the Eastwood family, by the name of Capes, who were living on this cattle station. One of their employees was a cattleman, the later notorious "Breaker" Morant. He showed the young seaman around the outback and they met again, purely

---

5   Wilfred Nash Bolton, d. 1930. After 1907 he joined the British Colonial Service and was a magistrate in Cyprus and Provost Marshal and Food Controller of that colony from 1914–18.

6   Morant occasionally even signed his letters as Tony L. In Oliver Goldsmith's play *She stoops to conquer*, Tony Lumpkin is a mischief-maker and heavy drinker in ale-houses.

Frank Eland's grave on Ravenshill.
(Louis Changuion collection.)

Morant and Handcocks's grave in Pretoria.
(Louis Changuion collection.)

by chance, in Pietersburg during the Boer War. Morant had joined up with the Australian contingent known as the "Bushveld Carbineers".

Returning to the meeting on the train, Morant recounted the events which led to his arrest: Captain Frederick Hunt had received information that some Boers were hiding in a house on the farm Duiwelskloof, not far from the present town of that name. When he approached the building together with his sergeant, Frank Eland, (whose farm Ravenshill was nearby) and some soldiers under his command, the Boers showed the white flag of surrender. Hunt and Eland accepted this situation at face value, but as soon as they entered the house they were brutally murdered. Hunt's tongue was cut out and his eyes pushed in. He had been a particularly good friend of Morant's who was beside himself with rage when he saw the mutilated body. He swore vengeance: "From now on every Boer I see I'll shoot. I don't care about the consequences."

He soon put this threat into ghastly effect. A donkey-cart with two men sitting in it, and six men on foot, was travelling through Buffelspoort to Louis Trichardt. Tony Morant and Peter Handcock stopped the cart, forced the men to dig their own graves and shot all eight.

This act of savagery had far-reaching consequences. At the time relations between Great Britain and Germany were strained and one of the murdered men, though a British subject by birth, was a missionary of the Berlin Mission Society. His name was Carl August Daniel Heese[7] who worked on the mission station Makapaanspoort, district Potgietersrus.

Lord Kitchener's intervention was sought on the part of the guilty men, with the murder of Hunt and Eland cited in mitigation. Lord Kitchener was adamant that they should face court-martial, which was held in Pietersburg from 17 January 1902 until 17 February of the same year. They were found guilty and were shot on 27 February in Pretoria, where they were buried. Morant left his personal effects to Dr Johnston of Pietersburg. Much has been written about this tragic event in which Morant has been depicted as both hero and villain. (5)

Shortly after the war Father was commissioned to deliver the first mail since the outbreak of hostilities from Pretoria to Komatipoort. His mode of conveyance was a scotch cart, which consists basically of a simple wooden box mounted on two large wooden wheels. A somewhat complicated mechanism of hooks and chains enables the driver to apply two blocks of wood to the wheels to act as a brake.

---

7   C.A.D. Heese, 24.2.1867 – 23.4.1901. [Heese was actually killed in a seperate incident and Morant and Handcock could not be linked to it.]

Towards the end of 1902 my father learned that the post of Forestry Officer at Woodbush, Haenertsburg, was vacant and he set his heart on being selected. He approached Mr Gilfillan, the Acting Surveyor General in Pretoria, and was given the job. His knowledge of surveying gained while he was a sailor, stood him in good stead. He was told to give top priority to the ending of the indiscriminate felling of indigenous trees.

During the war my mother and I lived with my grandmother, but we now joined Father in Pretoria and stayed with my Uncle Philip who had a comfortable house in an area which became known as Arcadia. It was situated against Meintjeskop where the Union Buildings now stand, overlooking the bare veldt. Although the house no longer exists, the street bears the family name and is called Eastwood Road. (6)

I remember Uncle Philip used to talk a great deal about "Sallies", a gold share which is still quoted on the Stock Exchange. It stuck in my mind because I had a rag doll called "Sally". I asked Daddy, "Why has Uncle Philip got Sallies?" and Daddy replied, "That is how you make money." I wondered at the time why Daddy did not make money! Uncle Philip loved gambling on the Stock Market but in an "easy come easy go" manner. At times he would own racehorses, or go to England on holiday and on one occasion he bought a yacht. He would then sell up everything and go through all his money. Through his work as Organising Secretary to the Transvaal Land Board, Uncle Philip met the author John Buchan, who used to visit his house and tell me long stories. I am sure he invented them on the spur of the moment – they were all very exciting.

At that time Buchan[8] was a member of Milner's Kindergarten, and was one of Lord Alfred Milner's bright young men trained for administrative positions. He was first concerned mainly with the post-Boer War refugee camps. Later, although he was based in Pretoria, he was constantly on the move inspecting settlement schemes for refugees as far a field as Rustenburg in the West, Machadodorp in the East and Pietersburg (with Woodbush) in the North. He loved Woodbush and his first impressions are faithfully recorded in his publication *The African Colony: Studies in Reconstruction*. Here he captures in lyrical terms the enchantment of the Woodbush country.[9] He became a celebrated author besides being a career diplomat.

---

8   1875–1940.

9   p. 113–138. A monolith in memory of J.B. was erected in 1987 as part of Haenertsburg's centenary celebrations. It is to the side of the Georges Valley road overlooking the Ebenezer Dam.

Shortly after we arrived in the Woodbush Father, coming from one of his surveying trips, noticed a fire in a humble, thatch-roofed house which stood where the bowling green of the Magoebaskloof Hotel (established in 1937) is now situated. Inside the hut was none other than John Buchan. The two men had a lively conversation and my father vividly recalls that Buchan said, "I want to retire here where in the summer I can catch trout, and in the winter enjoy the warmth of the Lowveld." Janet Smith in her biography on John Buchan quotes from a letter written by him at a Pietersburg hotel, dated 4 January 1903: "Here is the address of the note-paper of my Wood Bush residence.

"Station – Pietersburg 63 miles, Buchansdorp. Telegrams – Pietersburg 63 miles, Wood Bush. Letters – Haenertsburg 12 miles, Wood Bush"

John Buchan actually only spent two years in South Africa – from September 1901 to August 1903. It was a source of great disappointment to me that I did not meet his son, William, when he visited here in search of background material for his book *John Buchan. A Memoir*. He stayed with

John Buchan.

M. Williamson on Diepgelegen but I heard about it only afterwards. What a pleasure it would have been to me to point out the precise spot where his father had camped in Magoebaskloof.

John Buchan's famous novel *Prester John* bears the subtitle of "Adventures of David Crawford with Lowveld and Escarpment Background" and is dedicated to Sir Lionel Phillips who, together with his wife, plays an important part in my story.

The dedication shows his regard for the mining magnate whom he thought morally superior to many men of this turbulent time in the history of Johannesburg:

To Lionel Phillips:
>Time, they say, must the best of us capture,
>And travel and battle and gems and gold
>No more can kindle the ancient rapture,
>For even the youngest of hearts grows old.
>But in you, I think, the boy is not over;
>So take this medley of ways and wars
>As the gift of a friend a fellow-lover
>Of the fairest country under the stars.

The railway station Pietersburg, circa 1903.
(Louis Changuion collection.)

The Zeederberg coach in Pietersburg about to depart for Haenertsburg.
(Louis Changuion collection.)

II Arrival at Haenertsburg and Early Life in the Woodbush

On my eighth birthday in 1903 Father, Mother and I arrived at Pietersburg station on our way to Woodbush, where Father was to take up his post as Forestry Officer. We had been provided with railway tickets and in those days Pietersburg was a tiny *dorp* with unpaved streets and a few Indian-owned shops. While Mother and I had a rest at the Transvaal Hotel, Father bought a little donkey-drawn trolley, which was the sole means of transport afforded to the Chief Forestry Officer. All our worldly possessions were sent ahead to Haenertsburg in this conveyance, to await our arrival.

Father then arranged our personal transport with Zeederberg's representative, Jock Bannantyne, at his office at the Grand Hotel. All reservations on the famous Zeederberg Coaches were made in this way. Not only was Jock Bannantyne in charge of the stables and mules, but he was also Manager and Bookkeeper. The fare from Pietersburg to Haenertsburg was 5 pounds, if you required a seat with a backrest. The cheapest seats, comprising 18 inches' width of bare wooden plank, with hardly enough room for your knees, were sold at 2 pounds 10 shillings. The big advantage of travelling in a Zeederberg coach was speed! An ordinary wagon covered the distance in two and a half days, whereas a Zeederberg coach reduced the time to within a day. It departed from Pietersburg at 9 a.m. and arrived at Haenertsburg at 4.30 p.m. A break in the journey occurred at Smit's Drift, which boasted a hotel known as Smit's Hotel. This was situated on the left-hand side of the road coming from Pietersburg, just before the Wolkberg turn-off. There is a small concrete block above the culvert where the bridge is now and this marks the spot.

There were stables for the mules and a Mr de Villiers, who ran the hotel when we passed through, supervised the changing of the mules. He also ran a small pub and offered the travellers an adequate meal on the coach's regular run on Mondays, Wednesdays and Fridays. Sometimes nobody would be interested in the food provided and this had to be kept in self-made refrigerators. These consisted of a framework of wooden slats, covered inside and out with bird-wire. The intervening 9 inches space would be filled with charcoal all round. The contraption had a door also filled with charcoal. On top of this primitive fridge was placed a pan with tiny holes in each corner. Each morning this was filled with water which the charcoal

Smit's Drift, with the hotel on the far side, looking towards Pietersburg.
(Louis Changuion collection.)

Smit's Drift looking towards Haenertsburg.
(Louis Changuion collection.)

absorbed and its evaporation had the effect of lowering the temperature.

Today Smit's Drift has reverted to bare veldt, whilst the adjacent Boyne, built on the farm Kleinfontein is a thriving village with a sawmill, shops and a petrol pump. Sprawling over the hill beyond lies Zion City Moria, the headquarters of a prosperous religious sect under the leadership of Lekganyane.

Upon our arrival in the afternoon at the Haenertsburg Hotel, we transferred from the coach to our donkey-cart which was waiting for us. We spent the night in Stanford's Bush near the Fauconniers' farm, Waterval. The cart, covered with tarpaulin, had an inside framework with *riempies* drawn across, which served as an excellent bed for Mother and Father. This was known by the Boers as a *katel*. I slept under the buck sail in the front part of the cart on a small stretcher that was folded up during the day. However, I often preferred simply to sleep under the wagon, as did Father.

Father's main duty as Government Forestry Officer was to survey the rain forests of the Woodbush that were not owned by farmers, for transfer to the Department of Forests. The South African Republic had granted so-called "Burgher Right-" and "Occupation-farms" in an attempt to control the movement of blacks and settle the land. Those farms had already been surveyed. He had no jurisdiction over the indiscriminate felling of trees on such occupied land. However, there were patches of forest that was not owned by anyone and thus an area of about thirty five square miles was surveyed by him in about three years.

Our living conditions in the early days at Woodbush were primitive, to say the least. At first we camped, a small bell tent providing the only shelter we had against the elements. Joe Greenwood, a young policeman at Haenertsburg, taught my mother to bake cookies on a grid iron, as she had no knowledge of how to bake bread without an oven. Father sought in vain to find a house or some sort of dwelling that we could take over to improve our lot. The situation was particularly hard on Mother. In fact it was a dreadful shock to be landed in the wilds of the Northern Transvaal after the civilised life of an Eastern Cape provincial town where she had attended the newly founded Riebeeck College for Girls. She had always been very sociable and musical, and loved dancing. Now she faced a real pioneering life.

In February, the rains came and Mother and I were compelled to move in with the Hirschmanns at Houtbosdorp. Their house, a long building, still stands today behind their old shop. Hermann and Bertha Hirschmann, together with their children, lived in the one side and let the other side to us during the rainy season of 1903. Also living in a flatlet at one end of the house was a couple by the name of Arnot. Mr Arnot was the Chief of Police in Woodbush Village.

Mr Hirschmann[1] was clean-shaven, not very tall and rather podgy, but good-looking. Mrs Hirschmann was a kindly woman and we remained friends with both of them for many years. They had three children, Jack,[2] Hilda and a baby called Bertha. Later, when they moved to Pietersburg, they had two more sons, Charles and Moses. Jack was perhaps three years younger than I. I used to take him and Hilda to what we called *Platklip* in the river. This was a flat, smooth red rock and when the river was in flood we could slide down into a big pool. There was also another square rock in the river which was a little raised and under which lived a leguan. I used to tell the children long fairy stories with bloodcurdling details about dragons and often the leguan would come out to sun itself and I would say, "Jackie, there is the dragon, run!" The poor little devil would scream his head off. Mrs Hirschmann was a sweet woman, but she really got very angry with me for scaring her children.

While Mother and I stayed at the Hirschmanns, Father camped up in the mountains to survey the forests and fix up the house he had found for all of us to live in. Originally it served Jim Smith, one of the first woodcutters, as a goat shed. His own house, an elongated miserable shack, was now occupied by our goats! The goats had to be under cover because of the high rainfall. Jim's ex-goat shed was built from timber off-cuts and afforded poor protection from heavy rain and penetrating mist. On one such misty day Mrs Hemsworth, the resident Native Commissioner's mother, came visiting and complained about the damp "lounge". She took immediate action, asked the police "boys" wives to bring maraga, discarded her boots and stockings and showed Mother how to plaster the walls with that mud.

Divided lengthways, our house had two rooms, the front portion serving as the living-room and the rear as a bedroom. Father applied to the Department for the addition of a kitchen, but this was rejected on the grounds that no funds were available. Neither was there a bathroom; we washed and bathed in a tin tub in a little lean-to kitchen, which Father had built from off-cuts onto the side of the house. When the tin tub was not in use, it was hung conveniently outside on the wall. Water had to be carried in buckets from the little stream nearby. The extended roof of our abode rested on poles forming an open-air sitting area.

A banana tree growing in the backyard completed the picture of our

---

1   Hermann Hirschmann, d. 14.11.1922, age 56.
2   Jack Hirschmann, 26.9.1898 – 25.1.1977.

Hirschmann's shop at Houtbosdorp with their house behind it. Note the planks that were brought down the mountain ready to be loaded on the wagons.
(Photo: H.F. Gros, Louis Changuion collection.)

The village of Houtbosdorp with Schnellkop in the background.
(Photo: H.F. Gros, Louis Changuion collection.)

The Eastwood's home in Woodbush, 1903–1906.

A big Yellow being sawed into planks and carried down the
mountain to where the wagons are waiting.
(Photo: H.F. Gros, Louis Changuion collection.)

home, which we called "The Forest Home". Each African kraal used to have one such wild banana plant, *Musa ensite*, which has a red midrib. It takes seven years till it flowers and the bunch of fruit only ripens in another two years. It would then produce about a thousand pips, the size of marbles. They were used for ornaments, like necklaces and anklets and the Shangaans came and bought them from the locals as late as the mid-twenties for a tickey (three pence) each. Father also very soon had four rondavels built for the blacks who were policing the forest and there was a marquee which served both as Father's office and as a storeroom.

If you have a close look at the old photograph of our whole set-up you can also see a little wooden box on four white legs. This was a simple meteorological outfit, and next to this was a rain-gauge. Each day, at 8 a.m., minimum and maximum temperatures for the day were recorded, together with remarks describing the kind of clouds in the sky and whether or not it was misty. In Father's absence, Mother had to do this little job. Coming from the top of Magoebaskloof, all these buildings were situated just before the turn-off to the Forest Drive that leads to the Debegeni Falls on the left-hand side, in a square which today boasts high cypress trees. These were originally planted by Mother and kept trimmed like a hedge. Before we actually moved in, we spent a couple of months in two rondavels near the Helpmekaar Drift on Diepgelegen. These were known as Camp No. 2 and were intended for two of the four police "boys", but Father decided to leave them in their kraals and have the other two stay at Camp No. 1 in the Grootbos before they all moved into the rondavels below the Forest Home.

The gross inadequacy of our forest home received official comment in the 1905/06 annual report of the Transvaal Chief Conservator of Forests, Mr Charles Legat, three years after our arrival. By that time we had added a guest rondavel. The situation was described as follows: "The Forest Ranger is still without a house. The locality is very wet and misty and the miserable hut of thatch and slabs that he at present occupies is quite inadequate. The rainfall at this Station for the last season was very high, the gauge registering 72.58 inches. The biggest fall was 12.50 inches and was recorded on 17 and 18 December 1905".

A previous report by Sir David Ernest Hutchins,[3] Conservator of Forests in the Cape also drew attention to the necessity of "building a five- or six-roomed forester's cottage with two inspection rooms on account of the remoteness of the locality … I also recommend that native policemen be placed under Mr Eastwood's orders." Sir David Hutchins had toured the

---

3   1850–1920.

Transvaal and the forest country beyond Woodbush and Haenertsburg towards the end of August 1903 in order to determine which areas would be suitable for the establishment of plantations for commercial timber. Indigenous trees like bitter almond, ironwood, yellowwood, vaalbosch, assegai, boekenhout and waterwood were too slow-growing and he suggested eucalyptus and pines as an alternative. One of these early planted gums below our Forest Home is now regarded as the tallest tree in South Africa. A board is attached to it with the inscription: *Eucalyptus Saligna*, planted 1905/06, diameter 114 cm, height 82,6 m. This means its circumference is 3,58 m.

Of the three of us Mother found the adjustment to these uncivilised conditions hardest to bear. She was gregarious, missed company and longed to talk to someone other than Father and me. However, whilst staying with the Hirschmanns she made friends with them and we often camped at their place over a weekend. Mother and Father would ride there on horseback an I followed on a donkey. We took additional donkeys to carry blankets, pots and pans. Mr Hirschmann allowed us to shoot one duiker at a time and as many guinea fowl, of which there were vast numbers, as we wished. Other meat was hard to come by but from time to time a local farmer would slaughter an ox and send word by "piccanin" that he had meat for sale. The nearest butchery was in

Pietersburg, some two and a half days away.

Mr Hirschmann was some time later followed by several Jewish settlers to the district from Latvia and Lithuania. These included the Kallmeyers, the Perlmanns, the Paltes, the Israelsohns and a Mr Thal; the latter established a shop at Chief Mamabula's place. All these immigrants made good. I remember that the Joseph Kallmeyers[4] shared the Hirschmanns' house until they started a business of their own in Pietersburg. Mr Palte, on the other hand, hired a shop at Houtbosdorp that was owned by Mr Leo Victor von Reiche. His merchandise comprised mainly paraffin, blankets, sugar, soap and beads. He also profited well by supplying building materials such as timber and zinc by donkey-cart to Mr Lionel Phillips's newly acquired farm at Broederstroom (1906). After a visit to the United States, he gave up the shop in the Woodbush in favour of a more prosperous one in Pietersburg. He bought the shop with the clock-tower at the corner of Market and Vorster Streets in 1931.

In those days this building was the pride of the town. It had been erected as early as 1886 by a German trader, Hermann Möschke. Fire twice destroyed it, in about 1916 and again in 1930. When it was rebuilt by about 1925, Jimmy A. Jones[5] rented it from the Möschke estate and called it "The Irish House". You could get fine Irish linen there, as well as hats and other dress materials. This was the shop later owned by J. Kallmeyer and in 1931 taken over by Sam Palte.[6] Although it was rebuilt in a different style, to this day it is a handsome building and is now a National Monument [The Pietersburg Museum is today in this building].

Two other Jewish immigrants, Max and his brother Woolf Israelsohn[7] acting on Mr Hirschmann's advice, obtained a government loan with which they purchased the farm Turfloop, where the University of the North now stands. They built a small house on the main road linking Houtbosdorp and Pietersburg, where the pepper trees stand to this day. Woolf Israelsohn also owned a shop at Soekmekaar. The Israelsohn brothers built an earth dam on their farm, which unfortunately did not withstand the first rains. The banks burst and the waters flooded the road for miles. Undeterred, they struggled to fill the gap in the dam wall and toiled away for many weeks with their little wheelbarrows. These repairs only held until the following rainy season. The third year they had to undertake another

---

4   J. Kallmeyer d. 1.4.1931, age 72.

5   James Albert Jones, born in Castlereagh, Ireland.

6   Sam Palte, 22.5.1883 – 24.3.1958.

7   Max Israelsohn, d. 1.11.1934, age 63.

"wheelbarrow-exercise", and this time Sir Lionel and Lady Phillips happened to be passing. The sight of the two men labouring so hard moved Sir Lionel to acquire and donate four coco pans and tip lorries from the mines to replace the wheelbarrows. Together with the necessary rails they arrived by Zeederberg's Transport and as Max and Woolf had no foreknowledge of the gift, the Zeederberg's man had considerable difficulty in persuading them to accept delivery!

In the course of Father's duties he, accompanied by Mother and myself, travelled for three months in our donkey-cart surveying land in the Lowveld. I gained vast experience in handling spans of donkeys, at which I became very proficient. We went as far afield as the Louis Moore, the Giant Reefs and the Birthday Mines. The route we followed was down Buffelshill to the Brandboontjies River and on to the mines. Father also had the unique and difficult task of obtaining an agreement from Modjadji, the Rain Queen, that her subjects would refrain from felling and burning trees on State-owned forestry land. She was reputed to be unapproachable by any stranger, and Father was assured by her indunas that the Queen should not be seen by any white man. However, undeterred he replied, "I will wait here until either she or I die! I am not leaving before I have her signature and I am satisfied that she fully understands the situation and will abide by the agreement."

Surprisingly, he received royal treatment while he waited and mealie meal *pap*, spinach and meat were specially prepared for him. Finally, after ten days the Queen relented and sent word that she would grant Father an audience in her private hut, with two indunas in attendance. Father explained his mission through an interpreter, as he could not speak Sesotho. The Queen fixed her thumb-mark on a piece of paper and everybody was pleased. Father praised her foresight and assured her that the Government would reward her by leaving her in peace. The Queen was so favourably impressed by Father that she promised she would grant an audience to any friend that he cared to present. As a consequence the resident Native Commissioner at Haenertsburg, Mr Hemsworth, met the Queen. I myself was introduced to her only years later through Dora Graham, born Eland, who was the daughter of Frank Eland, of whom previous mention has been made. (7)

Dora Graham was a fascinating person and a good friend of mine. Although, as a child, I had heard a great deal about her from Mr Legat who, on his official forestry visits, stayed over at Ravenshill as well as at our forest home, I met her only after she married. She told me that during the war against Magoeba (1894–1895) Modjadji asked Mrs Eland to brand her,

Modjadji's, cattle – with her own cattle-brand to ensure that they were not stolen. When the Boer War broke out in 1899 Modjadji repaid her debt by burying all Mrs Eland's precious china safely in the bush.

One day Dora casually made the suggestion that she would take me to see the Lovedu Rain Queen. Of course I jumped at the opportunity and was well primed in advance on behaviour in the presence of royalty. "You must make obeisance when you receive the signal to approach, go on your knees and do not shake her hand". Modjadji III preferred to live in her *toro* hut and not in the special house built for her by the Government. A *toro* is a spirit represented by a wood carving of a little man affixed to the hut. The work is crude and unimaginative in contrast to the people's wooden eating bowls, which are beautifully shaped. When she appeared on the veranda of her hut, a kaross was placed on the ground and she sat on it unceremoniously. We climbed up the steps, went onto our knees and raised our hands above our lowered heads. This is called "go lótšha". The placing of the Queen's hand on your head is the signal to raise your head and look at her. We then engaged in a brief conversation and departed. The Queen was reputed to be over 100 years old when I was privileged to see her. She reigned from 1895 to 1959.

To return to this particular trip to the Lowveld, which must have been in the winter of 1903 or 1904, we also visited Mr Reuter's mission station Medingen. Fritz Reuter[8] had recently built and thatched his new house with the aid of untrained black labour. Mrs Elisabeth Reuter immediately urged us to spend the night and Daddy photographed Mrs Reuter and her three daughters Elisabeth, Maria and Martha on their veranda. The photograph is in my old album next to the one taken of our donkey-cart crossing the Shalot River. The Reuters offered us a lovely bread-spread which the eldest daughter had prepared and which was kept in a big stone jar. It was called *Apfelbutter* (apple butter) and I remember it well. I was never keen on food, but loved this so much that Johanna gave Mother a bottle to take home when we left. The book *Berlin Missionaries in South Africa and their descendants* does not list a daughter by the name of Johanna, but I remember the name well and can almost see her now – she was dark-haired (Maria was fair) and she was very strong. She often pulled the blacks' teeth, putting the patient on the ground and sitting on him during her endeavours!

The Reuters were kind and compassionate people. Fritz Reuter's attitude towards missionary work among the blacks seemed unique to me. He tried

---

8   1848–1940.

to instil in them the Christian ideal of giving without any thought of compensation; that true happiness was derived from manual labour, and that the development of physical and mental abilities was a reward in itself. He concentrated on teaching his blacks the art of building and many attained a high degree of skill. Most professional builders and thatchers available in the Lowveld were those trained by Reuter. I always understood that the Reuter home had been declared a national monument till I learned to my sorrow that it had recently been demolished.

After three months' absence we finally returned to our forest home. Mother and I busied ourselves unpacking our donkey-wagon, airing our bedclothes, washing our linen and blankets, and generally shaking out the dust of the Lowveld. Suddenly father shouted excitedly, "Look, the locusts are coming, grab the tins!" Like a vast storm, a big brown cloud appeared over the hill. Our small vegetable garden near the river, which was an important source of food during the winter, had to be saved at all costs. Beating noisily upon empty paraffin tins sometimes prevents the swarms from settling, but in saving the garden we forgot about the house. To our horror we found that our blankets were in tatters.

I remember that once Mother and I had spent a couple of weeks with Aunt Emily in Johannesburg and coming back by train, near Marabastad we got into a swarm of locusts. The rails got so slippery that the wheels could not grip. There was no shortage of sand around. The women passengers loosened the soil and the men carried it to the line in whatever they could find so that the train could move again. We drew into Pietersburg two hours late. This invasion occurred almost annually and was one of the most terrifying experiences of my early years. Mercifully, from about 1925 the locusts did not return.

There was trouble of another kind shortly after our return from the Lowveld: a leopard had killed one of our goats in the kraal. Our police "boys" whose duty it was to apprehend any unauthorised wood-cutters in the forests, fixed up a trap with the use of Daddy's shotgun. Instead of setting both triggers on one string, Frans used a separate string for each trigger and a piece of goat carcass was left as bait. In the dead of night a loud shot brought Frans rushing to the scene to investigate. On discovering the dead leopard, in his excitement he lifted the animal, accidentally triggering the other cartridge in the shotgun and fatally wounding himself in the chest. The other policemen panicked and secretly buried their comrade.

In reply to Father's enquiry into Frans's absence they said that he had gone home and would probably return in about a month's time. Father doubted this story as he knew Frans had not received his wages. Eventually the truth leaked out and one day the magistrate, Mr Beatty, came from Pietersburg and said to Daddy, "Eastwood, you're in big trouble. One of your police boys has been shot and we have got to go and dig him out." The post mortem was carried out by Dr Peter Parnell who was the district surgeon stationed in Haenertsburg, from about 1904 to 1914. Since the shotgun belonged to Father, the implications for him could have been serious. However, the Magistrate's finding was correctly put down as "death by misadventure" and the matter was allowed to rest.

Leopards were plentiful in those days. Their favourite prey was the young bush pig but bush pigs were also enjoyed by the early settlers. One of these settlers was Jan van Niekerk, a woodcutter originally from Knysna, who lived with his family in a hut in the Kaalbos behind Kromfontein. He also experienced problems with marauding leopards that went for his goats. One day he caught an animal by its forepaw in a *slagyster* and Mrs van Niekerk went to investigate. When she tried to beat the leopard to death, it tore her scalp right off! Dr Kermuir, the Haenertsburg medic prior to Dr Parnell, promptly stitched it on again.

I must now mention another long trip we undertook to the Lowveld early in Father's career as a "Demarcation Officer and Forest Ranger". We went down the Letaba valley. Traversing the Letaba Hills was a terrifying experience but eventually we ascended Mashuti's Hill and arrived at Mrs Strachan's Hotel at New Agatha. It is hard for me to believe that the journey, which took us two and a half days can now be completed in an hour by motorcar. Throughout these travels to the Lowveld I had my canary, Little Billy, with me, in a cage, and a cat. Like Mrs Strachan, who kept a pet otter, I loved animals. Unfortunately the poor otter climbed a bookcase, which collapsed on top of it, killing the little creature. I cried bitterly at the time.

Mrs Strachan had bought the hotel in about 1894 from Heinrich Schulte-Altenroxel, one of the early German settlers in the Lowveld.

It was originally situated on the farm Agatha and served as a staging post for the Zeederberg coaches, which travelled from Pietersburg via Haenertsburg to Leydsdorp. However, malaria took a grim toll in those days, with the result that the hotel and the stop-over were moved higher up the mountain onto the farm called New Agatha. Patients suffering from the disease were often brought to Haenertsburg in the erroneous belief that the cold air would effect a cure. The unmarked graves in the Haenertsburg cemetery bear mute testimony to the unfortunate prospectors and others who succumbed. The Africans had a saying that in March/April "the black man will wear the white man's clothing", meaning that those were the high mortality months. Many of these men may have been the cases which Dr Cavanagh, on the farm Waterval, was unable to help, although he dispensed quinine to his patients. This was diluted in water and taken three times a day. The potion was very bitter and dangerous when taken to excess. Too much quinine rendered the patient susceptible to the dreaded black-water fever, so called because it turned the sufferer's urine jet-black.

Mrs Strachan had a reputation for extreme severity towards her servants, who retaliated by naming her Maselepe, "Mother of the Pickaxes" (Battle axe)! She had arrived at New Agatha with her two daughters, Millicent and Molly. Colonel Richard Dagge, owner of the Magoebaskloof Hotel from 1947 to 1962, married Mrs Strachan's granddaughter Margaret and was told by his mother-in-law, Millicent Doogan, that her mother, Mrs Strachan had arrived from England in a sailing ship and had had a chequered career. She sang at the opening of the Feathermarket Hall in Port Elizabeth in 1885 and then started her life's ambition of following diamond and gold trails. She trekked to Kimberley and to the newly discovered gold fields on the Reef. There she owned a plot in the then sprawling mining camp, which was sold in 1893 for 100 gold sovereigns, a span of oxen and a wagon with which she decided to join the gold rush to Leydsdorp. The wagon broke down in the Brandboontjies Drift, between Munnik and Duiwelskloof and most of her belongings were swept away in a sudden spate of water. When the New Agatha Hotel was put up for sale, she took her chance, bought it and kept it for about 20 years. (8)

During the years that Mrs Strachan was proprietress of the New Agatha Hotel no alcoholic beverages were provided at the establishment, so that guests were compelled to bring their own. On one occasion my future husband, Louis, then the district surgeon in Leydsdorp, Mr Ward, the Inspector of Lands residing in Haenertsburg, and Mr Beatty, the Pietersburg magistrate, brought a bottle of whisky from which they enjoyed a nightcap before retiring. The next morning the three men were astonished to find that they had been charged for the half bottle of whisky that they had drunk the night before, and to add insult to injury, Strachan had taken possession of the remaining half! This, apparently, was common practice and guests seldom raised any objections. No doubt today we would find it unacceptable, but the old tartar was famous for this, and people used to laugh about it.

After the First World War she sold Cheviotte, the farm on which the hotel stood, moving to Haenertsburg, where her daughter, Molly Clark, was the postmistress for many years. The latter had married the same Mr Clark who

Haenertsburg in the very beginning.
(Louis Changuion collection.)

Rev. Fritz Reutes of Medingen Mission station.
(Louis Changuion collection.)

43

Sir Lionel Philips.

The Brits family of Koningskroon.

had escaped with Father from the Boers, only to be suspected of being spies when they reached the British lines. Mr Clark had died during the Boer War so the daughters must have been grown up by the time that Mrs Strachan actually bought the hotel[9]. When we saw it, it consisted of a big dining-room, a lounge with a fireplace, together with some bedrooms. It is the present site of a fine modern hotel called The Coach House which commands a magnificent view of the Transvaal Drakensberg.

Our relations with the local farmers, most of whom had previously earned their living as woodcutters, were on the whole friendly. An exception was Mr Terblanche on what was then called Mosterthoek, a farm later sold to Sir Lionel Phillips. He threatened Father when the latter interfered with his unauthorised timber cutting. Their house has disappeared but even right up to the present day you can recognise the site of an early homestead by old blue gum trees, cypresses and Spanish reed which was used to strengthen the dagha (mud) between poles and as laths for thatched roofs. On Mosterthoek, now part of the Woodbush Forest Reserve, there is also a graveyard with ten graves, including one that covers the bones of a very early settler, O.J. Botha, who lived from 1825–1887.

Another early settler, a Mr Brits, originally from Knysna, was a great source of information about the early woodcutters in the Woodbush area. He and his family lived at Koningskroon adjoining Mosterthoek for a long time. Father persuaded Mr J.W. Lengton, the teacher at Woodbush Hill School and an amateur photographer, to take a picture of the Brits family because he considered them a typical Boer family. Mr Brits eventually sold his farm to Harvey and Storey from Potchefstroom and they, in turn, sold to Mr Edgar Betton [now owned by Dr Jan Moolman's family].

On several occasions we were told by Mr Brits about the Sekhukhune campaign and its connection with the first settlers in the Woodbush. On 2 December 1879 the British Army under Sir Garnet-Wolseley routed and captured the Pedi Paramount Chief. Sir Garnet used a big contingent of Swazi soldiers, together with the 94th Regiment and the 13th Light Infantry from Perth. When the campaign was over, five soldiers from the 13th Light Infantry deserted and found shelter in the Woodbush. The names of these original five woodcutters were Woodward, Smith, Schnell, Ruthven and Taylor. They earned a living by felling timber which was badly required for railway sleepers, building houses and wagons. There was a great demand from the fast-growing town of Pretoria. The timber was also sold in

---

9   The farm New Agatha had been renamed Cheviotte and sold to a Captain Smith.

Pietersburg and to a lesser extent on market days at Houtboschdorp.

A few verses from Totius's book *Trekkersweë* seem to refer to our Woodbush:

Die hout was geelhout wat gesaag
is in die Houtbosbergse kuil,
vandaar met moeite uitgedraag
en oral in die land verruil.

The word of untold timber resources soon spread as far afield as Knysna, and not long afterwards the village was teeming with ox wagons, sellers and buyers. These arrivals swelled the number of white settlers, who had to buy sugar and material for clothing, but otherwise managed to live entirely off the land. They shot bush pig, duiker, bush-buck, gathered wild spinach and grew mealies from which they cooked their porridge. They even made their own coffee from the husks of mealies. The ground mealies were shaken in a basket and winnowed, an action known locally as *semel*. This allowed the lighter husks to rise to the surface and they were then roasted to a brown colour, ground in a coffee-mill and brewed for coffee.

Theodor Hermann Wangemann,[10] the Director of the Berlin Mission Society, came to the Woodbush in 1884 to visit the Missionary Knothe's Station Mphome. He records in his book *Ein zweites Reisejahr in Süd-afrika* (1886) that there were about forty families of woodcutters living poorly in little wooden dwellings either in the village of Houtboschdorp or in isolated locations throughout the forest. He observed that "the heaviest work is not done by the woodcutters personally, but by Blacks, who get fixed amounts of money for the felling of trees, or for sawing it into 23 foot long planks. Once this is done, loading planks onto ox wagons and transporting them is done by the woodcutters. Many of them refuse outright to pay taxes to the Government, which is too weak to force them to do so. The waste is tremendous. I myself saw the stump of a huge yellowwood and measured it. It had a diameter of 7 foot. Twenty-three foot of this giant, 5 to 6 foot in diameter, had been discarded by the woodcutters and left to rot. In this manner the indigenous forests were being ruthlessly devastated." In chapter 35 of his book, called *Ein Ausflug in den Holzbusch*, Wangemann gives a vivid and picturesque description of the dense forest with its beautiful flowers and orchids.

Of the original five woodcutters, I only knew and met James Smith, who

10 1818–1894.

was often called Jim. He tried to conceal his desertion from his descendants, and claimed to have been born in Graaff Reinet – in fact he came from the same city as my father, namely Bradford in Yorkshire, England. I liked the intelligent, refined-looking old man, and, as mentioned earlier on, our family took over the building that he originally occupied. By then he had moved towards Tzaneen to where Scholz's Sawmill now stands. He was a master craftsman in furniture and was used by Sir Herbert Baker as a carpenter for work in the Union Buildings. His trademark was a circle, enclosed by a larger one to be found on the armrests of the carving chairs of a dining-room suite. The chairs in our sitting room are evidence to this day of the high standard of his work. They were carried on the heads of blacks to our house from Smith's place.

Mrs Smith did the *riempie* work for her husband's chairs using goat skins which she cured herself. She must have learned the art at home because she was the daughter of Philip Botha from Nooyensboom who also made furniture from the local timber. In addition, she made boots, shirts, trousers and coats for her seventeen children. I remember her riding horseback with her youngest baby on her lap, together with a black girl on foot carrying the next child, all the way through Magoebaskloof to visit her father. The road was then nothing more than a footpath winding steeply up through the forest, past Taylor's grave. Mrs Smith was a wonderful woman. She died relatively young, while her husband lived to a ripe old age. One of his sons, Theunis Smith, ran a butchery in Tzaneen, later moved to Magoebaskloof to make furniture as well. He made our dining-room table originally intended for Willem Botha, a forestry worker and Mrs Woodward's brother. Fortunately for us the table proved to be too large to be moved into Willem Botha's house, was put up for sale and promptly bought by my husband, in about 1920, for 8 pounds. Willem Botha worked for many years at the Woodbush Forest Station. Barney McMagh, a young forester, taught him to read and write and after retirement he produced an excellent pamphlet on the names and uses of the trees that grew in the Woodbush Forest.

I remember well the wedding day of Philip Botha's son and Zina Page, whose father farmed on Nieshoutfontein. We received an invitation to attend but as Mother disliked these occasions, only Father and I accepted.

The house at Nooyensboom was freshly smeared with dung and was illuminated by many candles in little paper holders. Dancing took place in the voorkamer to the tune of a concertina. Despite the candles, visibility was reduced to a minimum because of the rising dust kicked up by the feet of the dancers. There were intermittent sing-songs and eventually the guests gathered in the kitchen for supper. The table was heavily laden with food and in the middle stood the crowning glory – an enormous three-tiered wedding cake. It was gaudily decorated, not with icing as we know it today, but with peppermint sweets, so-called *mottoes* or *vrylekkers*, popular in those days and procurable from the Haenertsburg Trading Store at four for a penny. Each sweet was different, some were round, some were heart-shaped and they were covered with coy messages in red lettering, such as "I love you" or "You are my best friend". As a curious and practical child, I asked Mrs Botha how the peppermint sweets adhered to the cake. She replied "Ons lek dit sommer!" (We simply lick them!)

There was a real crowd at the wedding feast. Babies seemed to be strewn all over the place, some were on the floor and others fast asleep outside, while their parents were partaking of the jollifications. From time to time the babies were breast-fed carefully rolled in clothing and placed in a corner, under a table or in any place out of harm's way from the dancing feet. Peach brandy purchased from Mr Leo Victor von Reiche at Houtbosdorp was served and for the more abstemious, there was tea and coffee. The celebrations continued for three days and nights, but Father and I left after the first night. We had had a very good time, had enjoyed the company and the food, particularly the pièce de resistance, the wedding cake.

Philip Botha's house is still in use. It contains a quaint wooden door leading from the kitchen to the bedroom. The outside doorframe, which bore the marks of a forced entry, was recently removed. The damage was caused by a group of Magoeba's warriors who had come to loot the place, but when they found Mrs Heiltjie Botha in bed with a newly born babe in her arms, they left her unmolested. The couple's graves are still well preserved at Nooyensboom.

We heard much talk about Woodward. He was a very large man, a typical hard-working labourer with a shock of red hair and ruddy complexion. He married a Miss Botha, however, she was no relation of the Bothas of Nooyensboom. They lived on Diepgelegen, now the site occupied by the Williamsons' cottage. It was well known that old Mr Woodward used to visit Mr von Reiche at Woodbush Village regularly, and return home somewhat inebriated on old Von Reiche's famous peach brandy. His behaviour used to annoy Mrs Woodward and she threatened to lock him out of the house if he continued to return from these weekends the worse for alcohol. This threat became a source of grief to her when she carried it out and he succumbed one cold and misty night.

Another of the deserters, Jock Schnell, we were told by Mr Brits, had planted the first two blackwood trees, *Acacia molissima*, behind Kwaaimansgat on Cloudlands. Schnellskop, the 6422 foot rise above the Dap Naudé Dam, is most probably called after him and was used as a signal station during the Boer War.

The fourth of the deserters, Ruthven, owned Botterfontein (Bellerive), now belonging to Steve Schoeman, the local saw-miller. [The farm still belongs to the family after Steve recently died.] Ruthven married a coloured girl and after his death, in about 1910, the widowed Mrs Ruthven was forced to sell up and move elsewhere. Early group restrictive legislation in the Transvaal was responsible for it. The same happened to the Southon family, who had to leave Broedersdraai. They should have left these people on their farms and by now they would be integrated and most probably have white skins.

The first five woodcutters were soon followed by others who had heard about the beautiful yellowwood planks which had been offered on the market square in Pretoria and a sort of "Timber Rush" set in. A ruthless decimation of the forests took place between the years 1880 and 1890. Apart from the giant yellowwoods, vaalbos, bitter almond (wagon wood), black and white iron wood, water wood – used mainly for furniture – stinkwood, boekenhout, many other trees fell to the woodcutters' axes. As soon as a tree was felled, it was marked and became the property of the woodcutter. It was reduced to boards by means of pitsaws. Two men operated these saws, one above the pit to draw the saw up and the other within the pit to draw the blade down. To ensure that the sawing was straight, a length of twine was plucked like a violin string and when released it left an imprint of charcoal. The entire log was marked in this way and reduced to planks of 3 inches or 1½ inches in thickness.

Trees that were too hard for the saw blades to cut into boards were left to rot on the ground. This applied particularly to iron wood. Father helped to enforce the law that made the felling of young iron wood trees in the forest strictly forbidden. However, in 1910 Sir Lionel Phillips wished to have his recently acquired farm, named Broederstroom Stud Farm, fenced in paddocks. It was specified in the contract that the straining posts of the fences were to be of iron wood with a minimum diameter of 9 inches at the base, tapering to a diameter of 7 inches at the top. Father at this time was farming at Clear Waters, after abandoning his work with the Forestry Department in 1907, but being anxious to earn some extra money he undertook the fencing job. He consulted old Mr Brits, who confirmed that there were indeed hundreds of unused felled iron wood trees in the forest. Father thereupon sought and gained permission from Pretoria to split poles from felled trees in the Longbos near Broederstroom. Old Brits was promised sixpence for

A saw-pit in the Woodbush.
(Louis Changuion collection.)

every pole that Father split. The trees had to be dug out literally from twenty years of mould and compost. After scraping away the cambium layer, Father was able to obtain no less than 36 poles from the heart core of a single tree. The mind boggles at the size of the trees which were doomed to rot by the greedy woodcutters. Some of the fencing poles Father erected still stand to this day.

Father's first encounter with the Phillipses was not very promising. Mr Legat, the Chief Conservation Officer, had requested him to establish a small tree nursery of *Pinus insignus*, blackwood, stone-pine, turpentine trees, Norfolk pine and others. It was situated slightly to the rear of the site of the present-day Forestry Officer's house at Woodbush Forest Station. One day a buggy drawn by six mules passed along the old road and outspanned at this point. Daddy observed the mules rolling in his little trees and he was furious. "What the hell are you doing here?" he addressed the campers. "You get right out of it. This is my nursery and just look at the damage you have done." Mrs Phillips apologised and offered compensation, but he still kept ranting on, "It's Government property and look at all the work that has been undone!" Father was certainly not one to curb his language. When he had gained control of himself, he faced a trio of women: Mrs Florence Phillips, her daughter, Edith, and her secretary, Miss Florence McLeod. Apparently their purpose was to seek and purchase a farm in the Woodbush. Father later showed Lady Phillips five farms belonging to Mr Altenroxel and Mr Plange. Sir Lionel promptly purchased all five at 100 pounds each. These together, bounded by Koningskroon and the forestry lands near Pypkop were renamed Broederstroom Stud Farm.

It was the intention of the Phillipes to use the land as a stud farm for the breeding of polo ponies and municipal mules. A number of mares were brought from Johannesburg, while a pony stallion and two Spanish Jacks were also imported. Mr Godfrey Newcome was appointed manager of the undertaking. Unfortunately it failed. The soil was totally devoid of the calcium necessary for the formation of strong bones in growing animals and the young foals died in this unsuitable country. The idea of a stud farm was abandoned and instead Aberdeen Angus and Shorthorn cattle were raised under the direction of a Mr Moir, a Scottish farmer. Harold Phillips, the eldest son, was to become the new manager.

On the veranda at the Haenertsburg Hotel, 1905. Seated: Miss Blair, Sir Arthur Lawley,
Lady Lawley; behind Miss Blair: Capt. Duff; standing: Capt. Jarvis, S.A. Constabulary.
Seated at back: John Adamson, Director of Education; S.O. Purvis, Inspector of Education;
Major W.N. Bolton, Magistrate and two unidentified men.

A Boer Long Tom 155 mm gun in action.
(Louis Changuion collection.)

III   Life at the Forest Home

Although our home was of the humblest kind imaginable, we used to get a continuous stream of visitors, mainly men connected with the Department of Agriculture and its subdivisions. However, in either October or November 1905, a most exalted personage was expected. This was Sir Arthur Lawley, Lieutenant Governor of the Transvaal, who was touring the Woodbush area. He was accompanied by Lady Lawley, and his party had taken the train to Pietersburg thereafter hiring a Zeederberg buckboard coach, drawn by six mules, accompanied by some riding mules.

Mother's hands were pretty full, for not only had she to prepare the food for Sir Arthur and his party, but also provide tea and coffee for all the local farmers who came to pay their respects. Clearly my presence was superflu-

Mogedigedi.

ous and Mother said, "Please Awdry, I don't want anybody under my feet, take Mogedigedi (my piccanin playmate) and play in the forest." She gave us some chicken sandwiches with the stern request that we did not return until the auspicious guests had departed. Understandably I was overcome by curiosity and Sir Arthur spotted me and remarked, "Oh, and here we have Robin Hood," to which I responded with indignation, "No! I am not Robin Hood, I am Awdry Eastwood!" He was very kind to me and so was Lady Lawley, who loved our indigenous flowers. She wondered whether it would be too much trouble for us to gather some seeds for her. These were shortly afterward despatched to her and Mother received a letter from Government House, Pretoria, in acknowledgement. This was dated Tuesday, 28 November 1905, and written by Lady Lawley's son, expressing her thanks "for the delightful collection". It was kept by Mother with many others in her old tin hatbox. That same box is now an absolute treasure trove for my nostalgic memories.

A dinner-party was held in Pietersburg in honour of Sir Arthur Lawley, to which well-known personalities were invited. Amongst the guests were Bernhard H. Dicke and Max Louis Marcus,[1] who subsequently owned the finest bottle store in Pietersburg. Apparently he was over attentive to Dicke's very pretty wife. To attract attention to his displeasure Dicke threw a small pie at him, making an awful mess. The episode was long remembered in Pietersburg but B.H. Dicke immediately and voluntarily resigned from all public bodies.[2]

Many of our visitors, who came in their official capacities soon became friends of my parents and these friendships lasted over many years. They played an important part in my education because at no time during my life have I attended school and I have always considered myself to be undereducated. My mother taught me to read and write and do some rudimentary arithmetic. She also taught me to appreciate the value of money, but above all, she instilled in me, at an early age, the love of reading. "You must educate yourself by reading good books," was her dictum. My parents' friends soon learned that the gift of a book gave me enormous pleasure. I was very young at this stage, but there were often interesting people in the house and Mother and Father encouraged me to listen to the conversations. Later they would explain to me the meaning of what had been discussed.

---

1   1930/31 Mayor of Pietersburg. His brother Solly was editor of the *Zoutpansberg Review*.

2   Verified by his daughter, Marga L. Dicke, 2.20.89.

Frequent visitors to the house were Charles Legat, who was Chief Conservator of Forests in the Transvaal from 1903; Arthur Grenfell, his second-in-command; H.O.K. Webber of Johannesburg; Justice Baines, a Johannesburg magistrate and Joseph Burtt Davy[3] who was the first agronomist and botanist in the Transvaal Department of Agriculture. He started the National Herbarium and I remember him well; he was a Quaker and had a large, thick, black beard.

I often used to take Justice Baines and old Mr Webber fishing. I would act as gillie and of course you cannot just sit there with your mouth open! They used to ask questions and as I was very interested in nature and native lore I was able to name plants and animals of our area and tell them about the rock gong and the bottomless pool, where Ebenezer Dam now lies. I told them too about old Neethling from the Department of Mines who, allegedly, after the Boer War, took the Long Tom cannon from in front of his house next to the butcher's in Haenertsburg and threw it into the Helpmekaar River near its confluence with the Broederstroom.(9) I would drive our visitors in the old buggy to fishing spots and I can tell you that those old jossers were terrified of my driving! On one occasion when going with the spider through Mapot's bush on the Cunliff's farm Justice Baines said, "I think I'll walk!"

Living in the forest we absolutely had to be able to get around on horseback. There were hardly any roads to merit that name, and so you depended on your feet, or on donkeys, mules and horses, with perhaps a buggy, if you were affluent enough to own one. Everybody used sleighs as half the places could not be reached with a cart. We brought all our produce up from the lands on these sleighs, which were made from the fork of a tree, poles and chains. You could carry big loads on them, and later that was how I transported stones for the building of my own house.

Charles Legat was a great tease and I remember one particular incident. Sir Aubrey Woolls-Sampson,[4] married a much younger woman, Violet Blaine. Her father, Jack Blaine, was sent by a Johannesburg mining company to assess the potential of the gold finds on the Iron Crown. Mr Legat was staying with us at the time and he said to me, "If I wait for you will you marry me when you're as old as Violet Blaine?" I replied "I've no intention of

---

3   1870–1940.
4   1856–1924. He was a member of the Reform Committee in 1896 and apart from Major Walter Karri-Davies, an Australian, the only one involved in the Jameson Raid who did not pay up or forswear politics and was imprisoned.

Two photographs taken at the Gold Mines near Haenertsburg during the 1890's.
(Photo: H.F. Gros, Louis Changuion collection.)

marrying an old man, if I marry at all." When he left us it was pouring with rain and he could not get across the Broederstroom, which was in full flood, so he returned to our Forest Home and said, "I've come back again to find out if you won't change your mind!" I believed him and was very upset.

When Arthur Grenfell arrived at our home he would invite me to unpack his clothes in the guest rondavel, and this would become an exciting game because I knew that the unpacking would reveal a wonderful book for me. The books that I liked best were those about nature and animals by Richard Jeffreys, who wrote about the English countryside with its hedges, birds and small animals. In those early days books were very precious and not as easily obtainable as they are today.

I used to spend a great deal of my time with the police "boys" and the piccanin Mogedigedi, whom Mother employed to look after me. I learned to speak Sesotho very easily that way. As a toy Mogedigedi made a little cart from two hollowed out stones for wheels, with a wooden box on top and a disselboom. Sometimes, at dusk, we would collect locusts in a sack, put it on the cart and take them to the police "boys". They boiled the locusts, removed the wings, legs and thoraxes and dried them on the lid of an iron pot. They tasted like biltong. I saw myself how Mogedigedi made the wheels and I don't think that these stones, which can be found in our area, are used as weights on digging sticks [as is commonly believed]. They were probably part of traps for bush pigs attached to a tree by ropes made from *miltiboya* (*Hypoxis rooperi*). For bird traps they used smaller stones. The piccanins dug with any old stick for *thabalala*, a sweet-sour tasting small bulb that comes up after a fire and has small white flowers. It's a kind of sweet potato, one of the *convolvulaceae* indigenous to the purple veldt.

Later on, when I was older, Mother replaced the piccanin with a girl named Julia. It was difficult to persuade her parents to let her work and live with us, as girls were not allowed to wander and always slept in a hut occupied by their parents. If a girl got pregnant it was considered a disgrace and the Africans would say "she is spoiled now". For this reason Julia slept in my room at the foot of my bed on a small mattress.

Julia's parents lived in a kraal on Kronenburg (Cloudlands). When I visited them for the first time I also wanted to have a dress like Julia's which was made of a German cotton material with a blue pattern, called "toitši cotton" by the women. The two of us hand-sewed the dress and the next day I happily bounced into their hut, saying "Dumêla". A torrent of disgruntled words poured over me because I had not shown the proper respect by "go lotša".

Rosina, Julia's friend, used to join us as we explored the bush and went swimming. Sometimes we would spend the whole weekend helping with the firing of clay pots. The red clay itself was collected near the Berlin Mission Station, Mphome, in the Woodbush. The graphite used for blackening the rim of the pots for decoration was also found in the area. Incidentally, *Phomo* means "graphite" in Sesotho and the mission station, founded in 1878 was called Mphome by their first *moruti* – Fürchtegott Johannes Carl Knothe.[5] We would collect a great quantity of wood, place stones on it and then twigs would be piled above and around the pots placed on the stones. Once they had been fired the pots would be watertight. On these occasions I slept with Julia and her two sisters in their hut and ate their food enriched with berries and locusts as a *sesebo* (relish) – when they were "in season".

By the time we arrived in the area, the old mission station was inhabited only by the widowed Mrs Anna Magdalene Knothe,[6] who had a most beautiful garden. We never actually met her, but we knew Mr Adolf Herbst,[7] who was the successor to Mr Knothe and Superintendent Oswald Krause.[8] The mission station had been moved in 1896 to drier ground next to Woodbush Village on Masealama. Later it was called Kratzenstein, after an Inspector of the Berlin Mission Society. Mr Herbst was very kind and visited Mrs Knothe regularly with his children. Unfortunately he died suddenly in March 1904, when the shed that he had put up for drying mealies collapsed on top of him.

Mphome eventually fell into ruins, but these can still be clearly seen. As late as the 1920's I used to take my children to the old mission station in "Grossmama's bush", which they loved exploring. A block of soapstone in one wall could be taken out and we called it "the secret cave". My father used to suggest that the Knothes perhaps concealed their money behind this block of soapstone. The building stones both for the house and the church had been transported from a nearby kopje and were of granite. As a matter of interest, Mr Knothe acquired the farm adjoining Mphome. He called it Tomaszow after his birthplace near Lodz in Poland. On our maps it appears as "Tomaszom" and even "Tomason".

As an only child I used to make up games for my own amusement and I

---

5   1838–1892 Buried at Tomaszow; gravestone later moved to Kratzenstein.

6   1843–1926.

7   1857–1904 His grave is at Kratzenstein.

8   1846–1915.

developed great self-reliance. One of my favourite games was one I called "Work on my little farm". Behind our house Daddy had prepared a piece of ground which I divided into paddocks with poles and string fences. The yard was inhabited by horses, foals, and cattle, and these were represented by various sized bottles with their corks decorated with mimosa thorns to indicate horns. Daddy taught me to make yokes and strops and every night I put my animals into the kraal. My farm also boasted an orchard with twigs for trees. Another "real" toy that I played with – apart from old Sally – was a doll which I had admired at T.W. Beckett's Store in Pietersburg and one year found to my great delight that it was my Christmas present. This Christmas must have been an exceptional one because usually presents were much less expensive. The main attraction on these occasions was a pudding with pennies in it.

To have a break from our solitary life Mother and I joined Aunt Emily and my cousins Bertha and Ethel on a holiday. Uncle Mannie Solomon who owned a house at the top of End Street in Johannesburg, next to the Pullingers, had hired the former seaside cottage of Cecil Rhodes for a month. Nissi, the Solomon's nanny also came along.

There was a big picture of Queen Victoria in the sitting room and Nissi, who was a staunch supporter of the cause of the Boers, said, "whoever pulls this picture off the wall will sit in heaven at my right side". We loved Nissi, and I, being the boldest, took a broom and pushed the picture down whereupon glass and frame broke into pieces. Aunt Emily was very cross. She and Mother obviously didn't share Nissi's political convictions and this became apparent in another incident.

We had heard of the siege of Ladysmith and asked about the meaning of a "siege". Mother demonstrated it to us on the beach by letting us build a castle. Around it clusters of shells stood for the Boer encampments, and we had a wonderful time charging and relieving Ladysmith. When we came home Nissi was upset that we were proud to have chased the Boers. We were threatened that from now on nobody would be allowed to hold her hand and sit on her right at table. She also gave up ending our prayers with, "Please God, save the Boers from the English".

In about 1905 my father bought the quitrent farm Broedersdrift of 343 morgen from Theunis Botha for the sum of 350 pounds.[9]

Theunis Botha had become heavily indebted to Mr Hirschmann. Farmers, unwilling to travel the formidable distance to Pietersburg, used to do

---

9   The Deed of Grant made in favour of Emma Mary Jane Eastwood born Bidwell was only registered on 16.12.1907.

their shopping at his general trading store at Woodbush Village, but being often incapable of producing cash they bought on credit. When the debt rose as high as 150 pounds Mr Hirschmann would apply pressure and the debtor would eventually be forced to relinquish his farm. Theunis Botha, finding himself in this predicament, came to Father and offered Broedersdrift to him. Father accepted with alacrity. Botha settled his debt and moved "behind the Mountain", meaning the Zoutpansberg. Many farmers, who could not make a living in the Woodbush after the timber resources had been exhausted, moved to the Zoutpansberg (now Soutpansberg) with high hopes. Koos (Jakobus Johannes) Brummer from Goedvertrouwen also went there, but most of them did not see their expectations fulfilled.

At the end of 1906 Father took three months' leave, which we spent on our newly acquired farm Broedersdrift. Before he left the Forestry Department, they sent up a man called Berry, who was a trained surveyor, to check on the work that Daddy had done. To our pride, he found that his work has been extremely accurate.

Father was succeeded by the first qualified forester in the Woodbush, Charles Edward Lane-Poole,[10] who had trained at the French Forestry School at Nancy and had spent 1906 at the South African Forestry School at Tokai. He had two assistants named Barney McMagh and Harold Lawrence Donnelly. Lane-Poole is easily recognizable on the photograph of our Forest Home, which was taken by Arthur Grenfell. He had lost his left hand in a shooting accident as a schoolboy.

Mr Legat instructed Lane-Poole to plant gum trees in the open space between the indigenous kiaat (*Pterocarpus angolenses*) in a forest on Middelkop, where the tea plantations are now. As an alternative Lane-Poole suggested young *Pterocarpus* or other indigenous trees like bitter almond, yellowwood, vaalbos or essenhout. It was a practice he had observed in Burma on a private visit before coming to South Africa; between the existing large teaks young teak trees were planted, and in time the old ones were felled. In this way the young trees eventually took over and the forests were re-established. However, he had to do as he was told. His annual reports of 1907/08 and 1908/09 make fascinating reading.

In 1910 a disagreement over introducing exotics brought Lane-Pool's work with the Transvaal Forestry Department to an end. Thereafter he worked in Sierra Leone and later, from 1916 to 1921, in Western Australia, where he became Conservator of Forests. Although he had disliked the

---

10 1885–1970.

Mphome Mission Station.
(Photo: H.F. Gros, Louis Changuion collection.)

Our forest home with Charles E. Lane-Poole, 1906.

introduction of eucalyptus as much as we did, living and working in Australia he began to appreciate them and wrote to Mother that they were magnificent. There is even a gum named after him – the salmon white gum (*Eucalyptus lane-pooleii*) which occurs south of Perth. I myself cannot believe that a gum tree can be beautiful!

Soon after 1907, when Father had resigned, he took on a special job entrusted to him by the Transvaal Forestry Department. He was asked to go to Elandshoek near Waterval Boven, where there were extensive indigenous forests, and give a report on whether they were worth preserving. Father stayed at Elandshoek for two weeks, making notes and when he came back to the Woodbush he cut down samples of the same kind of trees he had found there. He was told to take a 10 inch long piece, cut it down the middle and then across. These samples were sent to the Department and I saw them while I was with the army during the war [Second World War]. They might still be there.

While Father was away, Mother was very busy collecting ferns. Mr T.R. Sim,[11] a professional forest officer appointed as conservator in Natal in 1903, had approached Father for information on the ferns in the Woodbush. He was then preparing the second edition of his book *The Ferns of South Africa*.

Haenertsburg about 1908.

11 1858–1938.

IV   Village people

For all the farmers of the Woodbush area, Haenertsburg was the hub and centre of activities. The "Woodbush Gold Rush" to the Iron Crown mine that led to the founding of the village in 1887, was a thing of the past when we joined the community. However, Haenertsburg was still the "seat of government" for the district. The blacks called the village Matlalwe, "The place to report to", or "The place of the Law" – no doubt an allusion to the

Arthur K. Eastwood – the drawing by Miss Smith.

Carl Ferdinant Haenert after whom
Haenertsburg was named.
(Louis Changuion collection.)

Haenert's grave in the old cemetery
in Pietersburg.
(Louis Changuion collection.)

power of the Native Commissioner who collected the tax and represented the government. The people living in the area were the Batladi. *Tladi* means lightning.[1] Mr Neethling was the chief mining official;[2] Ernest Otway Ward represented the Lands Department with Mr Maurice Pascoe Everitt as Beacon Inspector. Harry Hemsworth was Native Commissioner, Col. A.P. Wolff acted as his clerk and Capt. Trevor was in charge of the S.A. Constabulary.

There was a hotel in the village, built in 1890, which was kept by Mr Sprungmann, a tall, big German with red hair and a red moustache who had welcomed us when we arrived in 1903. He had an English wife and two sons, Hugo and Oswald. He could well have been the Wilhelm Sprungmann from Essen, Germany, mentioned in H. Schulte-Altenroxel's autobiographical book as one of the shop assistants of Messrs Natorp[3] and Tamsen at Tweefontein near Warmbaths in the late 1880's. He was succeeded by Mr Burch. The hotel was situated in Kerk Street between Rabe and Kantoor Streets opposite the market square where a huge blue gum tree still spreads its branches next to Dan Symonds's house. [The tree was recently felled.]

Alongside stood the school and the little house of Mr Le Roux, who was the principal. His assistant was a Miss Smith, who had a special gift for caricature drawing. She boarded at the hotel and this gave her ample opportunity to observe its patrons. Her sketches of Messrs Neethling, Hemsworth, Ward, Everitt, John Swinburne and my father, Arthur Eastwood, were excellent and she presented them to the delighted men. At a later stage Mr Ward wanted to collect the set, but Mother would not part with her drawing of Father. It now has a place of honour in my son, Clifford's, house.

I know of only one other surviving sketch, that of John Swinburne. It was given by Mrs Joyce Parnell to Mrs Karin Iuel, who owns the farm Glenshiel, where Swinburne had taken up farming under the Land Settlement Scheme after the Boer War. John was a keen naturalist and had a most beautiful collection of butterflies. His passion was shared by a friend of his, Capt. Roy Hew Russel Stevenson,[4] who specialised in wasps and moths, particularly hawk moths. For a time the two men lived in a couple of rondavels diagonally across from the present day Mountain Butchery,

1   Confirmed in 1987 by Dan Symonds and Eva Human, his sister.
2   The first mining commissioner stationed at Haenertsburg in 1887 was Ds L.G.F. Biccard (1834–1900). Thus 1887 is regarded as the founding date of the village.
3   Carl Natorp, 1885–1921; Friedrich Wilhelm Natorp, 1889–1910.
4   1878–1968.

[today Blackburn Properties] where, later on, Mr Andries Grundlingh built a little house.

Swinburne and Stevenson worked as recruiting officers for the mines under Mr Erskine from Dalmada Farm near Pietersburg. For John, the additional income was necessary to supplement the little money he was able to make from the farm and the White Heather Mine which he owned on the Iron Crown. He was also employed by Mr Antrobus, the surveyor for the border between Rhodesia and Moçambique, to build beacons. Late in life John Swinburne moved to Rhodesia, where his friend, Roy Stevenson, had joined the Roads Department (in 1922) before he became Labour Supervisor at Selukwe Chrome Mines.

Roy was a huge man. He had been Captain of the 6th Dragoon Guards and fought from 1899–1902 in the Boer War and later in the Zulu Rebellion of 1906. I have been told that his treasured insect collection was left to the Bulawayo Museum.

The Native Commissioner, Harry Hemsworth, lived in a house below John Swinburne's huts. He bought the farm Rietfontein for his mother but she also built herself a house in the village. It stood opposite the Israelsohns' home and their butchery, where Barclays Bank has its agency now [today Linn's Hair Salon]. There was a furrow in the street in which the Israelsohns' ducks enjoyed themselves. Mrs Hemsworth, a mannish woman with knobbly hands and one of the first women I saw to ride astride, did not like the ducks and knew how to wield a sjambok: she made the poor ducks' lives a misery – and the Israelsohns' as well, I might add! She opened the Temperance Hotel in her new abode – however, legend has it that she quite liked a drop of strong drink herself. As late as August 1916 Mr Everitt mentioned Mrs Hemsworth's lively disposition when he wrote to Mother: "I am glad that old Mrs H. has got back to Haenertsburg; it will stir up those sleepy people a bit!" She actually stirred them up even after her death, particularly the Africans, who believed she was haunting the area on her big white horse.

Mr Ward, as previously mentioned, was in charge of the interests of the Lands Department. He was a tall, dark-haired, highly educated and very pleasant man who lived on Weighton. He was a relative of Rose Latouche, the daughter of a French aristocrat, who is mentioned in a book called *Ruskin and the Shelleys*. He inherited some money from her estate, subject to the condition that he changed his name to Ward-Latouche. He complied and with his wife, Feodora Daniel, Mrs Parnell's sister, they went to live in St Jean de Luz in Southern France, certainly a change from little Haenertsburg.

By contrast, Ward's Beacon Inspector, Mr Everitt[5] and his wife

Christabel,[6] made Haenertsburg their retirement home and were our much-loved friends for many years. We were still at the Hirschmanns when the newly married young couple spent a night with us on their way to Haenertsburg. There was no road between Pietersburg and Tzaneen but the one through the Woodbush and Woodbush Village. Mrs Everitt was a tall young woman, very religious and somewhat dogmatic and overpowering. She was reputed to be well-connected in England, where her father, a Mr Pigott, was a parson. I remember that she used to stay with us on occasion at the Forest Home and gave me some elementary drawing lessons.

Mr Everitt was a most entertaining, well-educated, very civilized and humorous man. He had studied at Oxford and could quote Shakespeare with ease. He was also a good sportsman and one of the most pleasant men you could wish to meet – an absolute dear! Both he and Mrs Wolff, the wife of Mr Hemsworth's clerk, were masters at quick repartee and we were often convulsed with laughter in their company. Mrs Wolff was a Cockney from the East End of London and so was her husband, whose father had been a hatter. He had come out with the Imperial Yeomanry during the Boer War and was very proud of it. He was not in the least amused when one day Mr Everitt showed him a cartoon from Punch, which depicted an Imperial Yeomanry soldier kneeling in front of a Boer. The caption read "I yield".

The Everitts lived in a couple of rondavels on mining land adjoining the Haenertsburg common. When all the Government Departments were moved to Pietersburg sometime during 1905, they also left, together with their baby, Christabel Lucy. She had been born on 3 September 1904 and was brought into the world by Mrs Page who lived on Reisigersrust. Sadly, towards the end of 1905, the little girl contracted enteritis, which was a cruel killer in those days. They brought her to the mountain and stayed with the Wolffs, but the child died on 29 December 1905. Later, they had another daughter whom they called Dawn, and whom they had brought up in England. Tragically, this child also died, at the age of fourteen. I remember Mr E.G. Ireland, who was married to Mrs Everitt's sister, Beda, bringing the message to me from Mr Everitt who had received a cable from his wife in England. The couple was heartbroken and we were of course exceedingly sad for them; they had at this time been transferred to Tempe near Bloemfontein. Mr Everitt had intended to retire to England in due course, but now they preferred to come back to Haenertsburg. The couple was friendly with Col. H. Mentz,[7] the MP for this area, who arranged for them to

---

5   Maurice Pascoe Everitt, 1874–1946.
6   Christabel Botry Everitt, 1879–1964.

Col. Hendrik Mentz.
(Louis Changuion collection.)

Maurice Pascoe Everitt.

Homewood in Haenertsburg – the house of the Everitts.
(Louis Changuion collection.)

acquire the ground that they had previously lived on from the Department of Mines. I believe it consisted of about 10 morgen. The house they built here, called Homewood,[8] had a large sitting-room cum dining-room, a kitchen, a bedroom and a front and back stoep. About 1935 Mrs Everitt asked me to help her to build on two extra rooms. There was a walnut table in their house covered with a howdah-carpet. It was supposedly given to Queen Victoria by an Indian Maharajah on the occasion of her coronation and presented by the Prince Consort to Mr Pigott. I inherited this table and howdah but gave the carpet to Dr Paul du Toit Burger, our doctor and friend.

To turn to other matters, Dr Peter Parnell[9] is regarded by most people as the first District Surgeon to be stationed in Haenertsburg. However, before Dr Parnell was sent from Pretoria, there was a Dr Kermuir who had a small hospital with living-quarters on the way up to the cemetery. There is a little rise with an acacia tree on it, and next to it were his "rooms" in a corrugated iron shack lined with matchboard. His wife, an Irish woman, was a half-trained nurse who looked after the patients. Cleanliness left a lot to be desired. They did not stay very long. Dr Parnell, on the other hand, became an institution in the district. He was District Surgeon from about 1904–1914 and again from 1924–1932. He built himself a house on the farm Hove just outside the village. His wife was Blossom Daniel the sister of Mrs Feo Ward. These two ladies, together with Mrs Christabel Everitt, were the pillars of Haenertsburg society.

Dr Parnell's frequent travels to fulfil his duties took him as far afield as Leydsdorp. One rainy and stormy day he was on his way home when he could not cross the raging Broederstroom which runs just below the village. His wife who had a terrifying night with the roof blowing off the house, went to the Haenertsburg side of the river and managed to convey these bad tidings over the torrent by wrapping a piece of paper round a stone and throwing it to him. Back came the answer that she should get a rope to pull him across. He plunged into the water, and after many long moments of anguish she heard him cursing somewhere downstream. He emerged, berating the rope-pullers for trying to drown him by pulling too fast; his voice however, was music to her ears. He had hoped to strike land at Tom Haenert's little mill with the wooden water-wheel which was at the

---

7   M.P. for Zoutpansberg 1.10.1910 – 9.5.1924; also Minister of Lands and Defence in Gen. Smuts's Cabinet.

8   Now again called Homewood.

9   1871–1953; married 28.10.1902.

spot where the pump house that used to serve the school is still situated, opposite the cafe.

The South African constabulary was under the command of Captain Trevor when we moved to Broedersdrift. He had married a Miss Crew whose father kept the stop-over at Smits Drift for a short period. She had been one of the Leonard Rayne theatre company in Johannesburg, and at times she must have missed life at [Leonard Rayne's] Standard Theatre badly. They had a little boy called Jack, somewhat younger than myself. I loved children, and when my parents went to the village he and I used to play together. Captain Trevor bought the Haenertsburg Hotel on retiring from the police force, but unfortunately the bar was too tempting for Mrs Trevor and in order to get her out of harm's way, he took on the management of the farm Ashmoledales on the Iron Crown. The owners were Cooper and Nephews of "Cooper's Dip" fame. There was no road, only a bridle path leading to the farm which necessitated riding on horseback. This was after the First World War.

During the Second World War, many years later, Professor Cyril Jackson,[10] the astronomer, who has owned the farm Hilltop since the early thirties, was stationed with the Intelligence Corps in Mega in Southern Abyssinia, where he had an amusing encounter with Jack Trevor. One day a lorry drove into the Professor's camp and a man jumped out. Cyril Jackson offered him a cup of tea and the two got chatting. The stranger, Jack Trevor, recounted that he had driven his lorry all by himself, coming all the way from Tanganyika and added that he wanted to get to Brindisi. He said, "I have two coffins on board which must go to England at once." Professor Jackson could not make this out and asked his visitor if he was an Englishman. Trevor replied, "My parents came from England and I was born at a small place of which you will never have heard; it is in the Northern Transvaal at the back of a mountain called the Iron Crown. I am now a Professor of Archaeology at Cambridge University and, as a matter of fact, these coffins are full of skulls and bones from the Olduvai Gorge in Tanganyika."

"Well", said Cyril Jackson, "I look at the Iron Crown from the back of my stoep every day of my life." No doubt lively reminiscences were exchanged that day in 1941 in the Abyssinian Highlands.

Returning to the Constabulary; apart from Captain Trevor, the two most memorable members of this little group of policemen were Corporals Joseph Greenwood[11] and E.J. Holyoake. They really became Haenertsburgers. Joe Greenwood had joined Lord Milner's Constabulary at the age of sixteen,

10 Died 1988.

had trained in Pretoria and was first sent to Pietersburg, being later transferred as a Police Constable to Haenertsburg. He was a big jovial man. After the First World War he and his wife, Florence,[12] bought the farm Wellstead which is named after Lt Wellstead, also of the Constabulary, from the Department of Mines. When the Greenwoods grew old they sold the farm to Robert Ambrose Turner,[13] and the father of my son-in-law, Robert Carver Turner. Thereafter, Joe and Flo lived in that little house which the Israelsohns had built. They are both buried in Haenertsburg and their gravestone appropriately reads, "Fondly remembered by all".

Corporal E.J. Holyoake, or "Holly" as he was affectionately known, was a big handsome Englishman who lived for a period in Australia and had come to this country during the Boer War with an Australian contingent. One day, after a party, he was on his way home to his farm Driekuil, when his horse, Ginger, threw him. Someone found him the next morning badly concussed. Holly was in hospital for a long time but never quite regained his mental capacity.

He lived with a black woman who had several children by him. This led to a legal problem in that an inheritance of immovable property to offspring resulting from this kind of union was not valid. The law did not allow land to be inherited by coloureds. Holly was friendly with the Everitts and must have trusted Mrs Everitt to let his old wife and children go on living on the farm, because he left Driekuil to her instead of selling it. I was present when she discussed with her husband and Dean Palmer what she should do with the farm. Mr Everitt was quite certain that Holly had left it to her under the impression that old Katie would be allowed to stay there until she died, but Mrs Everitt had different plans. She decided to sell all the implements and the cattle and give this money, together with 50 pounds to his children. The farm she wanted to sell and give half the money to the church. The Dean, the old devil, agreed, but honestly the incident still rankles in my mind. The late Rev. Charles Steer, who was our local parson in 1915 would be mad if he could hear me, but he is probably listening anyway!

However, there was some retribution, for when Mrs Everitt sold the farm Holly's son appeared threateningly on her doorstep. She felt haunted by the boy for the rest of her life. Mr Everitt was definitely the better Christian and knew that Holyoake had trusted her to do the right thing. The inscription on his gravestone reads "Mr E.J. Holyoake, died 2.2.1942 at Driekuil

---

11 1881–1970.
12 1886–1971.
13 1888–1969.

Farm, P.O. Haenertsburg. This stone was laid by his son A.P. Holyoake and his daughter, Gypsy Southern" [incorrect spelling of her surname]. Gypsy's real name was Mara who married Benedict Southon.[14] The steep winding part of the road to Pietersburg between the two Veekraal turn-offs which runs through Driekuil was called Holyoake's Neck by Mr Stanford, who was the Sub-Native Commissioner. Under his supervision the former Grobler's Hill road was replaced and built by prisoners. These prisoners never amounted to more than ten and were looked after by two police "boys". It will be appreciated that this was a considerable task for so few, but their efforts improved the gradient laid out by H.D.M. Stanford a great deal. Another place-name connected with Holyoake is a portion of the farm Wellstead which he acquired and named Cooyong after a town south of Melbourne in Australia. Trudi Schoeman's guest chalets are situated on it now. To end my story about the Haenertsburg policemen, I will only mention that Lt. Arthur Leach succeeded Capt. Trevor.

Finally, the one and only store in the village was owned by Major Egerton. He did not live in Haenertsburg and Mr Stephenson and Mr Harper managed the Haenertsburg Trading Store for him. On one occasion Major Egerton wanted to give me a parrot as a present, but Father objected, so he gave me a canary instead which I called Little Billy. It travelled with us to the Lowveld, as I have recounted earlier in this story.

Later Mr Wylie became owner of the shop but somehow he often happened to run out of essentials. When for instance a piccanin was sent to the store to buy basic items like matches, he would often come back without them because there were no matches in stock. Mrs Wolff once had a bag of mealie meal delivered to her which was full of weevils. She returned the bag with the request that she be sent another one without weevils. Mr Wylie's indignant reply was, "How can I? Weevils live on mealie meal!"

On one of my old photos, taken in 1903, Mr Sweeney, the blacksmith, and Capt. Neville of the SAC together with Mr Stephenson are standing in front of the hotel's store. Young Stephenson told us how his mother in England warned him always to wear a pith helmet against the African sun. When he wrote to her about frost in winter she sent him some skates! He showed them to Father and me; they were elaborately curved at the tips and puzzled me greatly as I had never seen any skates before.

---

14 This information comes from the descendants of the Southon clan who visited me on the farm. One woman works at Checkers in Pietersburg and another is a handsome nurse.

Sub-Native Commissioner Harley Stanford.
(Photo: André Strever.)

E.J. Holyoake.
(Louis Changuion collection.)

Clear Waters, about 1912.

The only remains of the old Woodbush Forest Station: the stables.
(Louis Changuion collection.)

V On "Clear Waters"

In 1907 we left our Forest Home and came to live on our farm. Our immediate neighbours were the Britses on Koningskroon, Philip Botha on Nooyensboom, Van Niekerk on Kromfontein, Captain Page on Nieshoutfontein and Mr Simpson, or rather his manager Henning, on Broedersdraai. The existing house was built entirely from *schaalplanke*, off-cut barked timber, with the exception of the stonework chimney at one end which was useless. At first we made do with an E.P. tent as a roof over our heads.[1] Father was able to borrow the one which he had used as an office from the Forestry Department. The tent was rectangular, measuring about 4 x 5 metres with a plank floor made of movable sections. This served as a home while Father built a house on the farm Broedersdrift which Mother now called Clear Waters after the little stream running below the house. Incidentally, Father's successor, Charles Lane-Poole, now lived in four newly completed rondavels, some way above our poor old Forest Home.[2]

It was Father who had made the bricks for these buildings from subsoil, but Jim Smith had advised him not to burn them as our soil contained too much humus and they would have consequently crumbled. They were just green raw bricks dried in the sun.

George Badenhorst from Kopje Alleen, a farm he had registered in his name in 1889, introduced Father to soapstone of which there was an outcrop near the river. Mr Badenhorst was a Master Builder and had used soapstone from his own koppie for his little house built in 1898. He knew the stone could easily be cut into shape with a crosscut saw and made excellent building material. For rafters, beams and floor planks, Father used one of the big bluegums which stood near the existing house that the Bothas had lived in and which Father had pulled down. He made a pitsaw to cut the timber and this was not expertly done, being kind of zigzagged inside – it rather reminds me of my legs nowadays! When we moved into our house it consisted of a front room, one bedroom, and a stoep; under a

---

1   European Personnel Indian pattern tent.
2   The ruins are still in evidence about 1 km from the O'Connor Memorial as well as a solidly built stable of soapstone ashlars possibly built by George Badenhorst.

lean-to at the back was the kitchen, together with a small pantry and two more bedrooms.

Below the house stood a beautiful walnut tree, which bore two full sacks of good nuts every year. Father planted more of them and the people of Stylbult, where the Lees are now living, bought some trees from him. [Stylbult is now known as Gem farm, owned by James Turner and his mother.] Unfortunately, the trees were attacked by a virus which made them shed their leaves in the middle of summer and they stopped bearing fruit. In addition, Father planted naartjie trees, but they were really no good and he replaced them with some Satsuma, Greengage, Burbank, Wickson and Methley plums. The latter he planted on Mrs Hemsworth's recommendation. It was a cross between a Satsuma and a Mira Bella, I think, having been named after her brother who recognized it as a worthwhile plum amongst a batch of seedlings. They did well on our farm but the Wickson and Burbank were not suitable for our climate.

By contrast, Father's apple-growing venture was a great success. Earlier on, even before we moved to the farm I remember the occasion when I accompanied Father to enquire about apple stock from Thomas Alfred Southon, who had farmed on Broedersdraai since 1890. His house stood where the De Hoek Sawmill's workshop is situated today. Mr Southon had begun his career as a gardener employed by a Mr Bunyard, a well-known nurseryman in Kent, England. He had brought with him, as an experiment, a selection of ready-grafted apple trees, including Orange Monmouth, Missouri Pippin, Sykehouse Russet, Blenheim, Cleopatra, Jonathan, Reinette de Canada, together with black as well as striped Ben Davis. He also had Red Caldwell, which subsequently became known as Versfeld. In addition to the apple stock, Southon introduced Friesland cattle from Britain (two heifers and a bull), as well as seed potatoes of the Scotch Up-to-Date variety.

Unfortunately, when we came to the house, we were unable to see Tom Southon, who was seriously ill and died shortly afterwards in 1905 at the age of 54. However, his wife, old Maria, was very friendly and generously allowed Father to take as much applewood of the black Ben Davis, later known as Barnack Beauty, as he wished. Maria Southon was a black woman from Mamabula's people. She showed us with pride the family photograph album which, amongst others, included a picture of Tom's family posing in the grounds of their double-storey home in Kent. At the same time she refreshed us with a delicious home-made brew of tea, made from leaves picked in the vlei. Tom and Maria had three sons and three daughters: Ross married a local black girl, John took to drink and Harry, a very pleas-

Mr and Mrs Eastwood on the stoep of Clear Waters.

Thomas Alfred Southon's grave at Broedersdraai.
(Louis Changuion collection.)

ant and capable man, moved to Buysdorp to join the coloured community there.

Tom Southon had brought out a friend from England by the name of Jenna who started a butchery in Haenertsburg which he was obliged to relinquish when it did not pay. Mr Jenna did Southon a special favour when, as requested, he reported Tom's death to his family in Kent long before he actually passed away. Southon did not want them to know that he had married a black woman and this was not revealed. When the father died the sons inherited the farm Broedersdraai, but coloured ownership was not allowed by the Government and they had to sell. It was bought in September 1906 by a Mr Simpson, a Pietersburg auctioneer whose daughter, as a married woman, Jessie Jacobs, became the Pietersburg District Nurse. Mr Simpson employed a Mr Henning as farm manager, and I remember that we used to take our cattle to his dip before Father built one for himself. A sad little gravestone may be seen in the small cemetery at Broedersdraai, marking the grave of Henning's infant son. It reads: "Hier rust in Vreede Onze Geliefde Zoontje Johannes Gerhardus Henning, geb. Julie, 19, 1914, ov. April 29, 1916, Veilig in Jezus armen. J.G. and E.S. Henning". Tom Southon and his daughter, Fannie Southon (born 21 November 1888, died 10 February 1904) are also buried there.[3]

Afterwards, Broedersdraai was bought from Mr Simpson by Edgar Betton, one of the earliest pine growers in the district. His sister, Marion, was the second wife of Mr Hodgson, a manager of Sir Lionel Phillips's farm Broederstroom. Mr Hodgson had four daughters who married men who established themselves on farms in the area.

To return to our initial farming at Clear Waters. It needed a great deal of hard work for a pioneering family such as ours to make a living. Father grew millet for home consumption and supplied oat-hay under contract to the police in Haenertsburg. This is, in effect, oats reaped shortly before it is ripe and, cut together with its stalks, makes an excellent horse fodder. It was my monthly task, with the help of a piccanin, to load six bales of this oat-hay onto our wagon and deliver it to Haenertsburg. We managed the journey from Clear Waters to Haenertsburg and back quite easily in a day, and were paid 7/6d a bale.

To increase our "cash flow" Father bought an old water-wheel from a farmer, whose name was Alberts, from either Klipspruit or Paardedrift, along

---

3 Many gravestones in local farm cemeteries were made of soapstone and engraved by George Badenhorst and his son-in-law, Jan Oosthuizen, both living on Kopje Alleen.

A typical scene in the Woodbush – wood ready to be transported.

what was later to be known as the Potato Road. The road was given this name because it was used by the old Boers to cart their seed potatoes to the Lowveld. It overlooks Kudu's Valley on the Woodbush side. Mr Alberts's enormous water-wheel was transported by means of a donkey wagon. Father made a large hole in the middle of the cart to accommodate the axle of the wheel as it lay on its side. In view of the fact that it overhung the wagon by a wide margin it had to be very securely tied. It worked on the principle of buckets along the circumference of the wheel, which filled with water that descended through a furrow from the river. Thus the weight of the water caused the wheel to revolve and this drove the mealie-mill. The cost of grinding one bag was one shilling and it took five hours to produce one bag. However, this was adequate because the mill was operated by a piccanin whose wage was five shillings a month! In these early days we could not afford adult labour.

The piccanin working for us at that time was called Mbaldi. Mogedigedi was not allowed to follow us from the Forest Home to Clear Waters. With Mbaldi and Father's help and advice I learned to plough with oxen. The plough was a special type made in England, and known locally as an *omslagploeg*, a hillside or contour plough. Of course, not having any practice or experience I initially made a pretty bad job of it. When my father came to inspect my work he said, "If you can't plough better than that you will never be a farmer, if that is what you want to be. You must be able to plough a nice even furrow yourself before you can teach others." I once rashly told

Father that I thought the herding of our 16 goats was an easy job, to which he replied, "Right! We will give the piccanin a holiday and you can take over." I was delighted, but soon changed my mind as the goats wandered everywhere. My time was fully occupied keeping these elusive creatures from straying and at sunset I took them home, locked them up and promptly relinquished the job. Father had taught me a valuable lesson, namely not to underestimate a job until you have tried it yourself.

I worked hard on Clear Waters and every morning Father and I milked no fewer than 22 cows. He had acquired our first heads of dairy cattle by a coincidence which has a good moral attached to it. When Mrs Ruthven had to leave her farm – she sold to Bertie Knott[4] – she asked a coloured man, Mr Pieters, the saddler in Pietersburg, to help her with the move. They were on their way from Botterfontein to Pietersburg and had to cross the river at Broedersdrift. We had had heavy rains which forced them to camp below the drift for two days. By this time the water level had somewhat subsided but they still could not get through with their donkey-cart. They turned to Father for help and he made his eight oxen swim the river while he himself carried the yokes and the drag chain over the "bridge", which consisted of a big gum tree, with a wire as a handrail. The school-children used it daily. The oxen then pulled Mrs Ruthven's two carts through the water and the donkeys swam over. All her provisions and furniture had to be carried over by means of the "bridge". Naturally, Mrs Ruthven wanted to pay Father for his help, but he replied, "You owe me nothing – we are in this world to help each other. It cost me nothing and I am pleased to have done it."

Some months later Mr Pieters delivered a cow, a calf and a heifer as a present from the grateful Mrs Ruthven. The cow's name was Lemonade, so Mother called the calf Sparklets and the heifer Rooi Meisie. They formed the nucleus of our herd and were good milkers. Incidentally, Mr Pieters worked for many years as a saddler in Pietersburg in the street below the Market, opposite the tinsmith, Mr Backman. He had bought his business from a Mr Carver, who was Robbie Turner's maternal grandfather. Mr Carver left Pietersburg to settle in Bulawayo, having first travelled all the way to Rhodesia on a bicycle to reconnoitre the business potential there.

Some years later Father wished to buy more cattle, but he could not obtain them up here because all the good cattle were owned by Bill and Bob Collins and Mr Simpson, and none of them were prepared to sell. However, he saw an advertisement in the newly founded *Farmers' Weekly*

---

4   A diamond digger in Lichtenburg.

(1911) indicating that a Mr Hallowell was selling his farm and disposing of Cape cows, a cross between Jerseys and Guernseys, Ayrshires, Frieslands and Afrikaner cattle. They were said to be good milkers. Father wanted 12 young heifers as these acclimatise more readily than older cows. Mr Hallowell wrote saying that his price would be 10 pounds each – a large price for those days – but they were young and some were in calf.

The cows were sent by train to Pietersburg and Father walked there with Moses – the grandfather of the Moses who now works for my daughter Sheila – in order to collect them. They stayed with the Everitts and when the cattle arrived they fed and watered them. For the return journey Father bought a bale of teff grass, which he halved so that he and Moses could carry a half bale each on their backs, whilst driving the cattle. They stopped at the Israelsohns at Turfloop [now University of the North], fed the cattle on the teff, and after some hours' rest, they walked them on through the night to Clear Waters.

On another occasion, when I was about twelve years old, Daddy and I visited Pietersburg in our cart drawn by four donkeys. We met Max Israelsohn in town and he suggested that we send Zacharias, the piccanin, ahead with our cart to his house on Turfloop, while we joined him in his faster Cape cart. The idea was that we should spend the night with his family and go home the next morning – a journey of some three or four hours. However, our plans went awry for on arrival at their home we found that Zacharias, after watering the donkeys, had taken them and the cart on to Clear Waters. There was no alternative but for Father and me to walk home. After a night's rest in the Israelsohns' typical little house, with lean-to pantry at the back, we set out early in the morning and arrived to greet Mother just after noon. About this time Father's cheese production really got under way, when we had this not inconsiderable amount of milk to use. Butter production was not profitable, as the current price was only one sixpence per pound and every farmer used to make his own. In addition, of course, there was no real refrigeration in those days and thus the butter could not be sent farther afield. However, before Father started his cheese production, he wrote to the experimental farm at Potchefstroom for all the available information on the subject. He was interested primarily in proper Dutch cheese. He bought vats and wooden moulds resembling truncated small barrels with metal strips round them. (Helen Stubbs, now on Clear Waters, still has some of them.)

The milk was first poured into the vat which was lined with a metal container and brought to the right temperature by pouring in hot water with a funnel. One tablespoon of rennet was then added, which set the milk

rather like junket, and a yellow colouring agent was also added. This is obtained from the juice of the pulp covering the seed of the annatto tree (*Bixa orellana* – West Indies). We obtained these additives in bottles from Mr Palte's shop in Pietersburg. The curds were cut into little squares and placed under pressure in moulds lined with muslin cloth. The pressure was maintained for 12 hours, steadily rising at a stipulated rate, and at two hourly intervals the curd was removed and placed in another mould containing a clean cloth. Eventually the maximum pressure was achieved and maintained overnight. The cheese was then left to stand in saltwater for several days and subsequently placed on shelves to dry and cure.

On one occasion, when Lady Phillips was visiting us, she showed considerable interest in Father's cheese production, but disapproved of the array of stones of differing weights which we used to achieve the increasing pressure – she thought that this was somewhat primitive. To our surprise and delight, some time later Zeederberg's Transport delivered to us a large professional cheese press, a present from the Phillips's who were always on the look-out for ways to help industrious and enterprising people. The cheese making then became much easier, as the correct pressures could be achieved simply and accurately by controlling the number of revolutions of the screw. The whey was fed to calves after being mixed with a little mealie meal, kaffircorn millet and some codliver oil, which Father also bought from Palte's store in gallon drums. Father's cheese was marketed locally as well as in Pietersburg and was also highly praised at the Johannesburg Rand Show, where it was awarded a first prize. [Nipper Thompson, Googoo's grandson, and his wife Sylvia, are today known for the best cheeses in the North.]

Another product we sent to the Rand Show was honey in the comb or in bottles. The first hive was bought from a Mr Sawyer from Johannesburg. Eventually we had 20 hives lined up along the hill where Mr Turner later built his house, all ten feet apart and painted in different colours.

Apples, dried apple rings, cheese and honey were sold in containers marked with a special label, consisting of a rectangular strip of paper and a diagonal line running from the top left to the bottom right hand corner. The legend in the top right hand white field read: Woodbush Mountain Apples, Black Ben Davis or Woodbush Mountain Cheese (or honey) respectively and the bottom triangle was coloured red. In accordance with Father's suggestion, Col. Wolff used the same kind of label with a blue bottom triangle and when I myself started sending boxes to the market from Wegraakbos I used the colour green.

We lived well enough, but there was never much money in the house, and we were just as poor as all the other farmers living around us. Mother enjoyed entertaining and as she had a vegetable garden and kept chickens, this was made possible. Father was always trying out various ways to eke out a living and in addition to his cattle, he kept sheep, but by September of most years the grazing was very hard and the animals had finished most of the food that we had grown for them.

One year there had been a fire on the purple veldt below Pypkop. Soon thereafter the grass was 3 inches high – all green and lovely. This was State Forestry land but nobody looked after it, so we drove our sheep and cattle up there and made a kraal. Every day early in the morning I used to ride up on my horse and let the sheep and the cattle out; they could not stray very far because there was indigenous forest all around and the cattle never ventured into it. I would turn them out into the area overlooking the Lowveld and by 4 o'clock I had to go up again and drive them into the kraal. Whilst riding up to the look-out above the Lowveld, I was enchanted by the sheet of blue scillas stretching all around me. In between the scillas were diorama and as the grass had not grown higher than they were, the whole scene looked like a paisley carpet. The countryside up to the 1940's was open grassland. Only where the streams ran down to the valleys was there indigenous forest.

One morning, riding up Pypkop, I accidentally came across one of the places where a circumcision school, *koma*, was held. When the elders and the witchdoctors chose a site for their initiation school, they put up two high poles with plaited grass rings around the foot of them a certain distance apart. Each morning the mothers of the boys had to bring food and leave it at the bottom of these poles. I had not noticed them and suddenly came upon a bare piece of ground where a number of piccanins were lying under ox and goat skins. One of them, his body all smeared with white and his face marked with black ash around his eyes and mouth, crawled out from under the skins. Then I remembered – *ba o wela*. My friends, Eva and Julia, had told me never to go near the boys when they were *wela*-ing! They were being circumcised although some had not necessarily reached the age of puberty. On one particular night the older men would make the boys run for hours. The witchdoctor would choose a victim who was lagging behind the others and then kill him. The body was then placed on a special big stone in the Grootbos. Old Eva did not know where this was and had never seen it. I understand that as the body decomposed, liquid was collected and used for medicine. The lungs, liver and kidneys were fried and the bones used for making muti (medicine).

I cannot vouch for the truth of all this, but it sounds as though it could be true – you have to accept what the blacks tell you. Old Paulina Magwele also knows about that "stone which rings". She would never go near it and recalls that when she was a child, a small boy and girl from the same family were poisoned by mealie meal, ground with a little stone in an indentation of the big one. I think the stone they talk about is the one which we call a Rock Gong. It stands about a metre high, has a surface of 90 x 150 centimetres and has grooves down one side. On the top is a small round indentation and a small stone lies in it. If you strike the rock in various places it rings out like a bell. This could well be the place where these sinister rituals occurred.[5]

There are many superstitions still in circulation. The Basotho of the Zoutpansberg will not let twins grow up and it is generally the grandmother who does away with one of the babies. Only five years ago there was such a case on a neighbour's farm. It is also a bad omen if a child's top teeth come out first. On this subject, John Butlin, who is my daughter Philippa's husband, did his housemanship at Elim Hospital and whilst he was there triplets were born. They were lovely babies and Dr Rosset told Johnny to keep the babies in the hospital and let the mother go home. Initially, the babies did very well, got bigger, could sit up and were feeding off Kaffircorn porridge. Later on a woman from the mother's tribe came and said that the mother wanted her babies, but Dr Rosset hid them in the washroom and would not allow the woman to see them. However, the woman hung around the hospital and one by one the babies died, despite the fact that no one was allowed to touch them, with the exception of the white sister. At the autopsy no abnormality was found.

At one stage we had two brothers working for us. Brothers do not attend the same initiation school, but when the eldest came back from the school Father and Mother, who were very respected in the district, were invited to the return ceremony. Before the boys leave the place where they have been training they have their heads shaved into a *dobo*. A three-cornered patch of hair starting over the forehead is left standing, and at the back of the head the hair is cut into a curve. At the sides of the head the hair is shaved off completely and they call this *go bêola dobo*. In addition, the body is smeared with red ochre. Instead of wearing just a piece of riem tucked into the belt at the back, they are now allowed to wear a *sestaba* or a *lekgêwa*, together with a *stertriem*, which consists of a skin with two plaits at the back, one on each side. The boys are marched in a square column, like soldiers, onto a patch of ground that the mothers have cleared. They are enclosed completely by their tutors and come in with heads down, chanting a most beautiful song, clapping hands and *go lotšha* greeting their parents by kneeling down.

It is then the mothers' turn to enact their part. Each mother, according to her wealth and position, has previously bought beads and made these into a necklace either in ropes or in *samaaka* – that is in a meander pattern. She

---

5 Female circumcision was also practised in our area.

now has to place her necklace on her son's shoulders. However, this can sometimes be somewhat confusing, as the children's heads are bent down and it is difficult to distinguish one from the other. If she puts her beads on someone else's son he has to wear them until his *dobo* has grown. It is deemed a great insult for the poor boy to have to wear another boy's beads, which in some cases are not as grand as his own would have been. The whole ceremony, with its beautiful singing is a lovely ending to the initiation school.

It will be seen that the witchdoctors used to be very powerful men, and to this day still wield a great deal of influence. My father was a great believer in witchdoctors. When he was on Uncle Phillip's farm at Zebediela, before the outbreak of the Boer War, a *ngaka* threw the bones for him and told him that in a few days he would go to Pietersburg on business and would never return. He also gave him a little calabash which served as a snuffbox, and said, "Open it when you are in really big trouble. Use the snuff and your troubles will be ended." In fact, Father never went back to Zebediela – and he joined up because the war had just broken out. I opened the calabash years later, but there was nothing in it.

On another occasion our washing disappeared from the washing line at Clear Waters. Because of the continuous mists, washing has sometimes to be left out for a number of days, but on this particular day, when we came to collect it, it had disappeared. Old Temma, who had been helping Father build a shed, suggested that both of them should go down to Malepo (Boyne) and ask the witchdoctor for advice. They took their horses and came back with Jan Vark, who wore a beautiful beadwork cloak, a big head-dress and other appendages, looking very grand indeed. He went into a little hut that we had and there followed a lot of belching and groaning, but when he came out he had the answer. "Go along the road at the back of the house, turn left at the vlei above which is a big rock. Behind this, if you walk a little way you will find an ant bear hill, and in it you will find your washing." We did as he said, and there it was! Surely he could not have got this information from anybody when he lived so far away?

On our property there was a provincial school – Woodbush Hill School. Between them the Botha brothers, Theunis and Philip had so many children that Theunis, before he sold to us, donated a morgen of ground to the Government for the erection of a school. It first opened about 1904, and the buildings were made up of two separate wood and iron structures. One served as a single large classroom, and the other as a teacher's cottage, which consisted of a bedroom, a front room with a sitting area, a storeroom and a place for a Black Davis stove, where the cooking took place. In addition, a large tank caught the rainwater from the roof.

The school's first teachers were two young women, Miss McIntosh and Miss McLeod. These ladies loved the area and enjoyed walking to Houtbosdorp to buy their groceries. Is it not amazing how Scottish brains, self-sufficiency and thriftiness penetrated even into the Woodbush, thus sowing some much-needed grains of civilization and education! To the delight of my mother, who became very fond of them, the teachers visited us quite often, but despite this Mother did not want me to attend the school. She must have thought that she herself could teach me equally well, and she regarded the other children as "very rough" – I was very precious! (10)

After these lady teachers left, a Mr St John-Lee took charge of the school. He was alleged to have come from Oxford and was a keen cricketer; unfortunately his appearance was marred by a crooked jaw sustained from a blow by a cricket ball. He also had the reputation of "lifting the elbow". He was succeeded by a Mr J.W. Lengton, who took the photograph of the Brits family, as I recounted previously. The last teacher of Woodbush Hill School was Mrs Johanna Betton,[6] who used to ride on horseback from her husband's farm Broedersdraai to the school. She was a good teacher and exerted an important civilizing influence on the area. She introduced the children to toothbrushes and taught the girls to sew nighties and pyjamas. Not all the mothers approved of these sophisticated innovations and quite often the boys' pyjamas were cut down to shorts while the hems of the girls' nighties were taken up to dress length. At Christmas time she gave each child a small present. Mother thought a great deal of her and admired the occasional articles that she had published in the periodical *The Outspan*.

The school ceased to function in about 1931 and the school grounds, which had been properly surveyed, were inherited by me. I gave that particular morgen to my daughter, Elizabeth, and eventually it was bought in about 1952 by Mr Furner to become, again, part of Clear Waters.

To digress, my first venture into donkey-riding was undertaken side-saddle and I wore a dress and bloomers. To ride astride would have been considered highly indecent. When Father decided that I had mastered the art of donkey-riding, he bought me a mule for 5 shillings, but old Piet Venter[7] who re-built the Veekraal road, warned him, "Don't let your daughter ride this mule. It has already killed somebody." So back I went to the

---

6   Johanna Frances Betton, 1888–1958, called Jack by her friends.
7   P. Venter is buried on R. Thompson's farm Veekraal near the present-day Veekraal shop.

donkey. However, quite soon, I was taught to ride properly on a horse or mule by Godfrey Newcome, the manager of Sir Lionel Phillips's stud farm. Mother and I spent a week at his home[8] for this purpose and during that time a magnificent polo pony named "Starch" was at my disposal. Mr Newcome said to me on the evening of our arrival, "Be ready at seven in the morning at the stables. I don't like the horses to be out late in the morning when it is hot." We knew that I was to learn to ride astride, so I had been fitted out splendidly with riding breeches, topboots and a smart jacket. I crowned it all with a beautiful pastel shade velour hat that Lady Phillips had given to me. Godfrey Newcome took one look at me and exclaimed, "Good God – this isn't a bloody circus!" I felt utterly crushed. The rest of the day I spent crying on Mother's bed!

The next morning my first lesson started in earnest. Godfrey Newcome explained, "Please remember when you ride a horse, you dress as quietly and as simply as possible. No colours, simply a good riding habit and a simple hat. Your beauty is your horse, not you. You insult the horse if you ride in colours. The red jackets are only worn for fox hunting, and your credit comes in the way you manage the horse. For show purposes your saddlery, your bridle, your clothes and your horse are the things that count, not yourself."

Under Godfrey Newcome's tutelage I made good progress, and frequently we rode together to Haenertsburg. I was very honoured to be allowed to ride Starch. Godfrey also gave me another lesson in good horsemanship: "When you get back, always remember that the first thing you do is to look after your horse – if it is hot, you don't put it in the stable, you walk it until it is cool, then you feed it, and when it has eaten, you give it water. Do not give it water when it is hot – this will give it colic." Later, when he considered my standard was high enough, I competed in Pietersburg and other agricultural shows.

On such occasions I wore a divided skirt, a jacket, a hat and a pinned scarf. A favourite event was the riding of "Ladies Hacks". I well remember a Miss Deetlefs from Pietersburg, who rode beautifully on a magnificent horse and presented stiff competition. At that time Jock Bannantyne was still in charge of Zeederberg's Transport, and he approached me with the order to ride Jolly Boy, a fine strong willed horse. His confidence in me gave me courage and he entered Jolly Boy and myself in the Ladies' Hacks. This meant first walking the horse around the ring, thereafter trotting and finally

---

8   Now the Broederstroom Hut on the Dokolewa hiking trail.

cantering. Mr Brothwick was one of the judges and he selected four out of all the contestants. Miss Deetlefs, in my eyes the most invincible competitor, was unfortunate when, during the trot, her horse left the ring. I was next and I was terrified – I had not even had a chance to try the horse before, but everything went well and the first prize, a pink rosette, was mine.

A good horse was often a status symbol – just as an expensive motorcar is today. It had to have a good appearance, be meticulously groomed and well handled. Mr Holyoake was an accomplished horseman. He suggested that the local young people hold a trotting race such as was popular in

Australia. The course was to be from Willie Thompson's place on Rustfontein down the old coach road to Haenertsburg and on to Letaba Hill. Down the steep inclines our mounts were walked. However, if the horse broke into a canter it was turned around thrice as a form of penalty. One year I happened to win and this was a considerable feather in my cap against such formidable male competition. The prize was an Australian stock-whip, beautifully made with a wooden handle weighted with lead and a lash plaited for nine feet ending in a *voorslag*. The length of the whole whip was 20 foot, attached to a handle of only 18 inches long. A man, adept at handling such a whip, can with a single crack lift a shilling coin from the ground. The action is similar to casting the rod for fly fishing.

I spent days practising and did not give up until I had mastered the skill. Mr Holyoake also admitted that I could do it perfectly. My cousin, Geoff Eastwood, Uncle Alfred's son, who was learning to farm under my father's guidance came out of the store room one day and challenged me to hit him. I did – and he bore a scar under his arm for the rest of his life. Well, he should not have taunted me!

As my father had been a sailor, he was a keen fisherman, and was intrigued by the fact that there were only eels and loach in the many streams of the Woodbush. These beautiful rapid brooks seemed to be ideal for trout. Harvey and Storey had established a trout hatchery at Potchefstroom and got the ova from somewhere in the Cape. They were the first to introduce trout into our rivers.

Later, Father and my husband wrote quite a number of articles about trout for the *Zoutpansberg Review* and I quote part of one because of its historical interest:

> After a preliminary inspection, which revealed the most perfect conditions, in 1907 two hundred and eighty trout were liberated by Mr C. Harvey on my farm 'Clear Waters'. Owing to transport difficulties, only a portion of these reached their destination alive, but a week or two later a further 250 were liberated without any loss. A little later 500 were turned in near Haenertsburg, in splendid condition, and another 250 on Mr Lionel Phillips's estate. Since then 500 have been turned into the Helpmekaar, a small tributary of the Broederstroom, and I hear are doing splendidly. To discuss the natural enemies. Otters are not numerous …

The "transport difficulties" were overcome by putting into effect Father's idea that a bicycle pump should be used to pump oxygen into the big milk cans which were used for conveying the fingerlings. The fish came to Pietersburg by train, where Zeederberg's Transport was ready at the station to take the cans to Haenertsburg, the journey taking a whole day. They were rainbow trout which can take a slightly higher temperature than the brown trout.

The Transvaal Trout Acclimatisation Society was founded in 1911. There are some records held by the present Haenertsburg Trout Association of a meeting held on Saturday 9 December 1911 at the hotel in Haenertsburg at 2.30 p.m. At this meeting were present Mr Evans, Chairman; Mr Swinburne, Honorary Secretary and Honorary Treasurer, and members of the committee: Messrs Stanford, Wolff, Leddra, Eastwood. Members of the general public: Parnell, Le Roux, Robertson, Cavanagh. Most of these names have already appeared in my story, except Mr Evans, who held some Government or Police job and lived at Wellstead. Mr Leddra (married to Laura Deneys), also worked for the Government and Mr Robertson, managed the farm Ashmoledale for Cooper and Nephews. Apparently the main point of discussion focused on their affiliation to the Transvaal Organisation, but I am afraid I do not know too much about that.

Only the other day Louisa Kidd née Fauconnier[9] told me that she had caught the first trout ever in the Helpmekaar River with a rod given to her by John Swinburne. Apparently he was a fervent admirer of hers. He proposed to her at a dance at the hotel, but she was spared the embarrassment of refusing him by her St Bernard dog, which bounced into the hall at the crucial moment! Louisa and her brother, Constant, were confirmed together with me in about 1911 by Bishop Furse from Pretoria in the Haenertsburg Anglican Church. The tiny church which could seat only ten worshippers was built in 1906 from funds raised by the congregation. Mrs Cornelia Johanna Fauconnier, or rather Cavanagh, after she married her second husband, had been one of the driving forces in collecting money, by organising bazaars, whist drives, etcetera. She was a kind, helpful woman who kept a hospitable open house. I remember that for some reason or other Father and Mother could not come along to my confirmation ceremony and I rode to the church on my own. I then changed behind some big trees into my somewhat creased dress of white crêpe (at sixpence a yard) which I had transported in my saddlebag! After I had been confirmed I used to ride to communion once a month, when the district parson, Mr Evans, who was stationed at Munnik, came to the village with his buckboard and four mules. He held services at Agatha, Leydsdorp, Munnik and

9   Born 6.10.1897.

Haenertsburg in rotation. Sometimes he stayed with us on Clear Waters and walked to Agatha where he would spend the night with the McCullums, the Fergusons or Harry Whipp. He would then walk back to us and go down by buckboard to Leydsdorp. The main reason for his walking all that way was that the road was too bad for his transport. Mr Evans was called "Good Evans" in contrast to "Bad Evans", the trout enthusiast, who in fact was not bad at all and was a very pleasant man. Occasionally the officiating pastor was Noel Roberts, the Anglican pastor of Pietersburg who had actually prepared me for my confirmation. His brother, Austin Roberts, was the famous ornithologist.

When Mr Evans died the Rev. Charles Steer became his successor and he also made use of our simple house. At times he would spend a few days with us and help with the farming activities. When he noticed that Father reaped the oats with a sickle, he suggested that a scythe would be much more efficient. He showed him how to handle the newly acquired tool, but Father could never manage it.

Constant Johannes Fauconnier and his wife, Cornelia Johanna née Campher[10] were the parents of Helen, Elizabeth, Constant, Louisa and Doris. They owned the farm Waterval on which we spent our first night on our arrival in 1903. It stretched from the Cheerio turn-off to Lakeside and included Merrick and Brackenhurst. The total extent was some 600 morgen. They also acquired the farm Uitkyk, later called Sandford Downs, which according to the Deed of Sale was "gemeten voor C.J. Fauconnier in April 1899, door F.S. Watermeyer, Landmeter, goedgekeur Johann Rissik, Landmeter-Generaal" and confirmed by W.H. Gilfillan, Acting Surveyor-General, signed Surveyor-General's office 24 November 1902.

The couple had come from Knysna by ox-wagon to settle in the Lowveld, but the fever drove them up the mountain, where, according to the family bible, they "arrived at Houtboschberg in February 1889". During the Boer War the family lived in their house in Pietersburg and Louisa remembers vividly a big patch of white violets in their garden. Her father had joined the Boer forces and was killed on 13 December 1900 on the battlefield of Nooitgedacht. At the time his neighbours, Bennie van Blerk on Bloemtuin and Frikkie Deneys on Westwood, were with him in the field, busy boiling some water for tea. Fauconnier got out of the trench to fetch the billy and was shot. His name is on the monument at Breedtsnek in the Magaliesberg, which was erected in memory to the Boers who died in this action.

_____

10 18.11.1865 – 24.6.1940.

When Mrs Fauconnier and the children came back after the war, the situation was still unsettled because of marauding blacks. Louisa remembers a day when a group of intruders armed with assegais and shields entered the house, plundered it and even took the washing off the line. During the incident, the children were told to go into the bedroom and keep completely still.

Shortly afterwards Mrs Fauconnier got married to Dr William Cordner Cavanagh, an Irishman whom she had taken in as a paying guest. He put a Red Cross sign in front of his house, but he often did not charge poor whites and railwaymen for his services. The articles he wrote for medical journals were mainly about malaria and its cure. He also enjoyed writing letters of complaint to the *Zoutpansberg Review* being a somewhat quarrelsome old man.

Dr Cavanagh died of cancer of the sinus in a little house at Veekraal on the Thompsons' farm in 1935. It was his plan to build a sanatorium on Waterval, but instead he erected near the house a factory which produced soda water, mineral water, gingerbeer, lemonade and champagne! The essence for the cool drinks came from Boots in England. The main outlets for his products were the hotels in Haenertsburg and Pietersburg and these drinks were really good. Later, in the 1920's, Constant junior built another factory nearer the Stanford Lake, where there is a good spring.

This information comes from Louisa Kidd and her niece, Helen Manderson. Helen Manderson is the daughter of Elizabeth Fauconnier who married Chichester Gould. The eldest Fauconnier girl, also Helen, married the forester Alexander James O'Connor, who for many years was in charge of the Woodbush Forest Station and became Director of the Department of Forestry from 1940–1942.

There is a memorial erected in his honour on the way to the Woodbush Forest Station amid towering eucalyptus trees. The inscription reads:

Alexander James O'Connor
22 Dec. 1884 – 2 Oct. 1957
Circumspice si monumentum requiris

This epitaph is the same as that of Sir Christopher Wren (1632–1723) which is inscribed on the floor of St Paul's Cathedral. It means: If you seek his monument look around you.

Awdry in Johannesburg, 1913.
(Photo: Marian Maxwell.)

VI Growing up

My closest and only real friend, that I had as a young girl, was Norah Devenish.[1] She lived with her widowed mother (who had been a governess), and her six sisters and a brother, Graham Mills Devenish, in the house on Cooyong.

Her father, A. Lennox Devenish,[2] had been a surveyor employed by the South African Republic. He surveyed 455 stands in the newly founded Pietersburg (1886) and demarcated many farms near the Spelonken and around Soekmekaar, Levubu and Louis Trichardt. The family used to accompany him on his official travels, but they also had a house in Pietersburg, the grounds of which bordered on Maré, Grobler and Market Streets. As President Paul Kruger often had difficulties finding ready cash to pay for work done, Mr Devenish was given the pick of a number of farms for services rendered and he is supposed to have owned no less than twenty at one stage. According to B.H. Dicke, "these free grants were called 'quit-rent' farms because an annual nominal rental was payable for them at the rate of 15 shillings per thousand Cape morgen". Lennox Devenish and his eldest son, Leister, died of enteric fever before the Boer War.

The family was left very well off. Mrs Devenish[3] wanted the girls to learn German and French and she consequently sent the two eldest, Winnie and Anne, and later Lilly and Irene, to a German family in Berlin and also to a convent in France. For some time there was talk of sending me along with Dolly and Norah, but Mrs Devenish died suddenly of heart failure. Shortly before her death she mentioned to my father that she had not yet made a will, and he prevailed upon her to do this. She had a big estate which could not be distributed because the youngest daughter, Gwen, was under age. She, in fact, turned twenty-one during the depression, when land prices were very low, and even their large farm, called Mannamead, near Bandelierkop, realised less money than expected.

Norah was about five years older than I. She was a mature girl, kind, humorous, with high principles, as well as being a devout follower of Chris-

1   27.7.1889 – 31.3.1971.
2   Anthony Lennox Devenish, d. 3.5.1898, age 45.
3   Eliza Frances Devenish, d. 26.2.1914, age 56.

tian Science. She had a very great influence on me and I remember my mother once praising her, to which she replied, "You treat me as if I was a text on the wall!" She coined a nickname for me, namely "Mrs Flint" – I was made of tougher stuff and I was hard on her when she fell off her horse. I simply made her get back onto it and get on with things. We went for long rides together, and she often stayed with us for a few days at a time. Our friendship lasted all our lives. She met her future husband in Kenya, where her sister, Dolly, lived who was married to an engineer on the railways. Norah took on the job of assistant matron at a boys' school in Nairobi in 1923.[4] John Twells was one of the masters at the school. Norah had a son, Devenish, and a daughter, Melanie, who married Angus MacDonald – a farmer at Bandelierkop. When Norah's husband retired they went to live in Kent, but she did come out to stay with us here on one occasion. However, at that time she was a very sick woman and she died of cancer soon afterwards.

To revert to the farm, we had various outbuildings put up and I even had a little house of my own. This came about because I was very fond of dogs and at one stage had fourteen of them, a fact which definitely interfered with comfortable living in the main house! My love of animals and plants was very much encouraged by my parents and particularly by a guest who came to spend a holiday with us for the first time in December 1910. Mother had received a letter from Mr Legat, dated 29.11.1910, which read: *I hope you will not think me very rude for writing to enquire if you could put up at your house for a few days a young fellow called Methuen, a son of the General's, who wishes to come up to Woodbush with me when I go there next month. He is a keen biologist and would probably be out all day hunting for specimens.*

Paul Methuen wrote to thank us for the kind invitation. At the time he was working at the Transvaal Museum in Pretoria and by taking him around the Woodbush I learned a lot about how to collect specimens systematically. Paul was particularly interested in orchids when he first came here and I used to take him on horseback to the parts of the forest where he was most likely to find them. One day our horses ran away and we had to walk a long way back to the house. He really was not very used to hard walking and he collapsed on the kitchen floor on arrival. I thought he was asleep and I said to Mother, "Thank goodness I'm not a beautiful orchid. I would hate to be taken to Pretoria by him." Unfortunately he overheard the remark and was somewhat upset! I appreciated his mind and he sent me

4   Letter Norah to Awdry 10.10.1923.

lovely books, but I did not think that he was one of my admirers.

My admirers were the local farmers' sons like Ikey Collins, a prize-liar, who used to arrive on horseback, hair smoothed down with brilliantine. The boys knew I liked horses so they made them prance by digging the spurs into their sides. I was not pretty, but it never worried me. The following jingle could have been very well applied to me, I thought.

As a beauty I am by no means a star
There are others better-looking by far
But my face, I don't mind it, because I live
Behind it, the people in front get the jar!

Paul Methuen was nine years my senior, good-looking, and I was grateful to him when he helped me to end my "musical career". Mother played the piano beautifully and was very keen to teach me music. This was a bugbear to me, especially when I had to practise for an hour a day. On these occasions Paul had to wait until I had finished before I could take up my job acting as a gillie for him. He told me later that it had been purgatory to listen to my efforts and said that if he were I he would implore my mother to stop my lessons. After that remark I never played again!

Apparently I started collecting specimens very soon after he left, because in January 1911 he wrote to me acknowledging the receipt of a crustacean which I had found in the vlei. It was a small creature shaped exactly like a flea, about the size of a thumbnail and it could jump amazingly. Paul Methuen wrote up a description of this *Talitriator eastwoodae*.

Tetradactylus eastwoodae.

From then on the museum regularly sent me boxes containing jars, test tubes and formalin. I captured a plated lizard with a skink-like form (stunted legs) at Clear Waters in April 1912 which is also called after me, namely *Tetradactylus eastwoodae.*

According to Dr Alan Kemp[5] of the Transvaal Museum, *This good species is still only known from this one type specimen and has yet to be rediscovered. It is interesting to note that a small gecko collected by Googoo in 1916, as Mrs L.C. Thompson, and named* Afroedura pondolia multiporis, *was only rediscovered last year somewhat east of the original Woodbush locality. We also have* Graphiurus platyops eastwoodae, *now recognized as a race of this dormouse, collected by Miss Audrey Eastwood at Woodbush on 30 October 1912. It was a male and was kept in captivity for a year becoming the specimen that is still in our drawers.*

Eastwood's Dormouse.

Returning to 1911, I must mention that we were also hosts to Paul's father, Lord Methuen,[6] who was G.O.C. South African Command from 1908–1912. He had initially spent a fishing holiday at the Phillips's Broederstroom Stud Farm when Father and Mr O'Connor had tried their best to find suitable mounts for him and his wife. However, the fishing season had not yet opened and Lord Methuen wrote later from G.H.Q. Roberts Heights:

Dear Mr Eastwood,
I cannot say for certain, but I think I could manage to come to you on Sunday, 10 December for about a fortnight or ten days. This much depends on circumstances, and I could equally manage one week earlier, as

---

5   Letter Dr Kemp to B. Wongtschowski 6.8.1986.
6   Lord Paul Sandford Methuen, 1.9.1845 – 30.10.1932.

long as I get a few days' notice. Will this suit you? I can bring a servant, or not, as you like. I shall bring some pints of Pilsener beer, and some Riebeecks water.

Perhaps you could get me two dragonflies suitable for the river. I had luck with the "Yellow Woodcock", getting a fish on Monday.

18.10.11

Yours truly,

Methuen.

P.S. I shall be vexed if you do not treat me as simply as possible.

Eventually on 25 November 1911 a telegram arrived from Lord Methuen addressed to "Eastwood, Clearwaters, Haenertsburg, Transvaal" which read, "Lord Gladstone not now going to Mr Phillips – so please expect me on 4 December as previously arranged."[7]

He arrived bringing his pointer, Nell, but Mother had declined to accommodate his servant. His stay with us was pleasant and informal. For his fishing I used to take him to the Helpmekaar River where the Ebenezer Dam now is. We walked there from Clear Waters although he was very lame owing to a wound in one leg sustained during the Boer War. On some occasions we would have to come home in the dark. He thoroughly enjoyed his stay and his "thank you letter" brought a special surprise for me.

It read: *Dear Mrs Eastwood, I cannot thank you and your husband and the good Miss Awdry half enough for my very happy fortnight. I feel all the better for my rest, but shudder when I see the papers in my basket! If ever you and Mr Eastwood thought of letting your daughter come to England for her education – and I should have thought it wise – my wife could fix up everything at Corsham Court as we are only twenty minutes from Bath. The cost should not be great but if you ever thought anything of our offer perhaps you would have to let me know how much you could afford.*

Mother replied: *Dear Lord Methuen, your kind note came last evening – shall I ever be able to express my gratitude to you for the very kind interest you have taken in Awdry! At present we do not know whether we will be able to take advantage of your wonderful offer. I can hardly realize that it has really happened for it has been my one ambition to try and*

---

7   Lord Herbert John Gladstone, 1854–1930, was the first Governor-General and High Commissioner from December 1909 – July 1914 and invited Gen. Louis Botha to form the first South African Government. He was the youngest son of the British Prime Minister W.E. Gladstone.

get her away from the farm and all the work that it entails for a little time. We will do all we can to give her this wonderful chance and if you do not mind, will write to you later on. Your visit was the greatest pleasure to us and a very great event in our quiet farm life.

I was to attend the Slade School of Fine Art with their youngest daughter, Seymour. To study in England would have been wonderful, but we did not have the money for the fare. We wondered if there was any way in which we could raise it. There was the amount of 3000 pounds which my grandfather had left to each of his children. The sons could borrow from the estate provided they paid Grandma Eastwood interest in order to maintain her income. Until that time Mother would never hear of letting Father get into debt but she now thought, this is the time I am going to ask him to borrow 120 pounds; it would mean so much to Awdry's life.

Grandmother's answer was a shattering blow: *On no account would I like her (Awdry) to spend three years with Lord and Lady Methuen and then come back and despise her home. Her life would be ruined and I feel, therefore, that I must not lend the money to you.* After that I hated the old woman – how dared she say that I would despise my parents, she did not even know me and had never seen me. I was 16 and old enough to realise what a wonderful educational opportunity had eluded me.

A few more letters from Lord Methuen arrived over the years, the last one being dated 8.1.1917 from "The Palace, Malta". In it he acknowledges Mother's "charming letter telling me of the death of dear Nell" – he had left his pointer in our care when he was transferred. He also writes that he is too old for fighting and is looking after the wounded and sick "having increased the hospital from 262 beds, 14 nurses and 32 doctors to 27 000 beds, 630 nurses and 272 doctors, which means a good deal of work." He then goes on to mention his children and a P.S. runs, "The news of the death of my old friend, Selous, has just come – as straight, simple-minded and fine a character as I have ever come across."

Before going any further with my life story, I must talk about a camping trip which took place in November, 1912. My father suggested going to a place called Arthur's Rest near Olifants Gorge. We had a little donkey-wagon with eight donkeys for carrying our provisions and blankets. Mother used to sit on the cart while we all walked down through Buffelspoort. In our party were Norah and Graham Devenish, Kenneth McGaffin and Barney McMagh. Over the weekend we were joined by Dr Louis Clifford Thompson, the District Surgeon in Leydsdorp and a friend of his, Mr Parker, who had bought the farm Wegraakbos, which he called Cosy Corner, from Percy Kent. We camped out for a week and then came back via Tzaneen. At the

Our camping trip, crossing the Selati.

time there was a big party going on to celebrate the opening of the Selati Railway from Komatipoort to Tzaneen. (Incidentally John Swinburne had been employed to supervise the clearing of the survey track.) Messrs Pauling & Co. gave a luncheon for the more important citizens on 9 November, but we ourselves camped out on the Bennett's farm, Yamorna, and came into town for the general party. It was held in a sort of prefabricated building which normally served as a hospital and living quarters for the two nurses employed there. There was plenty to eat and drink, a dance took place, and all the old prospectors from near and far attended, getting gloriously drunk! Mica-Bill and Paraffin-Joe who lived in the baobab tree near Leydsdorp must have been part of the crowd.

Doc [Dr Louis Thompson] told us a funny story about another prospector, old Valentine, who used to cadge meals from Mr Wilson, an engineer working on the railway. The latter got a bit annoyed with this and one day when Doc and he were having a drink, Valentine appeared, but he was only offered a pot with salt water. This must have been food for thought, because he did not bother Mr Wilson after that. However, Dr Thompson had a more positive attitude towards Valentine, because he had once been presented by him with a little copper dish, which I still use as a vase, but which, according to Clarence van Riet Lowe, the late Director of the Archaeological Survey, is a small Arabian measuring cup. Valentine had found it between the roots of a blown over knoppiesdoring tree together with some bones. Louis, being the local District Surgeon, looked after the railwaymen working for Pauling & Company Ltd. George Pauling, in his autobiography *The chronicles of a Contractor*, gives a vivid picture of this period. A close associate of many of his engineering undertakings was James Butler, whose daughter, Katie, married G. Newcome, my riding teacher.

Returning to my personal life, the chance of obtaining professional drawing and painting lessons which had evaded me when I was 16 came my way again when Lady Phillips saw some of my watercolours. I loved drawing animals and under the watchful eyes of my father, who, like his brothers Philip and William, was a fine amateur artist, I made reasonably good progress. I had painted a watercolour of my two little black spaniels, who were observing a feather in the air – a typical genre piece. On seeing this, Lady Phillips remarked to my mother that I should have art lessons. When Mother replied that we did not have the means to send me to Johannesburg, and even if it was possible there would be nobody to look after me, Lady Phillips offered to take me down and let me stay with them for a while until the Parliamentary session started, at which time they would have to leave for Cape Town. She said she would see me safely placed with her aunt, Mrs Soames, or her sister-in-law, Mrs Mascall. I would then be able to attend the School of Art, which had been founded early in 1913 and which was situated at the station-end of Eloff Street. Lady Phillips's role in the establishment of the Johannesburg Art Gallery and Art School is well known.

I arrived at Villa Arcadia on 4 February 1913. When I rang the bell a footman answered the door and this opened a totally new world for me. The splendid Herbert Baker house, now a Jewish Orphanage, in Oxford Road could have accommodated our whole house at Clear Waters in one room. It contained a music room where Sir Lionel had his organ, brought from their home Tylney Hall in England, and there was a library which I was allowed to use. Surrounding the house were lovely orchards as Lady Phillips was an enthusiastic gardener. She was very fond of our indigenous flora. Feeling that if one was to have flowers it was essential to have butterflies, she planted special flowers and herbaceous borders to attract them.

One day, at an early stage in my stay, when Sir Lionel and Lady Phillips had gone to a dinner-party, the butler asked me what time I would like dinner. Being straight from the bush I was very much out of my depth, and so I asked, "What time do you usually have it?" "About half past seven" was the reply. I am sure you can imagine the scene – there I sat all by myself a butler in attendance and a footman standing behind my chair. I was so embarrassed by the whole situation that I could hardly eat anything, let alone enjoy it. The butler then offered me coffee and brandy or liqueur in the library. Needless to say I only had the coffee, but in spite of it I must have fallen asleep whilst reading, because when I woke up all the lights were out and it was the middle of the night. I did not know my way back to my own room in the dark in a house with so many rooms and corridors, so I stayed in the library and slept on the sofa for the rest of the night!

At that time Lady Phillips was writing a book entitled *A Friendly Germany – Why Not?*, and as she did most of her writing in bed and did not get up very early, I had to take messages to her. I have never known such a wonderful woman. She gave so much of herself, helping so many people and initiating so many projects in Johannesburg. However, she could be very tactless at times. One of her friends in describing her said, "She is like a cow, she gives a big bucket of milk and then kicks it over!" This remark describes her very well. I loved her dearly and could never be grateful enough for all that she did for me.

Shortly after my arrival, her secretary, Miss McLeod, took me to my art teacher, Mr A.E. Gyngell[8], who lived with his mother in a tiny house in Yeoville.[9] Perhaps it was at 39 Harley Street because, on the first page of my sketchbook this address is written in his own handwriting. He gave me this to use for my homework and advised me to make little sketches of anything that I might see during the course of the day. "Animals can't sit for you, take a pencil and draw their outlines even if it is only a portion of them." One day he told the class to draw a picture depicting early morning. My effort of a house with two bottles of milk on the front step was awarded full marks. He also approved of my drawing of the old St George's Church, Parktown. Mr Gyngell gave us lessons in portraiture and I made dozens of charcoal sketches of an old man, who earned a little money by sitting for us. He had a strong bony face and made a good model. The other Art master was George Salisbury Smithard.[10] He was somehow deformed, but I cannot put my finger on what was actually wrong with him. Perhaps he had had polio and I always looked upon him as a much older man than Mr Gyngell. Mentally, he was very alert, very interesting, and a wonderful painter; in fact, I think, a better artist than Mr Gyngell. There is a painting

8 Albert Edmund Gyngell 1866–1948.
9 Letter Awdry to Mother 4.2.1913.
10 1873–1919.

Awdry's drawing of the St. George's Church in Parktown.

of the Woodbush by him in the tearoom of the Pretoria Station, which he must have done after he had been to stay with Lady Phillips at the Stud Farm, while she was up there trying to rehabilitate her eldest son Harold.[11] Mr Smithard taught us landscape drawing and under his guidance, I drew willows at Zoo Lake at all seasons of the year. I don't know why he took me alone – perhaps Lady Phillips paid him for special lessons in order to help him financially. He was such a kind old man.

I used to buy my crayons and charcoal from a little art shop opposite the school, but did not know at the time that it belonged to Pieter Wenning,[12] who became a well-known South African artist. I had to work awfully hard at school because I knew nothing of proportions, and of course there was also plenty of homework to do as well. During the day we would have only an hour's break for lunch and often I went to a bioscope, where the entrance fee was a sixpence; with the addition of a cup of tea and two buns the expense amounted to nine pence! The films were silent ones in black and white and I sat there for an hour before going back to school.

11 Letter Audrey to Mother 11.2.1913.
12 1873–1921.

104

I do not have many memories of the other students except a very clear picture of Joyce Ordbrown who had had lessons in London and was not a beginner as I was. She was tall, fair, very reserved and a very good artist. Her speciality was painting designs on pottery. She had brought out from England an unglazed tea-set, onto which she painted *bobbejaan* crocuses. She painted the leaves on the saucer in brown and dull green as they are in nature. The cup with its mauve-white flower rose like a real flower from them. I admired her for this unusual idea, and when it was finished and glazed, I thought it one of the most beautiful things I had ever seen. Later on in her career she did many murals on tiles for official buildings throughout South Africa. The only other girl I became friendly with was a Miss Martin, whom I mentioned in one of my letters to Mother as "one of the few who had any time for me". Fortunately, I had close ties with the families of two of my mother's sisters, Emily Solomon, and Edith Eastwood and her husband Bill Eastwood. In addition there were numerous cousins, who helped me to get over my initial stages of homesickness. I was always assured of a sympathetic ear and a jolly weekend.

I lived with Sir Lionel's sister, Mrs Florence Mascall and her husband, in Pallinghurst Road, Parktown West. The house was very near Villa Arcadia and there was a bus stop nearby. Mrs Mascall was a great musician and used to get up at 3 a.m. to practise on her grand piano. She was a keen gardener and would fill up her wheelbarrow with manure, digging away enthusiastically, despite the fact that she was a small slender person, very like her brother, who always reminded me of a scruffy pigeon! I think Mr Mascall was active on the stock exchange, but they were never well off, and I was a little frightened of him because he "lifted his elbow" a bit. When he tended to get tight, once or twice, I had to snub his familiar advances. In fact, right from the beginning, this situation was something of a problem, but after a talk with Uncle Bill I got good advice and was able to handle things.[13]

I was very naive, younger in my ways than I was in years. Lady Phillips had given me and a young niece of hers, Mirri Poultney, a little talk when I went to live with the Mascalls. She said, "You must be very careful, especially you, Awdry, coming from the country. You don't know how wicked men are. You must never let any man take liberties with you and never kiss anybody. If you get married you must be able to tell your husband that you have never been kissed by any man in the world!" This was the gist of the lecture that she delivered and I really did not know what she was talking about. I thought that the men she was referring to were pickpockets, and on my tram rides I would clutch my purse with my couple of shillings in it, tightly in my hand. I knew nothing at all about the facts of life – I had seen horses and cows taken to be covered, but did not connect this with human beings. However, I managed to get through life quite well.

I met all sorts of interesting people at Lady Phillips's dinner-parties, and enjoyed listening to her social gossip. My letter to Mother, dated Thursday, 11 February 1913, mentions that, "Last Sunday Lady Phillips had such a lot of people to dinner. Amongst them was Mr Irving,[14] the actor. He is a very clever man with a beautiful voice." He suggested that I should come and see him at Leonard Rayne's Standard Theatre in "The Bells". This well-known play by the French writer, M.M. Erckmann Chatrian, adapted by Leopold Lewis from Le Juif Polonais was popular at the time. It is still performed and I am told, that in December 1984 it was relayed on the English Radio Service. I do not remember the plot, but Irving came onto the

---

13 Letter Awdry to Mother 11.2.1913.
14 H.B. Irving was the son of the famous actor, Sir Henry Irving, 1838–1905. H.B. Irving died in 1919.

snow-covered stage on a sledge drawn by live Shetland ponies and I was greatly impressed.

I was staggered at being with all these grand people, as I had not had much contact with people at all. I never spoke unless I was spoken to and never came out with any subject of my own. Mother had taught me always to listen to what all these great people had to say, take it in and remember it. I felt my life was a very ordinary one of not much interest. I would only reply if I was asked questions about it. My cousins, Ethel and Bertha Solomon, were much in advance of me concerning the "ways of the world". Their parents were very well off and whenever they cleared out their wardrobes, I inherited some of their cast-offs.

While on this subject, on the very first day of my arrival at Villa Arcadia, Lady Phillips's secretary, Miss McLeod, also took me to a dressmaker, who made me a dark-blue coat and skirt. Then we went on to Blenman, Helwell and Islop for a dress. Blenman had the loveliest material, of very good quality and very expensive; their shop served as a landmark whenever I got lost in town. I had a few dresses, of course, which I had brought with me, and particularly my confirmation dress that Mother had made for me. I would often change into it after my daily bath before dinner. Grandmother Eastwood also supplemented my clothes with the occasional parcel. Hats were indispensable in those days when going out. The straw-hat I am wearing in an old photograph had been given to me by Paul Methuen. Miss McLeod did my hair and we arrived rather grandly in the Phillips's car with chauffeur at the studio of Marian Maxwell.

To illustrate how naive I was, once when staying with the Solomons, I was invited to go along to a dance at the Langebrinks and young Langebrink, who was very good-looking and about my age, when I asked if he would dance with me exclaimed, "Good heavens, you don't invite a gentleman!" Obviously that put me right off and I never again went to another dance. I did, however, see some shows and was taken to the Palladium, where I loved the various acts, particularly the graceful "Diving Girls". Bertie and Ethel Solomon were absolutely in the swing of things – they had dancing lessons and later became performers themselves. They lived with their mother, my Aunt Emily, who was by then divorced from Mannie Solomon. She was a great friend of the painter Heinrich Egersdörfer,[15] who was her neighbour for a while, when they lived at 24 Honey Street, Berea. I thought he was quite a "nice josser". One day we visited him and he gave Bertie one of his drawings of a lion's head. I admired his skill as an animal painter. He was also famous

15 1853–1915.

for his gentle caricatures of colonial life. It was my ambition to draw animals well, but at that stage this was a distant dream, and I wrote home: "I do pray that I will one day be able to draw."

Some years later my husband bought one of Egersdörfer's paintings, a Bateleur eagle with a springbok in its claws. Egersdörfer was dead by then, but my husband had been to Johannesburg, where he ran into Mr C.R. de Laporte, one of J. Stevenson-Hamilton's game wardens in the then Sabie Game Reserve, who took him to an art exhibition. Louis was supposed to purchase a bed, but he came home with the painting, for which he had paid 13 guineas, a large sum of money for us at that time. However, we both agreed that it had much more value than a mere bed. Later, Mr Bridgeman of Weltevreden Farm offered us 100 guineas for it, but we preferred to keep it.

Although I definitely acquired some social polish, had a good time and loved my lessons, I did not take to the social set and I think they not to me. In a letter I wrote home[16] I said, "People here seem to have no time for others unless they throw money about, especially for motor-cars. I really will be thankful to get home again. I hate this place and everyone in it. This is my present conclusion." Villa Arcadia was always a place of refuge. On one of my "blue days", Christine, a ladies' maid at the Phillipses, lent me her shoulder to cry on and cheered me up with a cup of tea. About forty years later, two funny old people arrived at our house on Wegraakbos, and it transpired that they were a Mr and Mrs Guyt. The latter turned out to be the ladies' maid, Christine, now riddled with arthritis. Her husband, Mr Guyt, was supervising the gardens at Joubert Park and he had heard that my daughter had a whole bank of *Haemanthus catherinii* behind our annex. When he saw the mass of pink flowers he was extremely excited.

The Phillips's children were grown up when I came to Johannesburg. Edith was married in England, and Frank had a job on the mines. Harold, the first-born son, lived with his Canadian wife Hilda (née Hills) on Broederstroom. Harold had been sent to the Ontario College of Agriculture in Canada to learn farming, with the intention that he would take over Broederstroom Stud Farm and so get away from the wild and dissipating life of Johannesburg. It did not work, but for a time he enjoyed his role as gentleman-farmer. Once he organised a hunt in his own bush, with Africans as drivers, for Mr Beatty,[17] the magistrate of Pietersburg. It was more of a slaughter than a hunt and my poor father was made to take part in it.

---

16 Letter Awdry to Mother 29.4.1913.

17 Later Sir Kenneth Beatty. He was Chief Justice of the Bahamas in 1930. Letter Mr Everitt to Mrs Eastwood 23.11.1930.

Barney McMagh and Kenneth McGaffin, 1914.
(Louis Changuion collection.)

When I look at an old photo of the hunters and their kills, I'm ashamed of it. Father was disgusted with the proceedings.

For a while, after Harold and Hilda's son, Lionel Frances, called Bobkin, was born in March 1914 it looked as if they would settle down, but it was not to be. Mother and I often joined them for a game of tennis before I left for Johannesburg. The tennis court was on their farm and we went there on horseback. The players used to meet on a Saturday afternoon and sometimes for the whole day on Sunday, if there was no rain. Mr Badenhorst, from Kopje Alleen, often watched us on these Sunday afternoons when he was on his way to the Stud Farm. He had taken on the job of building the stables and had to start work early on Monday morning. The stables which now house the Woodbush Forestry Station's mules look as solid now as when they were built in 1912/13.

The other members of the little tennis club were Kenneth McGaffin, who managed Koningskroon, Barney McMagh and Harold Donnelly from the Forest Station, Mr Muir, the Phillips's manager, and a nephew of his who was helping him. We had a rondavel built, where tea and sugar were kept and we each took our own sandwiches. I was never any good at tennis, and much better at riding, but these young men became my firm friends. In my letters to Mother, I regularly asked her to give them my regards, and to pass these regards on to my cousin, Geoff, who was still staying at Clear Waters and to Mbaldi, my former "co-worker" on the farm.

When Barney McMagh gave up forestry work, he joined the Department of Native Affairs and later became Assistant Mining Commissioner.

109

Spaniels looking up at floating feathers and watercolours of pointers, by Awdry, 1909.

He was a well-known character in Pietersburg. He had lost his parents when quite young. His brother took on the post of Stationmaster at Komatipoort – a death trap of a place – but this enabled him to pay for Barney's training as a forester, and for the education of a sister. They were a lovely, close-knit Catholic family.

Mother took all these young bachelors under her wing. They used to come and have supper with us on Sunday evenings and after the meal Mother played some hymns while we all sang. Then followed some Bible reading, after which we had tea and cake and they rode home again. Usually I would be responsible for making the pudding. I could not bear cooking or working in the house but Mother said, "You jolly well have to learn until you can do it with a smile." She also acted as an older friend to Hilda Phillips whenever the young woman felt lonely. This was especially so on the occasion when Sir Lionel had been the target of an assassination attempt towards the end of 1913, and Harold was summoned urgently to Johannesburg.(11) At the time I was still at Art School and I well remember that straw was put on Hospital Hill to soften the noise of traffic as his room was near the road.

110

VII Back on the Mountain

Towards the middle of 1914 I returned home from what one might call my "Finishing School" and my first encounter with the big world. I am sorry that I gave up drawing and painting in adult life, but one cannot have babies, run a farm, and still go on with one's painting. On the other hand I did neglect a talent which ran so strongly in the family. For example, there are my father's lovely watercolours of sailing boats, now in my daughter Gub's house, and about a dozen paintings by my grandmother, Emily Anne Eastwood, who was a pupil of Whistler's. These are scattered amongst various members of the family. In addition, my own children and particularly my grand-children, Carol Butlin and Louis and Julie Thompson, are quite good amateur artists. Carol, under her married name Cally Mail, did the paintings for the 1984 Wild Life Calendar *Plovers of Southern Africa*. My cousin, Dermot Morgan, a brigadier in India, even exhibited in London.

I was very happy to be on the mountain again and back with my old circle of friends. In 1914 when war broke out, we went to the Lowveld on a last camping trip, and then all the young men I have mentioned above joined up. During the war they kept in contact with us by writing to Mother. I think Kenneth[1] McGaffin's letter, is worth quoting as it gives one an appreciation of the esteem in which these young men held her.

Pretoria Hospital
17 November 1914

Dear Mrs Eastwood,
I have just finished a letter to Miss Eastwood giving her all the news so there's no use repeating it. But, I have been all along awaiting an opportunity to write and thank you most sincerely for all the great kindness we received from Clear Waters.
I wanted to do so when we left but somehow or other, and as usual, I got stuck. I do hope you understand how we appreciate what you have done

---

1   He was a half-brother of Trevor McGaffin from Crown Mount, Magoebaskloof. Kenneth became a teacher and was headmaster of Union High School in Graaff-Reinet from 1935–1944.

and are doing for us. I really cannot put it into words. McMagh and I have many a time agreed that we have never met or were likely to meet people like the Eastwoods. This looks ambiguous and I know you will take it the wrong way – out of sheer cussedness – but it's true and I can't help it or put it otherwise. Please remember me to Mr E. if he has not already left you. Why is he not coming to join our mob? It will be very hard on you when he has gone. I think it splendid of you to let him go. We are having the time of our lives, but it is a very different matter for those at home. I do hope all goes well with you and with everything on Clear Waters. Please remember me to Mrs Everitt and say I made enquiry after the cow and calf. We have not forgotten about those photos,[2] but first Mc was away and now I am stranded in hospital with a touch of dysentry (sic). However am practically fit again and feeling very much ashamed of having left the column, which I hope to rejoin immediately.

Now I must close. Good bye. I shan't forget your offer of a time at Clear Waters when this affair is over. Again I wish you every success and may everything that is yours go well.

Yours very sincerely,

McG.

Mother was regarded as a very special person by friends and acquaintances. The coloured saddler Pieters from Pietersburg, who had helped Mrs Ruthven move her cattle, said of her, "She always leaves you with many good thoughts to think about."

At the outbreak of war the police camp was moved from Haenertsburg, opposite the butcher shop (where later a tennis court was laid out) [at the back of the Post Office] to Wellstead. There were rondavels for the men and barracks with trenches dug around them. They wanted to collect all the women and children from the farms because the men had joined up and the rebels and the Africans could have become a danger to them. Mother would not go, nor would most of the other women either. In the end I do not think that any of the women actually went to live there.

I was kept busy with the usual farm work and my fourteen dogs. Most of them were mine, but I also looked after numerous others belonging to McGaffin, Barney and Harold Phillips and I took on Dewdrop and Warrior for Dr Thompson. I also had Lord Methuen's old pointer, Nell, which he left in my care when he became Governor of Malta. Nell was a wonderful, faithful dog and often on a Sunday I would go riding, taking the pack along

---

2   See adjoining photo.

A drawing of Nell, by Awdry.

with me. One particular Sunday I left early in the morning and went to Spitskop, where I collected some specimens for the Transvaal Museum. On returning home a little late, and when I was feeding the dogs, I did not see Nell. I called and called for her but she did not return. So I said to Mother, "If you hear me getting up early in the morning when it is still dark, don't worry. I'll saddle the horse and go back looking for her where I was yesterday." When I got to the top of Woodbush Hill, there was old Nell on my jersey which had fallen off my saddle.

Usually she never left my side and slept next to my bed, but on one occasion, when Paul Methuen was staying with us she was not with me. Mother asked him in the morning whether he had had a good night. He replied, "Fairly good, but that awful pointer kept jumping over my bed, licking my hand and waking me up!" "Heavens Mr Methuen," I said, "the dog must remember you – she is Nell and she belonged to your father." During his whole stay, Nell never left his side; she was a lovely, intelligent dog.

In November Father could no longer stand taking no part in the war and although he was then in his late forties, he joined up with Hunt's Scouts. Messrs Holyoake, McGaffin, McMagh, young Bob Collins, Geoff Eastwood and Dan Allan[3] belonged to the same unit and because of Father's age the young men called him Oubaas. They were attached to Col. Hendrik Mentz's Column to fight the rebels in the Klerksdorp area and later they fought in South West Africa.[4] He left the running of the farm to me, but this was no hardship as I had learned the job from the bottom and enjoyed the responsibility.

---

3   Daniel Allan, 1864–1939, prospector and farmer.
4   Letters Arthur to Emma 17. and 19.11.1914.

In February 1915, in order to give me a break, Mother allowed me to go with Norah to visit her sister Winnie, who was married to Colonel Davie, and lived at Military Headquarters at Roberts Heights in Pretoria. They had splendid horses and some days I used to ride from early morning till dark. Doc Thompson [Louis Clifford] was also stationed there as he had joined up with the S.A.M.C. and I saw a great deal of him. He and Mr Legat went to much trouble to entertain us, taking us to the zoo, the bioscope and the Transvaal Museum, which I had not seen before. Doc must really have been courting me at the time, but I did not realize it.

I had met him initially a couple of years earlier, when he was camping on our farm while on a fishing trip. I had gone over to Philip Botha's to get some butter, when I saw a man by the river. He asked who I was, and I enquired where he was camped, because he was not on the outspan near the river. "Oh", he said, "I have got my mules and things up on the hill there." When I told Father that there was an Englishman camped on the farm he went to see him and said, "You can't camp here, this is a terrible place; it's the middle of winter and there is no wood nearby for a fire. Come down to the house and take potluck. Stay with us and tomorrow morning you can find out whether there are any fish in the river." So Doc came and put his four mules in the camp with our cattle.

He had an arrangement with Bob Collins, who rented the farms belonging to the estate of the late Mr Naudé, whereby he could fish in the Helpmekaar River and also keep some cattle under Bob Collins's care. The farms of this estate were Rondebult, De Kroon, Boschhoek, Kaalfontein and Groblers Rust, and I only mention this because at one time Doc thought of acquiring them before the Cunliffs bought them in the 1920's. There was some controversy as to the way the late Mr Naudé met his end. His grave is on Groblers Rust and the headstone reads "Hier rus Pieter Johan Wighardt Naudé, gebore 16 April 1861, gesneuwel 30 April 1901, ons sê Here U Wil geskied." This sounds as if he died in some kind of action during the Boer War, but Mrs Dorothea Collins told us that he was stabbed by a black. She herself then went with the bereaved Mrs Naudé and her two little boys to Woodbush Village from where they were taken to the Pietersburg Concentration Camp.

Doc's cattle, looked after by Bob Collins, somehow never did well. One of his letters that I found in my husband's document box reads, *Randfontein 18.11.1913 ... Dear Doc, yours of the ... re bull. I think we had better take him, he is good. Could not get a permit down the hill for oxen on account of losing two little calves three weeks old. I got the packets of seeds, the bulbs are growing with only a few not yet up, so I think they will grow. We had good rain. I have done a good bit of ploughing. Got about a bag of seed mealies or more in the ground and six bags of potatoes. Will put in another bag of mealies. Hope you are keeping well. Kind regards from Mrs and kiddies. Yours sincerely, Bob Collins.*

Doc and Bob were great pals. Whenever they planned a fishing weekend Doc slept on a stretcher in the Collins's goat shed, with his otter hounds next to him.

The permit Bob mentions must have had to do with the dipping of cattle and the sporadic outbreaks of East Coast Fever. His brother, Bill Collins, who had a most beautiful herd of cattle, had lost a few head. He sent some blood smears to Onderstepoort whereupon the government inspector came and shot the whole herd. Compensation only covered half the value of his animals and for a number of years the unfortunate farmer was not even allowed to restock his farm Lunsklip (now called Grey Mist). The origin of the name Lunsklip is derived from the Afrikaans word *luns* i.e. "linchpin" which keeps the wagon wheels attached to the axle. The old road which passed through this farm somewhat to the left of the present one, coming from Clear Waters, had a rock which stuck out and occasionally tore out the *luns* of wagons – hence the name Lunsklip.

Actually the outbreak of East Coast Fever had started in Woodbush on Alwyn Botha's farm near Klipspruit beyond Woodbush Village. There was such an outcry after Bill Collins's loss that the farmers were now obliged to take three blood slides per cow. The farmer kept one and two went to Onderstepoort. When another of Alwyn Botha's cows died he took two slides from the beast and on the third slide he put blood from his own finger, remarking, "These people don't know what they're doing, they think they are clever. Let's see what they have to say if I send one from the cow and one from myself." The Veterinary Research Institute returned the verdict that slides No. 1 & 2 came from a beast that had definitely died from East Coast Fever, but slide No. 3 was from the blood of a baboon in the advanced stages of senile decay! Old Botha said, "Man, daardie mense is slim!"[5]

The brothers Collins had gone through a severe disagreement during the Boer War because Bill had become a National Scout. This was a unit comprised of Boers who had surrendered to the British and joined action on their side. They were also known as Khaki Boers and were very much ostracized by their own people. After the war they sought the patronage of Sir Arthur Lawley whose support resulted in further bitterness. [Bob, although English speaking, fought on the Boer side.]

---

5   Man, those people are clever!

115

At this stage I must relate more about my husband up to the time he came to our farm and I met him. He was born on 24 June 1877 in Bristol, England and was the third child of Dr George Thompson and his wife, Mary Egan. Louis told me that when he was born one of the nurses in the hospital was in love with his father and her name was Louise. As his mother and father already had boy twins, named Clifford Clifford and George Clifford, they wanted a daughter whom they intended to call Louise. Rather sporting, I think! When the baby turned out to be a boy they called him Louis, spelt the French way but [initially] pronounced with the "s" at the end. There were eleven children in all, and the second Christian name of all of them, boys and girls, was Clifford, an idiosyncrasy of the family.[6]

Louis's mother's father was a Dublin surgeon. Mary Egan had two sisters – one Phoebe, who did not marry, and the other Elizabeth. The Egan girls' aunt, their mother's sister, Henrietta Galvin, died as a very old lady in my sister-in-law Dorothy Davy's house and left Louis some pieces of silverware. There is an ink-stand of silver and brass and a big tea urn of Sheffield plate at my son's house, together with a little silver tray for visiting cards which is kept on my walnut table. He brought these heirlooms home in his kitbag after the Second World War. Louis went to the grammar school in Bristol and then he won a scholarship to Epsom College, where the sons of impecunious doctors had the chance of getting a good education. He studied medicine at Guy's Hospital in London, and qualified in 1905. Whilst he was doing his housemanship at the Great Ormond Street Hospital for Children, he contracted polio, which left him lame in his left leg. He was then the dresser for Sir Victor Horseley, the surgeon, who said to him, "Thompson, you will never do your finals in surgery because of this leg." However, Louis did not give up easily and promised that he would do his surgery even if he had to do it from a bathchair, which he did!

His first job, as a ship's doctor, took him to Jamaica, but he was not very keen on travelling, nor on voyaging – at any rate he never told us much about it. After this, when his brother-in-law, Dr Val Watts, who had married his sister Winifred and was practising in Barberton, asked him to do a locum for him while he went to England on leave, Louis eagerly accepted. Val had also mentioned that the Transvaal urgently needed doctors and that there would be no difficulty in finding work and establishing himself there. After applying to the Transvaal Medical Council and paying the

6   Mary Egan's grandmother's maiden name was Phoebe Clifford m.
     Bartholomew Galvin (sic) a solicitor.

sum of 10 pounds, "being the amount of the fee payable for Registration as a Medical Practitioner", he received a certificate dated 16 June 1909 which stated in black and white that "Louis Clifford Thompson, Member of the Royal College of Surgeons of England, 1905, and Licentiate of the Royal College of Physicians of London, 1905, is registered as a Medical Practitioner in accordance with the provisions of Section 18 of the Medical, Dental and Pharmacy Ordinance, 1904, and is hereby authorised to practise as such within the limits of the Transvaal."

In 1911 Louis went back to England and on returning in 1912 he did a six months locum for Dr Perkins, who was the District Surgeon at Mbabane in Swaziland. He managed very well, even to the extent of keeping an old lady as a patient who had nothing much wrong with her, except that she was neurotic and needed to be humoured. He achieved this by giving her a very special bottle of medicine, which had to be kept upside down in a bucket of water! I presume this kept her pretty busy! Another of his patients was a piccanin destined to become King Sobhuza II.[7] He had malaria and my husband pulled him through. The Queen Regent was very grateful, which became very important when shortly afterwards he got into trouble with her tribesmen.

Louis was very keen on trout fishing and, like my father, he loved to stock rivers with trout. The rivers there were so beautiful, and always so clear and cold that, noticing a lovely pool half way up the escarpment, Doc conceived the idea of diverting the river into this lake and out again along its own course. This would entail digging a small canal from the river to the lake and another one out of the lake to rejoin the river. He felt that this would increase the possibility of trout-fishing, but he needed the consent of the Resident Commissioner. Robert Coryndon, later to become Sir Robert, agreed that the project could go ahead and provided the labour by supplying prisoners to do the work.(12) When the Queen Regent found that the lake was no longer an inland lake she said to Sir Robert, "Dr Thompson has spoilt my rain medicine and if my Swazis find out that I cannot make rain any more they will definitely kill the man who did it." Sir Robert, therefore, had no alternative but to ask Louis to move to Bremersdorp, now Manzini, where he would be safer than at Mbabane. Because he had saved the life of the royal prince, the Queen was willing to protect him, but for the rest of his time in Swaziland he always had two policemen at his heels. As soon as Dr Perkins returned, he had to leave and was never allowed to return. It is interesting to note that a few years ago there was an article concerning this

---

7   1899–1982.

incident in *The Star*, trying to trace "the Englishman who spoilt the Queen's rain medicine." I never told them!

The next job that Louis took on was as Resident District Surgeon in Leydsdorp from 1912–1914. Here he had a small hospital with Sister Gatt as his assistant. When war broke out he offered his services, but was advised that, "in the event of the Government deciding to take advantage of your offer you will receive a further communication." Col. Knapp who was chief medical officer with the recruiting staff at Pretoria had told him he would be useless because of his lame leg. Louis replied, "I can walk you off your feet any day. I can't run, that's all, but I'm not running away from anybody – if they catch me they can have me." He was later called up and posted to the S.A.M.C. at Roberts Heights and then to Wynberg in the Cape.

In 1915 he was sent to South West Africa. There was a famine raging in Ovamboland and people on their way to Tsumeb looking for work, died at the water holes. It was Louis's job to visit and check these watering places to ensure that they were not contaminated. The drought of the previous year had broken that summer in 1915, and the troops with whom Louis was travelling towards Grootfontein, where he was going to be stationed, had great difficulty in finding a dry patch for an outspan in all the morass. The main force of the army had already off-saddled their horses and stopped their transport wagons when Louis came along with his ambulance, pulled by six mules. He then encountered Billy Scarth, a fellow officer, who agreed to a place where he could put his little outfit. They erected his bucksail and cradling under it he tried to get some sleep.

Colonel Judd was in charge of the transport and was something of a martinet. All carts had to be parked in one line and the fires started in a proper place with nothing out of order. When he found the ambulance completely out of line, he lost his temper and burst out, "Who the hell put this wagon here?" Louis replied, "Hold on Judd, don't use that sjambok so easily, I am trying to sleep here." However, old Judd replied, "You get the hell out of here; this isn't your place and it's a disgrace." I was told this story later and could well imagine it. Louis was the most disorganised person imaginable. He did not check if his mules were properly fed and, at Roberts Heights I noticed that his horses were badly tended. He was quite hopeless and I already thought then that if ever he got married, his wife would have to take over most things and jolly well do everything for him!

Doc wrote long letters to me and also kept up a correspondence with Mother. In his letter dated 13 April 1915 he talks "apples" to her, mentions that Dr Parnell was with him in Wynberg and that he had heard about heavy rain in Haenertsburg. This is borne out by Mother's letter to Father.

Wednesday Clear Waters Farm
14.4.1915 *Haenertsburg*

My dearest Arthur,

Your two charming letters from Swakopmund were censored. Names of officers and places being erased – so do not risk too much information as they might not send the letters at all. Your description of Swakopmund was most graphic and I am keeping every letter as a sort of diary. Do try and paint some little sketches. They would be invaluable. I have pictured you in my mind, sitting alone (like Napoleon who was a corporal once) in the moonlight watching the stately and dignified breakers rolling in one after the other and oh! how I would love a little sketch of it. Keep it in your mind, dear, and when you have your colours again put it on canvas for me to keep.

Your letters were lovely. I am so pleased you went to the Service on Good Friday and Communion on Easter Sunday. Arthur dear, you are just my style – there is no other like you. How grand the organ must have been! And how you must have enjoyed the music!

Magoeba's Kloof was closed for about two months on account of the torrential rains we had. Capt. Wolff came up on horseback and said he had the utmost difficulty in getting through even the bridle path. The road was quite blocked with great boulders which had piled up the drains and so causing the embankment to wash away. No one can have any idea of the terrible rains and weather we had and it is marvellous that the road was not 50 times worse. Had it not been so very well made and engineered it would have been quite impassable even now. I have never heard anything but the greatest praise for it.

When I tell you Mr Roberts caught a four pound barbell on the road from McKechnie's farm "Orange Grove" to Woodbush, the whole road being one huge river, you will form some idea of the destruction and havoc caused. He had to be dug out of great ponds in the road and I believe Geoff was delayed 5 hrs in the coach helping old Isac to dig the coach out. I did not see Magoeba's Road but all these items will assure Mr Hawker that the damage done to Magoeba's was insignificant compared with other less well constructed roads.[8]

I always reproached myself with never having been to call on Mrs Hawker and felt I deserved the reprimand he gave me and liked him for it. It is nice to meet these people in a strange land.(13)

Much love, dearest, from Emma.

---

8 One page of letter dated 14.4.1915 got lost, notice gap in continuity.

119

Magoebaskloof road, circa 1910, seen from the bottom.
(Louis Changuion collection.)

A few years later looking down the valley.
(Louis Changuion collection.)

Thursday 15.4.15
Here am I still writing to you – have just filled three sheets and enclosed them in different envelopes.

Awdry has just heard that the seed oats have arrived at Palte's so she is going down to fetch them tomorrow. We are paying 24/– per bag and they are very inferior. It is dreadful but we must have them and I feel sure you would have done likewise. Poor old Awdry is looking quite old with all her cares and worries. She is always busy, works very hard, but she is happier busy than otherwise. It is much hard lines having all the boys either away working or down with fever. She got her face and hands very much burnt and very sore dipping the cattle – it has to be done again in a fortnight's time.

We are anchored with a vengeance now and do not even care to go to the Tennis Court. Mrs Lengton has just presented old John with another son! Woke us all up last night at 1.30 a.m. to run for Mrs Woodward – rather trying.

I think Awdry has written to Barney – our one extravagance is stamps and it is worth it, for we live for post nights and if there is not a letter from you it is sad for me.
Very much love and God bless you always
Emma

In connection with the building of the Magoebaskloof road it is worth recording here that there were quite a number of big trees where the Rest Camp is now, and when the men were ordered to cut them down the "boss-boy" came to Mr Hawker and told him that the men refused to do it. Hawker argued with them but they just would not do it, saying that they were God's trees and must be left standing. He therefore decided to ride to Pietersburg to discuss this impasse with the Native Commissioner, Mr C.A. Wheelwright. Mr Wheelwright came back with him to try to break the strike, but to no purpose.

Hawker then decided to alter the course of the road to where it is now. It was thought that perhaps Magoeba was buried there, but we were never able to find the grave. I am told that Mr Menno Klapwijck, the road builder from Tzaneen, when doing some extensions to the camp, found a "burial pot", which is now in his private museum.

By May 1915 I received the following letter from Mr Everitt to the effect that the South West Africa campaign was over:

On the Magoebaskloof Pass, circa 1920–1930.

A drawing by Awdry of her mother, Mrs Eastwood.

My Dear Awdry

I saw a cable at the "Grand" this evening which says that our troops have occupied Windhoek[9] (apparently without any bloodshed), and that troops there were Botha's, Mentz's and Myburgh's. Botha addressing the troops, said that Mentz would be in command of army of occupation. Cable goes on to say that heavy Anti-German rioting took place in Johannesburg this morning and that 51 places of business, belonging to Germans, were looted and destroyed – estimated damage a quarter of a million. The cable also stated that 3 000 whites and 12 000 natives were found in Windhoek.

---

9   11.5.1915.

I know this news will interest you all at "Clear Waters", so I will try and get Mr Shirley to send this letter through for me tomorrow morning.

The Johannesburg rioting is no doubt the result of the "Lusitania"[10] incident, and between you and me I am jolly glad they have smashed up some German property – it will teach the Germans in this country a lesson and perhaps prevent them from smiling at me when they meet me in the street! I only hope English Insurance Companies will not have to pay out on damage done by rioting.

I think the "Lusitania" murder sickened everybody. It did me, and as soon as I heard of it, I wrote to Loeffler,[11] my butcher, (who is a Hun), and told him I didn't want any more meat from him. I am going to have no further dealings with Germans, business or social, till the War is over, and have even sworn off the "Empire" bioscope, which is run by a German Syndicate.

After the "Lusitania" affair, one can't have dealings with these brutes and still retain one's self-respect. I am seriously thinking of smashing Möschke's plate-glass windows for him and should advise you to heave a brick at old Lengton next time you see him!

I wish I was in Windhoek this evening – I can see your father there, talking to his old friend (!) Lock, with a long glass of German beer in his hand, saying, "I can assure you, Lock, this is the pleasantest evening I've spent since I left Woodbush. Bring another bucket of beer, please."

I haven't heard from or of you for ages, and am getting quite anxious. I do hope none of the young Dutchmen of the district have been round "keering" (sic) in your father's absence. If so, they "want shooting." Also tell me what you're doing to improve your mind nowadays – or are farming duties so heavy that you have no time for anything else?

I am going out to Haenertsburg on Saturday week, and shall shoot there on the Sunday and Monday. Any chance of seeing you there? I have missed my annual shoot with your father very much.

Now no more but kindest regards to your mother and Mr and Mrs Sutton, and with best love to yourself, I remain yours affectionately
M.P. Everitt
P.S. I have been teetotaling now for ages, and though good for the Soul, it is most infernally cold for the tummy!

---

10 British liner sunk by German submarine.
11 Hans Loeffler's Pietersburg Cold Storage, founded in 1910, developed into the firm Enterprise Butchery. He died 31.10.1941, aged 65.

A drawing by Awdry of her father, Arthur Eastwood.

In July 1915, when Hunt's Scouts were discharged, Father came back to the farm. He took over the reins again and Mother went on holiday to Johannesburg, where she stayed, as usual, with Aunt Emily while I looked after Father. If I did anything wrong on the farm he made me work on Saturday afternoons instead of going for a ride – like killing locusts in the apple orchard, which I hated. One day he put me on to weeding carrots because, he said, "That's all part of your education – we grow vegetables and who do you think is going to weed them?" He was a hard taskmaster, but he knew his work and I am grateful to him now. I hated gardening and much preferred to work with the animals such as the oxen, the horses and the mules. I'm afraid my attitude led to a big row, the upshot of which was that I said, "I'm not staying another minute, I'm off. Goodbye."

I got on my horse and rode up to see Lady Phillips and there and then asked her to give me a job. I said, "You are keen on land-girls running farms and I have been well taught by my father. I don't care what I have to do as long as you give me food and a roof over my head." She hesitated. "I can't do that Awdry, your father is a friend of mine and I wouldn't dare take his daughter against his wishes. We'll all go down tomorrow and have a talk with him." So we went to Clear Waters the next day, but Daddy was still very angry with me and said, "Do what you like with her, I don't want to see her again." And that is how and why I left home – all because I did not want to weed the garden!

Mother was still in Johannesburg and I implored her to stay and have a good rest there. I assured her that Father had had a good time with Hunt's Scouts and could very well look after himself. However, it was not very long before Daddy and I were pals again, but I had made up my mind to accept Lady Phillips's offer to work on their farm Sterkloop as from 1 August. The farm is just below Schnellskop along the Houtbos River. I lived in two rondavels, and earned 8 pounds a month working under Mr Julius Reinecke. Mainly we planted lucerne and mangelwurzel – a sort of turnip (corrupted from the German *Mangoldwurzel*, a beet of unknown origin). We used this as additional cattle-feed, as the grazing up at Broederstroom was not very good. He was a very pleasant old man, and he taught me a great deal. When the Phillipses gave up their farm, Mr Reinecke worked at the Schlesinger's orange plantation at Letaba. Later, he bought a farm near Duiwelskloof, where he established a nursery.

My working hours at Sterkloop were long, but I got on very well with the manager, Mr Munro. Then Norah [Devenish] came visiting. She had ideas of getting a billet with the Phillipses and we dreamed dreams about having wonderful times together. However, on one occasion we did not feel altogether safe, when three shots were fired and the bullets passed close to the huts.[12] We put out the lights, but did not apparently worry overmuch because, a couple of days later, we gave a little dinner party for Father, Harold Donnelly, Mr Vivian Baragwanath and Mr Reid from The Downs. We walked back from Clear Waters, arriving home at about 1 a.m. Norah thought "it was the greatest sport".[13] We had told the men about the mysterious shots and Vivian Baragwanath presented me with a Baby Browning. I do not think that I ever used it though.

All the time after I left Roberts Heights, letters were going forwards and backwards between Louis and me and, seemingly quite out of the blue, there arrived one in which he proposed to me. It appeared as if he was jolted into action after he had a letter from me in which I told him of the Rev. Steer's suggestion to take me and Mother to the Victoria Falls after the war. I had become very fond of Louis and loved his long missives and parcels, many containing books. Although the proposal came as a great surprise, I knew immediately that I would accept him. To my utter dismay, Mother was not as enthusiastic as I was.[14] Perhaps she doubted my feelings for Doc.

---

12 Letter Awdry to Mother 27.8.1915.

13 Letter Norah to Mrs Eastwood 30.8.1915.

14 Letter Awdry to Mother 28.8.1915.

Norah had seen it coming all along, and had written to Mother somewhat disparagingly, "Doc is a hopeless crock." She would have loved me to marry her brother Graham.

Another friend who did not want me to marry just then was Kathleen Morris. Her father had some position in Pietersburg but her mother had died and she and her sister lived for a short time with Mrs Evans in Captain Leach's old house on Cooyong. We had planned that she would buy the farm Wegraakbos, I would run it, and perhaps become a partner after I had made a success of the farming operations. Naturally, when I got engaged to Louis the "deal" was off. Later, whilst on a boat trip to England, she met a parson, Vernon Ford, and she wrote to me, "Just to spite you I'll marry him – I will live in England and you can buy the farm on your own." And that is exactly what happened.

Dr Louis Clifford Thompson, 1916.

Picture of Awdry in SWA (today Namibia) with the rifle of Davies, 1916.

VIII Early Married Life

Louis asked me whether I wanted to go overseas or have a farm for a wedding present. I did not hesitate in choosing the farm. At first we thought of buying Nieshoutfontein from Harvey and Storey, but the sale fell through. Then Wegraakbos came on the market again when Louis's friend, Parker, who had owned it for a few months, went back to England. The Woodbush climate did not agree with his tubercular hip. He still owed most of the sale price to Percy Kent, so Louis took over his debt. Louis sold his shares in Portland Cement and paid 320 pounds for the 207 morgen farm. The deed of transfer came through only in 1921.

For the rest of 1915 I kept on working at Sterkloop, and even became godmother to Sarah Munro, the manager's baby who, according to the baptismal certificate, was born on 17 July 1915. The baby was baptised at Broederstroom on 3 October 1915 by the Rev. Charles Steer. The other godparents were Norah Charlotte Devenish and Edward August Kietzmann. Thus my working career, hardly started, came to an early end and Lady Phillips wished me well for the future, hoping "that Dr Thompson would be worthy of me!"

I thought this a very strange remark as he was such a cultured, kind person, the picture of an English gentleman. When I asked him one day how he came to choose "a *nagapie* out of the bush" although he had "the pick of all those intelligent girls in Europe", he replied that he had looked for a companion and not a demanding town girl.

We were married on 25 January 1916 on a pouring wet day. Mr Steer, who had joined up, wrote to Mother, "I am sorry not to be able to perform the wedding, but that will not prevent my hoping and praying most earnestly for God's blessing on the union." Louis had hired a car from Zeederbergs (they were running cars then as well as coaches) to collect the minister, Mr Lewis in Pietersburg, but they could not cross the Broederstroom at the drift at Clear Waters. They therefore had to go round via the Helpmekaar River, where the Magoebaskloof Hotel stands today, and consequently Mr Lewis was late. We did not think that he would be able to make it, and Louis suggested that we go fishing and if the car came Father could send out a piccanin to fetch us. Eventually the piccanin arrived and said that the motorcar had come.

We quickly went home where Mother got out of her bed – she was always ill and very delicate – while I changed into a skirt, shirt and coat, and that was my wedding-dress. The chauffeur and my parents acted as witnesses. The whole ceremony took only about five minutes and after that we had tea and sandwiches.

In my letter dated 26.1.1916 on some notepaper headed "Carlton Hotel, South Africa Limited" and addressed to "Darling old Mother and Daddy", I told them how we had got to Pietersburg at twenty minutes to seven, just fixed up our luggage and had gone straight to the Wheelwrights who gave us dinner before the train left for Johannesburg. Louis had forgotten to book seats for us; however the parson, Mr West, made the necessary arrangements. There were many friends to see us off, but fortunately Mrs Wheelwright would not allow them to throw streamers at us.

In Johannesburg we had a visit from Bertie and Ethel Solomon and Phyllis Eastwood. They came for tea only, but in the evening Bertie and Ethel returned for dinner and brought with them a friend named Ted Collins. When he heard that Louis had a month's leave and that we were going to The Bungalow Hotel near Nottingham Road [in Natal], he offered us his farm Rathmines nearby. He told us that he had an Indian couple looking after it, and that we would find everything we needed there, including bedding. Naturally, we jumped at the idea as a good stretch of the Umgeni River flowed through the farm for us to fish, and in addition, by staying there, we would have no trouble keeping my little dog Wanda. On arrival at Nottingham Road we left my trunk at the station and simply took my suitcase and Louis's two kitbags to the farm.

The house at Rathmines was comfortable, although there were rats running around in the roof and a "dear little bat" was hanging from the ceiling in our bedroom.[1] The promised linen had been taken by Ted's brother to Durban and we had to make do with Louis's two blankets until the neighbours lent us some sheets. These neighbours were named McKenzie and turned out to be "awfully nice people with a gorgeous farm and a lovely paddock with springbok, eland and blesbuck". We had a couple of meals with them and Sir Duncan[2] rode all over the farm with us showing us his South Devon cattle. He had been a transport rider during the early days in Barberton, Johannesburg and also in Rhodesia. In the second Anglo-Boer War he served with the Natal forces and he also took part in the South West African campaign of 1914–1915.

---

1   Letter Awdry to Mother 3.2.1916.
2   Duncan McKenzie, 1859–1932.

The countryside was very much like Haenertsburg, with mists and rain, but we had a wonderful time and were awfully happy. [She wrote to her mother:] *When I was at home I had a ripping (sic) life and never thought it was possible to be happier, and I never wanted to change it, but really!! I think I am the luckiest girl I have ever heard of. Don't you think so? Louis is so sweet to me and most frightfully unselfish. I do love him.*[3]

Our honeymoon ended on 9 February when we took the train via Ladysmith, De Aar and Upington to Windhoek and then on to Grootfontein. We managed to miss every connection and ended up going by goods train; it took us three weeks to reach Otavi from where we travelled the last lap to Grootfontein by a mule-drawn wagon. When I finally retrieved my big leather trunk into which had been packed my whole trousseau, I found it completely empty except for the case of a set of brushes, Louis's wedding present from the Wolffs! My grandmother in England had made a lovely point-lace tablecloth for her first grandchild to be married and I was extremely sad at its loss. I was glad to have kept with me my Henry Heath hat and a pair of Sparks boots. They had been given to me by Sadie Butler, the daughter of Jimmy Butler who built the Selati Railway with George Pauling.

We lived in the house of the German veterinary surgeon who had left the country. There was laboratory equipment of all kinds and he had a number of brass trays and copper kettles, the latter were very limed up and the spouts did not work. Col. Scarth said, "Take what you want or chuck them out", but we sent them home together with a table we bought from a German lady.

I spent a fair amount of time swimming because it was so very hot.

Grootfontein has an eye [fountain]. Before we arrived the Germans had made the English POW's dig a swimming pool into the limestone and little cabins to change in.

Meeting Louis's friends of the South African Mounted Rifles was great fun. One of them was Sergeant C.G. Davies[4] whom Louis had introduced to H. Boyd Horsbrugh. This led to Davies illustrating Horsbrugh's book, *The Game Birds and Waterfowl of South Africa* (1912). [Obviously Louis must have introduced them at a much earlier occasion.] The four volumes according to an account I found in my husband's papers, dated 16 July 1913, from Witherby and Company, 326 High Holborn, London, cost 4 pounds 17 shillings and 9 pence. No doubt they fetch much more than that nowadays.

---

3 Letter Awdry to Mother 6.2.1916.
4 1875–1920.

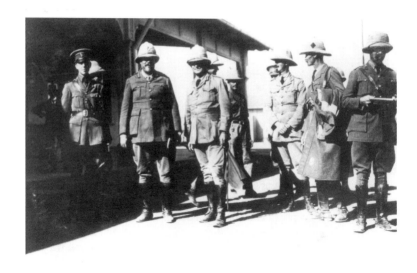

South African troops in South West during the invasion, 1914–1918.
Gen. Louis Botha second from the left.
(Louis Changuion collection.)

A.K. Eastwood (second from left) on military service during the First World War.

Claude Davies, besides being a soldier, was a good ornithologist and artist. One day, Louis, Davies and I went by mule cart into the flats below the village. As we reached some koppies, we saw a bird skim over a rock and Louis said, "Davies, supposing that is a Hartlaub francolin – go and see." At that moment the bird flew up again on to the rock and Davies shot it. He thought he had not killed it properly, so he gave me his collectors' rifle to hold and ran round the other side of the rock where he found the dead bird. Hartlaub's francolin, named after a German who lived in South West Africa, is very rare and here Davies got his chance to paint it exactly as it was. He always carried a paintbrush and paint in his pocket. He marked the colour of the francolin's eyes, its beak and legs. Every scale on those feet is correct; he counted every single one and painted it with a camel-hair brush on the spot, because all colours change very soon after the bird is dead. I said, "You'd better hurry up, because that's all we have for dinner tonight." Before we left my husband took a photo of me holding the gun and I still have it in my old album. Claude Gibney Davies was married that August 1916 to a Miss Aileen Singleton Finch and he added her surname to his. When [in the 1970's] Dr Alan Kemp from the Transvaal Museum prepared *The Bird Paintings of C.G. Finch-Davies*,[5] he interviewed me several times. Then one day last December [1984], a stranger came to our house and told me that his name was Finch-Davies. He had been brought out by the publishers from England and he was delighted to hear my old stories about his father, who had died suddenly in 1920. None of his children really knew him.

While we were in South West Africa my husband received a business letter from Lord Walter Rothschild[6] asking him to collect certain birds, particularly larks and warblers, for his private museum at his Christopher Wren-house in Tring. Lord Rothschild is famous for assembling the biggest collection of natural history specimens ever made by one man. He approached travellers, medical men or men serving in the army. In our case he most probably got to know about us from R. Ogilvie-Grant from the British Museum. Mr Legat had brought him [Ogilvie-Grant] to our house and he taught me to skin birds.

As soon as the bird is dead you take careful measurements from the tip of the beak, over the skull, down the neck, to the end of the Pope's nose, without stretching, and also around its breast. To skin the bird needs some dexterity and takes about fourteen minutes. You must not prick the eyes

---

5   Winchester Press, 1984.
6   1868–1937.

because the liquid spoils the feathers. To preserve the skin and wing bones you then have to brush on arsenical soap, resembling brown soft-soap.

We sent three SAGI-boxes[7] full of skins to Tring. The postage was paid at the receiving end but we did not accept any payment for ourselves. Lord Rothschild wrote such nice appreciative letters. He remarked on how well the birds were skinned and packed and that he would be most grateful for a pair of African ostriches – but that was beyond me!

In May 1916 I had a miscarriage[8] and was very depressed about it. After I was strong again, we went on several "treks" as both of us loved camping out and enjoyed the beautiful scenery with its profusion of birds and game. Norah would have loved to visit us, but Mother advised against it. On Monday, 14.8.1916 she wrote to her:

I think it would be unwise of you to go to Awdry just yet. I know Awdry often feels terribly lonely and longs for you, as she has not one woman friend up there. She loves you as her very best and truest girlfriend, but I have always thought it a mistake to go to a newly married couple, till they have quite settled down to such other ways. You see Norah! I do not know Louis so very well. I love and admire what I do know of him, and feel sure he will make Awdry happy – but she is a most difficult girl to manage, as you know, and I should think it wise to let them learn to know each other thoroughly before going to them.

By August I was expecting again and I would have had my baby in SWA but the Ovambos were restless. They used to steal cattle from the Portuguese beyond the Kunene River, and the South African Mounted Rifles under Major Fairly tried to prevent this. Louis put me on the train in Windhoek. I met Mother at some railway junction further south and we went together to Durban where we spent a couple of months in a rented flat. We then meant to go to the farm, but, while staying over at Wakkerstroom with Aunt Minnie and Uncle Carl Rose I became ill. Louis did not want me to be far from a doctor so Aunt Emily Solomon took me in and I spent the months before my confinement with her, Bertie and Ethel. Louis, in the meantime had to go back to Ovamboland.

At this time in Ovamboland there was a man called Brodkos, a Norwegian, who was running arms to Chief Mandume's people. A detachment

---

7 S.A. Garrison Institute supplied provisions to the Army; boxes appr. 40 x 20 x 30 cm.

8 Letter Awdry and Louis to Mother 20.5.1916.

under Colonel Billy Scarth was discussing their next stratagem under some enormous fig and marula trees, when suddenly there were shots and Louis's horse and that of Capt. Chisholm were shot and killed under them. There were blacks hiding up in the trees and down they came, while a wave of others was rushing towards the South African troops. By chance they had a machine-gun and they caught Mandume right across the chest. That was the end of the uprising. I had a photograph of Mandume lying on the ground but this has now been mislaid.

I also had several curios, like a skirt of ostrich shell beads which Charles Manning presented to me. He had been Native Commissioner in Pietersburg for a time and later became the first Administrator of Ovamboland, stationed at Ondangwa, after the war. He had to organise food supplies to the starving Ovambos and was given all kinds of royal regalia by the Queen Mother as a token of gratitude. He in turn offered many of these memorabilia to the Windhoek Museum, though he regarded them as junk and had no feeling for their intrinsic ethnological value. He lived very primitively in a little square grass hut which was still there when I passed through about 35 years later with my son Clifford and his wife, Eva, on our way to Angola.

Life in Johannesburg was not boring. My cousins Bertie and Ethel were dancers and performed at the Empire. I believe they were good, but I never saw them on stage. They received good salaries, but this sort of life did not appeal to me. Both cousins also performed in London and Bertie played the leading part in the silent film *Lorna Doone*[9] which was shot in Devonshire. Bertie had a lovely personality. She later married Eric Bell who was an electrical engineer with the well-known Inn of Reunert and Lenz. Ethel was quite different. She once said to me, when I was sewing for my baby, "If I have a baby I will smother it in lace and ribbons." Appropriately she married the rich Glenham Davis who ran a stevedoring business in Durban. His father was T.B.F. Davis who, in memory of his fallen son [Howard], built the Howard Memorial College which houses the Faculty of Engineering of the University of Natal on the Berea in Durban. As an additional gift to the nation, he bought the British cruiser *Thames*. Refitted and rebuilt in Simonstown and renamed *General Botha*, she served from 1921 as a training ship for Deck Officers in the merchant marine.[10]

---

9   Book by R.D. Blackmore.
10 Now renamed *Howard Davis*, serving as a naval training ship for boys and girls.

My baby, Sheila Clifford Thompson, was born in the Colwyn Nursing Home, 47 Kaptyn Street, Johannesburg, on 23 April 1917. We had expected a little Louis, but I wrote to Mother: "I have quite forgiven her, she is fearfully plain, the image of Louis, with a huge chin and turned-up nose, and very fat. She weighed seven and three-quarter pounds and is the biggest baby in the home." Her godmothers were Bertie Solomon and Norah Devenish and Mr Legat was her godfather. We first wanted to call her Norah, but Louis's brother, James, in Brazil had a daughter by that name, so Louis chose the Irish name of Sheila – he was three-quarters Irish himself. The Home was run by Sister Elizabeth Kirtley and Sister Simon who was a Welsh woman from Colwyn Bay [Wales]. They were wonderfully dedicated women and whenever I came to have another baby they gave me a real holiday. Dr Mudd, a doctor friend of Louis's, had delivered me.

Another friend, Dr H. Temple Mursell and his wife, asked me where I was going before returning to my husband. I had thought of spending a couple of weeks at the Orange Grove Hotel, where Lady Coryndon was staying with her children and a nanny, but Mrs Temple Mursell would not hear of it. She said, "No nanny is going to teach you how to look after your own baby. It's ridiculous to go to a hotel. You are going to stay with us." As I wanted to make things as easy as possible in a strange household, I thought I would get a Chinese laundry recommended by the Coryndons' nanny to do the washing, but again I was put right: "With the laundry you get all sorts of diseases. What is wrong with you? Why can't you wash? You'll do all the baby's washing yourself, my girl." She was a woman who loved organising others and had no children of her own. We lost contact with them and were only reminded of them years later, when my husband bought Mrs Heckford's book, *A Lady Trader in the Transvaal*, from the antiquarian bookseller Heffer in London. This turned out to be a copy signed by the previous owner H. Temple Mursell. Isn't that a coincidence?

At last, at the end of May, I was well enough to travel with Louis and the baby up to Mother. I was very excited to go back to the dear old berg again. Mrs Mursell has given baby the loveliest little dress, most beautifully smocked.[11] We stayed on the farm for four weeks before Louis had to report to Roberts Heights in Pretoria.[12] The next day I wrote to Mother: *Do let me know how you are, I just hated leaving you yesterday! I cannot believe that it was only yesterday that we ended this happiest month of my life. I was so homesick when I left, but I am glad I came down with Louis;*

---

11 Letter Awdry to Mother 26.5.1917.
12 Letter Awdry to Mother 30.6.1917.

it is so much easier with a man. Louis has gone up to Roberts Heights to see our house, and we have to hire furniture. We will be settled tonight, more or less. I rather dread The Heights, but we met General Berrangé this morning and he said, 'You will have a lovely time up here. They have dances and parties nearly every night'. Do you know that they have 'Unie Gebouw' on the front of the trams and 'Union Buildings' on the back, and 'Spoorweg/Station'? The Boerness of this dorp is too awful. Nowadays [1980's] I find this kind of derogatory remark quite unacceptable but it was typical of English attitudes and my upbringing.

I never took to the social life at Roberts Heights and was very happy to be with Louis in our own home. Believe it or not, all my children slept for the first few months of their lives in a string cradle which Queen Victoria had used for her babies. I got it from Mrs Everitt, whose father, Mr Pigott, had received it as a memento from Albert, the Prince Consort. Mrs Everitt had used it for her little Christal, but when the child died she was too superstitious to use it for her second daughter. The netting was all perished but Father knew how to net and he repaired it. It is still in the attic at our farm Wegraakbos. The frame is of iron, and at the head there is a long rod for the canopy. It is dreadful to look at now, but originally it was probably quite grand, covered with satin and lace.[13] It is junk now, but I was reminded of it the other day when I read Anthony Burgess, *On Going to Bed* where he says, "The division between lowly and high born children was marked by the use of wood for the cradles of the first and metal for the latter." Mrs Everitt also gave me a few other curios. There is a fishing rod which had belonged to Charles Kingsley and the whip that was used by the driver of the Royal Couple at their coronation, together with the Indian howdah mats that I mentioned earlier.

The Great War was raging in Europe and was always at the back of our minds. Grandmother Eastwood wrote long letters from Seaford, and one day we received the sad news that my cousin Harold, Uncle William and Aunt Edie's son, had fallen in the East African campaign in 1917. Harold had been born with a cleft palate and had been taken to England for an operation, which was performed by Sir Arbuthnot Lane. He was actually brought up by my Aunt Emily Eastwood, who lived with Grannie. When he came back to South Africa as a teenager he showed a great deal of pluck, but was very depressed at times. He was killed at the age of 19. Another casualty which grieved us was the loss of Moseped, one of our African workers. He had joined the Native Labour Contingent and was sent to

---

13 Letter Mrs Everitt to Mother 25.3.1917.

France on the troopship *Mendi* which sank after a collision with the *SS Darro* south of the Isle of Wight in February 1917. Our driver, Moses, came to me the other day and asked me to name a new baby of his, a boy, and I told him about his mother's uncle Moseped, and suggested that he should call the boy after him. At the time I felt it would be better if the blacks could be taught more of their own history rather than about the Greeks and Romans.

My husband, in his capacity as Medical Officer, was sent to various towns in short succession. I sometimes lived at home, but also spent some time in Pietermaritzburg and East London. Louis was a very successful gambler and used to win such large sums of money from the other doctors that all the other wives looked down their noses at me! It came to the point where I threatened him with "going home to Mother". He also played a good game of bridge, but thought that the only people worth playing with were the Jews because they were really good. We liked the Jewish people; they were always so kind to us.[14]

When Louis was transferred to East London and I was going to join him, Mrs Betton recommended to me a little maid called Martha, and because I was pregnant again, I could take her into my compartment. This was in October 1918, and I remember that the train stopped somewhere for hours, because the fireman and engine-driver and guard were down with influenza. The steward was the only one on his feet. I was allowed to go to the kitchen to cook the baby's food. It was quite an experience. When I got to East London in the morning I found that my husband had received a telegram saying that he had to go to Potchefstroom at once as they had so many patients down with 'flu. He left in the evening and arranged for Dr Nangel to look after me.

I was alone in that rented house near the cemetery and I frequently sat on its tiny stoep, knitting. Sometimes I used to see trolleys going past piled up with coffins. I did not know a soul there, except a very kind old lady, who also lived near the cemetery, and often came to visit and talk to me. Dr Nangel had the house next to the one that we had rented, and he arranged a midwife for me, as there was no Maternity Hospital in East London. My bad luck was that the midwife was seconded to another place, and Dr Nangel found a dreadful old woman to replace her. Fortunately Louis came home two days before the birth, on 6 December 1918, but I had a terrible time because Diana, nicknamed Tiny, was such a big baby. I remember I was still in bed, and I think Tiny was only three or four days old, when this

14 Letter Awdry to Mother 11.2.1918.

Market Street Pietersburg looking south, circa 1925. The tall clock tower is that of the Irish house, today housing the Pietersburg Museum. The smaller tower just left of it is that of the old NG church, today housing the Hugh Exton Museum.
(Louis Changuion collection.)

Awdry saying goodbye to her husband setting off on a vaccination trip to the Lowveld in 1923.

woman arrived one morning with a bucket which she dumped in the corner of my bedroom and then went off to the kitchen. I heard a scratching noise coming from the bucket and then an enormous crab, the size of a big plate, climbed out and walked along the floor. If there is one thing that I am terrified of it is a crab. I pulled up all the bedclothes and I really cannot tell you how frightened I was. I suppose the woman had caught the crab before coming in that morning.

When I was well enough to travel, I went home to Haenertsburg. Mr Allison from Boyne [next to Moria, the black Zionist Church] ran the post from Pietersburg in a small motorcar each Monday, Wednesday and Friday and he gave me a lift from the station to Veekraal Post Office. There I saw old Moosa who ran the shop on the farm which belonged to Reg Thompson's parents (bought in 1918). From Veekraal Martha and I walked to Clear Waters. I carried my new baby and Martha had Box [the eldest child, Sheila] on her back. Incidentally, Box got her nickname from "scoff-box" – she always loved eating. A couple of days later, when I had some shopping to do, I was shocked to find old Moosa lying prostrate and ill on the counter and his wife and daughter dead on the floor. The influenza epidemic had struck here too!

As far as I can remember, the first motorcar in Pietersburg belonged to Percy G. Louw. When he came to Haenertsburg in his car, about 1912, it really was a great occasion. On his way back home down Grobler's Hill, the brakes failed, but fortunately for him at the bottom he ran into a bank and stopped. Grobler's Hill was a hazard that you had to accept in the rainy season. Percy was known as quite a character around here. As a young man he had worked with John Buchan as his clerk but later, according to a photo taken in 1905 by Pietersburg's famous photographer, Hugh Exton,[15] he advertised above the entrance of his business premises, "Transport Agent, Mining, Forwarding, General Agent".

After the war, my husband was appointed District Surgeon at Tzaneen, and he held the post for five years. I lived on our farm Wegraakbos which he renamed Otterholt, and he used to come up once a fortnight. Louis's district stretched from Boyne to Komatipoort and from Mafefe's Location to Soekmekaar and Leydsdorp. To get to Chief Mafefe, he used a little cart drawn by two oxen. The scene is beautifully captured in a photograph

---

15 Hugh Exton 1864–1955, had a photographic studio in Pietersburg from 1893–1945. The old NG-Kerk in Market Street next to the new City Hall houses the Hugh Exton Museum since 1986. Built by T.F. Vinnicombe, opened 18 October 1890.

where I am saying goodbye to him at Clear Waters. He often travelled with the Sub-Native Commissioner of Haenertsburg, Mr Harley Dale Maurice Stanford.[16] The Commissioner would hold court and collect the Native taxes, whilst the District Surgeon vaccinated the Africans against smallpox. Mr Stanford had been the Sub-Native Commissioner in the Pilansberg District of Rustenburg from 1902 to 1910, and he was then transferred to Haenertsburg in January 1911 to act in the same capacity. At that time Haenertsburg included the larger part of the Letaba District.

Mr Stanford held this position until 1924, when he retired and settled on his farm, Good Hope. The Africans called him "Mtabaleni", "The One That Must be Beseeched". His other appellation was "The Lion That Never Misses" because he was a keen big game hunter. My husband always called him "The Lion" after he had been severely snubbed by Mr Stanford on one of their trips. They had passed many Africans on the road and Louis had answered their greeting of "Morena" with the raising of his hand in a friendly wave. Stanford said, "You mustn't do that! I am the most important man here and I must return their salutes." However, the men became good friends on their joint tours and often went fishing together.

When Tiny was six months old I accompanied my husband to the Lowveld and we stayed at Jimmy Porter's Hotel in Leydsdorp. He also owned the store which was manned by Mr McCusker, a degenerate old josser. I was very fussy about the milk that my babies drank, because of the high incidence of enteritis, and so got his permission to milk a cow myself. His receptionist and housekeeper, Mrs Carol, said, "What's all this trouble about the milk? I've had six children and three are alive!" That didn't encourage me at all. I went regularly to the open kraal to milk the cow myself, and I kept a little basin with milk in it in my room to give to Tiny.

Mrs Carol was a real battle-axe; if the guests didn't get up early enough for her "boys" to clean the rooms she would make them get up. Jimmy (James Frederick Watson) Porter had been nursed by my husband, when he contracted blackwater fever. In order to show his gratitude, Porter put 100 pounds into Louis's bank account in Pietersburg. Louis could not accept the gift. At the time, Jimmy was starting a farm and was going in for thoroughbred cattle and the Aberdeen Angus breed that was in great demand. Louis bought him a pedigree bull which actually cost more than the 100 pounds. It came by train to Gravelotte and from there it walked. By then the once thriving gold mining town of Leydsdorp had been left high and dry because the railway [built in 1912] did not pass through it.

---

16 2.7.1871 – 8.1.1941.

Harley Stanford on one of his hunting trips in the Lowveld with a lion he had shot.
(André Strever collection.)

As a rule we were a healthy family, but I remember when my husband contracted what was called relapsing fever. This was much worse than malaria. Louis had been to do vaccinations at Mafefe's Location, and there had been a violent thunderstorm. He was offered the guest hut, and having to sleep on the floor, he put his blankets on the mat. A tampan, which is not a tick (generally found in poultry houses), must have bitten him. Tampans hide in cracks and come out at night. Louis would be well for one or two days, then he would go down with a temperature of 104°F. Silas Maldea, the witch-doctor who lived on Waterval, and to whom Louis often referred as his colleague, promised that he could help him. Louis would have to order him (Silas) to go back to Mafefe's and draw some blood from the tampans there. He would then inoculate Doc with the "serum"; however, Louis wouldn't hear of it because he feared to get blood poisoning. I myself would have tried this "progressive" cure.

Eventually he went to Pietersburg, where Dr P.A. Green and Dr Johnston treated him for malaria in Pietersburg Hospital for two weeks. When this

142

did not help, Louis consulted Dr A.J. Orenstein in Johannesburg, who diagnosed his condition as relapsing fever. During the First World War Dr Orenstein had been Chief of the South African Medical Corps, and his orders were that any soldiers arriving at a deserted village must on no account take refuge there, but must rather burn it down. This sickness had caused much trouble in the army – the only cure then was a course of injections of 606, which was usually given for venereal diseases. After a course of these, Louis was all right.

The furthest point in Louis's travels relating to his job was Komatipoort. He used to phone the stationmaster to find out whether there were any sick people needing his attention. If there were no patients, he often went up to see J. Stevenson-Hamilton in the Game Reserve for a day or two, and they would have a good chat. Louis was surprised to find that all he was offered for lunch or supper in the way of meat was tinned bully beef. His host did not eat venison. Stevenson-Hamilton suggested once that Louis and I should accompany him on one of his annual complete inspection trips through the Game Reserve, together with pack donkeys and police "boys". Nothing came of it as I couldn't leave my children but I did meet him and his wife, Hilda, sometime in the forties. She was a wonderful artist and showed me a dinner service from the Doulton Pottery Works, which she had ordered. It was unglazed and she had started to paint different animals on every piece. There was a giraffe eating from a bush, warthogs having a bath in the mud, or some impala crossing the road.

It was nearly finished when her son, Jeremy, got malaria. A great friend of Hilda's, a nurse from Pretoria, Ruth Baber, fetched him from Skukuza and later Hilda was called to Pretoria when he became really seriously ill. While she was away, members of the Parks Board, like old Knobel, arrived and were staying with Stevenson-Hamilton. The cook was asked to produce something out of the ordinary and, realising that the guests were "something special", he took out all the dinner plates Hilda had painted and served dinner on them. Then, when he washed them, all the paintings were washed off! One can imagine how upset Hilda was when she returned home.

Clifford, our son, was a baby at this time. He was born in Johannesburg on 29 February 1920 and was baptised by Bishop Neville Pretor. His godparents were Mr and Mrs H.P. Wolff and Mr Stanford. His Sesotho name is M'Pateng, "the little man with the big chest" – the same as my father's – because it is the custom of the Africans around here to call the first son of the eldest daughter after the grandfather. As it turned out there developed a strong physical resemblance between them and Clifford moves and talks

A painting by Alida Stevenson-Hamilton, which she gave to Awdry.

just as Father did. Years later, when we lived in Messina, our friend Lucille Kehew, said, "I can't remember the name M'Pateng. I'll call him 'Potty'," and that name stuck. However when I send a message to Clifford with an African I always refer to him as M'Pateng.

My husband's salary was never more than 60 pounds a month. In the early days he got 36 pounds, sixpence a mile for travelling, and free transport on the railways. During the week he lived in the Lowveld but he hated its heat. However, when the Tzaneen Estate was cut up into small farms of about 120 morgen each, he bought one next to Roger Mills, a former sergeant in the Police. Returned soldiers from the First World War were encouraged to buy these farms because the Government wanted the area settled. Louis employed a manager, Jackie Mahon, who built a splendid big house there, which is still in existence today. One winter I came to stay with him for a few months.

After living, for a change, in a decent house, I got angry when I had to make do with the dilapidated old building that had belonged to Bezuidenhout, a previous owner of Wegraakbos. It had only two rooms and a kitchen built of big unburned Kimberley bricks – quite useless in this climate – and it was falling down anyway. I said to Louis, "Why must you have a good house which you hardly ever live in, whilst I, with three children, have to live in this dreadful place?" He tried to defend himself by saying, "You can always come down in the winter while there are no farming activities," but I just got more and more furious, and pushed down the outside wall. Now he *had* to build a new house. The old one was down where the silo is, above the mud dam from which we got our water.

I built the new house higher up with a beautiful view towards the Iron Crown and the Wolkberg. There was no one else to build it, so I did it myself. Two "boys" did the quarrying, I brought the stones by sleigh to the site, and Kleinbooi helped with the mud. I put all the stones together with my own hands and it took me six months to do the outside and the middle wall inside. The other dividing walls were built later on with bricks. Everybody can see how badly it was done. The roof has two gables and down the middle there is a gutter to catch water from the roof. This gutter which I had put in was really too small, and when it rained hard it overflowed.

All this happened in 1922 when the miners staged a strike[17] on the Rand and General Smuts had the unrest quelled by the army. To get imprisoned ringleaders out of the way they were put into a camp near the Debegeni Falls. (Debegeni should really read Dibodiba, which means "The Pools" in Sesotho.) These men had nothing to do down here, so it was decided that they should be made to build a road up the mountain to where it would link up with the Veekraal Road, not far from the top of Magoebaskloof. My husband was the Medical Officer who had to look after them. One day he asked some of these miners if there was anyone amongst them who knew how to solder and put in a gutter properly. [More than one accepted to do the job.] One of them said to him, "Doctor, who the hell built this damned house? He must have been drunk all the time that he built it!" My husband replied, "You mustn't say that; my wife built it and she is just not a builder."

During the building the children and I lived with Mother. I used to get up at 4 o'clock in the morning and would walk to Otterholt [Wegraakbosch]. There I had my breakfast and did my work, and I walked back in the evening. All the furniture we had I stored under the wattle trees on the lower drive to the old house; it stood there for six months with a bucksail over it. Those Jimmy Smith chairs have been roughly treated and yet they still have the original riempies. When we realized I had built the house too near the border, we bought a piece of land of about 16 morgen from Koos Brummer's farm, Goedvertrouwen. Later on Brummer wanted to move behind the Zoutpansberg and asked Louis whether he wouldn't like to buy the whole

---

17 The "Rand Revolt" began in December 1921 and lasted until March 1922.

farm. We bought another 72 morgen of which we sold 24 morgen to Col. Wolff when he wanted to retire. Louis didn't really want to sell this land, but I persuaded him to do so as the Wolffs were friends of my mother.

I have mentioned earlier in my story that Capt. Philip Wolff had come out during the Boer War and during the First World War he was in charge of the Africans in France who did camp duty. They called him "Magumeledi" or "Mastulela" – "The Quiet One". He and his wife, May, both came from London. She was very humorous, and she called their place Cheerio Halt. Another part of Goedvertrouwen, now called Peasant's Perch, changed hands from Brummer to Roodhuizen, then to Savage and finally to Davidson. Field-Cornet Roodhuizen, an old Hollander, had been stationed in Duiwelskloof, but on retiring, came to live on his little farm in a brick house with a thatched roof.

One hot day in 1923 or 1924, locusts appeared in such a big swarm that Roodhuizens' neighbour, Schalk van der Merwe, on Kromdraai, set the grass alight around his wheatfield to protect it from the locusts. At the time the Roodhuizens were visiting their son in the Lowveld I, with my husband and Uncle William Eastwood, was on our way to see the Bettons. When we arrived at the top of the hill we saw the smoke and I noticed a piece of bracken catch alight and settle on the Roodhuizens' thatched roof. Before we could get there to save their possessions the house was burned down. We went home quickly and beat this fire along our boundary until dark. In the meantime, the locusts had come and settled on our apple trees. The next day there was a misty rain and they could not fly away. They just sat there for two days and ate until the sun came out again. The apple trees were about eight years old, nearly full-bearing. They were completely ruined and I had to prune them very severely.

Schalk van der Merwe [grandfather of the two present Schalk van der Merwes] was an honest man and a good farmer, so there was no question of his denying his guilt. He just came and rebuilt and refurnished the whole house at his own expense. This nearly ruined him, especially as he replaced the thatch with an iron roof. Our own roof had been thatched by Reuter's "boys" from Medingen, but after this fire I did not rest until we also had an iron roof. Thatch may look better, but you only want to live under it, not look at it! Every night in wintertime I used to get up and have a look round to see whether or not there were any fires in the offing. Nowadays, of course, people are so conscious about fire hazards in their plantations that they have watch towers on the hills and proper fire-fighting equipment. I remember Constantine Fauconnier's sheep running around with their wool on fire. Many people planted wattle strips around their boundaries. This

Picnic at the Debegeni Falls.
(Louis Changuion collection.)

Tea party at Clear Waters, 1923. Seated: Uncle William Eastwood, Awdry, Mother with Tiny, Norah Devenish. On the grass: Nora's niece Mary Irvine, Sheilah (Box), Joan Eastwood and Philippa.

The Cunliff-family. Richard Cunliff is the man with the bow tie.

checked the progress of the fire, but in later years wattle became a dreadful pest. It is said that the first wattles were planted by Jock Schnell, who owned Cloudlands, the farm which has that deep depression on its ground, locally called "The Devil's Bowl" or "Kwaaimansgat".

Burning the veldt to encourage the new grass to grow is still practised in this country, and after the fires the veldt is like a paisley carpet. I have spoken about our spring flowers, but I would also like to mention here the abundance of orchids that we used to find. The vleis opposite the Magoebaskloof Hotel and on Appel were full of them. All the edges were full of *Schizostylis* and these were followed by little red disa, *Disa extinctora*, pink satyriums, agapanthus, arum lilies and eucomis. Prof. H.A.Wager of the Botany Department at Pretoria University found over 200 species of orchids in this area.

The building of the house at Otterholt took quite a number of years, but by 1922, when Philippa was born, we were living there. At that stage there were no partitioning walls, so we managed to move in the big kiaat dining-table made from handsaw planks by Theunis Smith, Jim Smith's son. We replaced the thatched roof quite soon after the Roodhuizens' house burnt down, and Mr Cunliff put the zinc on. He also did the plumbing, and as late as 1955[18] he wrote a letter to me from Springs in which he gave me detailed instructions about some plumbing problem or other. Richard Steadman Cunliff owned five farms – and the farms bought from the estate of Mr Naudé mentioned earlier. One of them adjoined Wegraakbos, and on the lower one, Groblersrust, he ran his Limber Lost sawmill. Originally he had a contract with the Forestry Department to mill their timber, but round about 1936 he lost his contract to Edgar Betton on Broedersdraai, and took on a job with the mines. He was a very helpful, gentle kind of man. His wife, Dorothy née Mogg, was quite a good painter, but was regarded as somewhat eccentric. She always wore jodhpurs and a long smock, which was very unusual at that time.

In March 1924, our fifth and last child was born in the Colwyn Nursing Home. I called her Jane after my mother and also gave her Sister Kirtley's name, Elizabeth, which the blacks changed to "Little bits". However, her other nickname, Gub, stuck all her life. This came about when the children were bathing in the river at Clear Waters. Harry Brawn, my cousin Grace's husband, who was visiting us, carried the shivering little girl to the house and handed her over to Mother. Mother said, "What a plain baby, isn't she?" To which Harry replied, "Yes, she looks like Mrs Gub, our midwife."

---

18 Letter Mr Cunliff to Awdry 4.11.1955.

By contrast, Philippa had been very beautiful, and it was quite a joke in the family that I spoilt Philippa's fortunes by refusing an offer by a Mrs Quinn, a baker's wife, to adopt her. Mrs Quinn had seen this particularly pretty baby at the Nursing Home and promised to give her all the things we would not be able to afford. I loved having a big family and would have had more children, except that we had to think about their education.

In 1924 my husband gave up his work as District Surgeon in Tzaneen. By that time the Drs Pat and Bill Adams were practising there, and Dr H.W. Burman had become District Surgeon in Duiwelskloof, whilst Dr Peter Parnell took over Haenertsburg. While Louis was DS for the Letaba District he also acted as medical officer for the SA Railways and we used his free ticket during this last year, 1925, to make an extensive trip, first to the Victoria Falls and then right down to the Cape. We stayed for a whole week with Sir Lionel and Lady Phillips on their farm Vergelegen [near Somerset West], which they had bought in 1917 and were busy restoring and furnishing. The previous owner had cut down some of the old camphor trees about which Lady P. was very indignant. There were also old oaks on the banks of a little stream, the Lourens River, and in a particular bend erosion threatened their roots. I suggested iron standards be hammered into the bank and across that bend and ruled in with stones. Later she confirmed in a letter that this plan seemed to work. She had said to me earlier on, "Awdry, you should have become my manager instead of marrying." It was the last time I saw them both.

Lady Phillips loved trees and maintained that if you stayed somewhere for longer than a week you must plant a tree. As a young girl I would often arrive on my mare "Pet" at their farm, go for a ride with her on her very tame chestnut Basuto pony, "Hurry-hurry", have a good talk and sleep over till 3 o'clock in the morning, when I had to return home to help with the milking of the cows. On one such weekend, in about 1910, we planted twenty swamp cypresses (14) near to the Broederstroom, just below the stables. They form an avenue of tall stately trees now and are a feast for the eye in autumn with their gold and red needles. Her young relative, Miri Poultney, and I also helped her to plant acorns in the "thicket", now a camping place near the Dap Naudé Dam. We all got hot and had a swim in the nude below the Swallow Falls, later incorporated in the dam (1956–1958). When it came to dressing we had to help her with her corset. She herself could close the front but to do up the back she asked us to pull it tight, and while we pulled she put her hand on her stomach and "it all came up". Miri said, "Oh, cousin Florrie, you make your bosom so big", to which she answered, "Of course, my dear, it has to go somewhere."

Louis did various locums during the following two years, first for a Dr Lynch in Johannesburg, and secondly for Dr Harry Brawn, in Uitenhage. He also had a short period in Carolina [Eastern Transvaal, today Mpumalanga]. I stayed on the farm for those years, but the separation was felt keenly by both of us.[19] The bringing up of the children rested mainly on my shoulders, and for most of their childhood their father was a rather distant figure.

From very early on I made camping trips with them, and one of the early ones was with Box and my father. At that time zebra and wildebeest were plentiful on all those farms around Dendron on the way to the Blouberg. There were thousands of them, and because they were a problem to the farmers, the Government declared them to be vermin. When we got there we arrived right in the middle of the carnage – it was too terrible. When a farmer shot a wildebeest and did not kill it outright he would hamstring it, so that it would keep alive while he would cut up for biltong the ones he had killed. Then he would turn to the wounded ones, slaughter them and proceed to make biltong out of those. The trees were hanging full of biltong and all the old farmers up here, like Theron, Schalk and Gert van der Merwe, Van Aswegen, Van Wyk en Viviers went there and came back with their ox-wagons piled high with biltong. Even today, Box says, "I will never forget the scene. My grandfather, Bego [A.K. Eastwood], shot all the hamstrung animals he could find. I was only five and was crying bitterly. People won't believe this now, but it was in my lifetime, only sixty years ago." Farmers obviously used to go shooting on their own farms, but what we witnessed was wholesale slaughter!

My parents, Mr and Mrs Everitt and Mr and Mrs Ireland came back from one such camping and shooting trip on the Irelands' farm, Concordia, in May 1921. This lay 120 miles [193 km] north-east

E.G. Ireland.
(Louis Changuion collection.)

---

19 Letter Louis to Awdry 1.8.1925.

of Pietersburg, and according to Mother's letter "it is the wildest country we have ever been in. Some people call it the breeding ground of the lion."[20] Father got lost one day and had to spend a night in the open.

Mrs Beatrice Ireland, called Beda, was Mrs Everitt's sister. Mr E.G. Ireland first kept a store with Mr H. Möschke. Later he ran a little native shop together with Mr Carl Natorp, where the recently pulled-down old town hall was. He also owned the farm [stand?] where the Pietersburg bioscope is now, and for a while the family lived on their portion of Goedvertrouwen, now Dr Holloway's, or rather his children's place.[21]

In the late 1920's their two sons, John and Bo (Botry) [Ireland], as well as the Savage twins, Philip and John, were taught on the farm by a Mrs Fridjhon. Mrs Fridjhon and her daughter, Ruth, had come from Pretoria where the late Mr Fridjhon had owned a furniture shop. She was Percy Louw's secretary for a time and later lived for many years in Haenertsburg. Now, 60 years on, Mrs Leonie Nel, née Holloway, still talks about the "school-room" when referring to a particular room in the annex that Mr Ireland had built for the widowed Mrs Everitt.

The Irelands are a well-known family in Pietersburg. Ernest George Ireland,[22] became the town's first Mayor in 1903 and a sculptured bust of him has stood in the gardens laid out around the newly built town hall since its centenary year, 1986.

---

20 Letter Mother to Awdry 27.5.1921.

21 Dr J.E. Holloway was Director of Census and Statistics from 1925–1933. Thereafter Secretary for Finance, 1937–1956, and High Commissioner to the UK from 31.8.1956 – 23.10.1958.

22 1866–1942.

IX At Modderbee Mine

In 1926 the whole family moved to Modderbee Mine [between Benoni and Springs], where Louis had taken a short-term job. Dr Alexander J. Orenstein,[1] who was Medical Consultant to Rand Mines, offered him a permanent post, but Louis wanted to "grow apples on the mountain and specialize in pomology!" Dr Orenstein said, "You're a fool – you'll never make a living that way." We did, in fact, in the end make a good living out of it, but it took a long time.

I hated leaving the farm, but it was for the good of the children. They had not gone to school yet, and Box and Tiny were teased by the piccanins, who knew that white children had to go to school. Box was really in fear and trepidation that the authorities would catch up with her. On the occasion of Princess Alice's (15) visit to our area, when she had to present her with some flowers, she was scared that she would be asked where she went to school. She thrust the flowers at the Princess and then disappeared, running all the way home! "Mother didn't know what she did to us by not sending us to school," she remembers. After moving to Modderbee, the girls even joined the Brownies and M'Pateng [Clifford/Potty], at 6½ years, became a cub in the Boy Scouts. As usual I off-loaded all my troubles on to Mother's shoulders and gave her a vivid account of my feelings in the following letter.

Dear old Mother,
I simply dread the mail from H'burg now. Each time it brings awful news about the poor cows, oh dear! It was mad for me to leave them. Still I have only done as I was told but it is a fiasco, isn't it? I can't think what the Capes [friends who looked after their farm] *are doing to my poor cows. I simply can't think. They all looked so lovely when I left. I wish to heaven we could sell the whole lot soon for 200 pounds because what does not die now will surely die next winter, oh! dear oh dear! What am I to do? If only Louis had let me stay on the farm till next year, how different things would have been. It would have put us out of debt and left no cattle to*

---

1   1879–1972; he was the supreme authority on the health of mine workers.

worry about. Daddy does not know how hard it is to come out on the right side of 50 pounds a month. I will just tell you how the money is spent:

insurance	*10 pounds*	*vegetables & fruit*	*2/10*
Louis's mother	*5*	*groceries*	*5*
house	*8*	*Jim*	*3/5/–*
milk	*3*	*boys at home*	*3/10/–*
butcher	*2/10/–*	*school*	*2*

That comes to 46 pounds 15 shillings, which leaves us three pounds five shillings for extras, not much to go on the bust on, is it? You see he gets 10 pounds extra for the car, but as that is used on his duties I don't count it. You need not tell anyone, and don't mention it in your letters – I'm just telling you why it is so different when you have to buy every morsel you eat. Still I have nice vegetables coming up and we have had a glorious rain. Please God, you will get one soon too.

I am feeling too depressed to write more now. I do hope your next letter will bring a little more cheerful cattle news with it. The kids are all well and flourishing, thank heaven.

God bless you both, love from us all, Awdry.

However, then we bought a cow and finances improved. The firm of Drysdale and Watson owned the best Ayrshire cattle in this country, and won all the prizes at the Rand Show. When they dissolved their partnership, because Drysdale was going to live in England, Mr Watson bought up most of the good cows, and then organised a sale. Louis suggested that I attend this sale, but I was absolutely staggered at the prices. The auctioneer started a beautiful heifer in calf at 200 pounds and of course we did not

Buttercup.

have that sort of money. I had thought that the cows would go for about 5 or 10 pounds, so my eyes really came out on stalks. Then "Buttercup" came on – she was about 13 years old, was in calf, and they started the bidding at 45 pounds. I came home rather dejected. Louis said, "Why didn't you buy her? The calf would have been worth that amount." He phoned Mr Watson, bought the cow, and we sold the calf for 50 pounds when it was six months old.

I kept Buttercup on the golf course, not on the fairway but in the rough. The man who looked after the golf course offered me a little shed near the clubhouse. I used to go up there in the evening, milk my cow and feed her, and then in the morning, when I milked her again, I used to leave the stable door open. She gave enough milk for all my family, and I also supplied Mrs Gilchrist, who ran the little private school that Box and Tiny attended and I put some butter on the local market as well. Buttercup was a pedigree Ayrshire cow, dark red with a white star and white feet. She gave seven gallons of milk a day. Oh she was a beautiful cow and you have no idea how I loved her!

I also looked after the Jersey cow belonging to Mr Pam, who was the manager of the Modder East Mine.[2] The animal had broken a hip and I put three slings around her, hanging from the rafters. After a long time she recovered and was not even lame. He was very impressed with that and I think he also wanted to help us financially, as he asked me to look after the mules that were working underground. Edgar Pam was not satisfied with the condition of the mules. I insisted that the animals be brought up into the sun at least once a week. This improved their condition a great deal. We got very friendly with the Pams, and I particularly with Millicent Pam, who was a qualified doctor, and loved coming to visit us on the farm. She was a genteel person, but enjoyed the camping trips that I took her on. Mr Pam was also a very kind man. He put me right off fishing when he said one day, "How can you say fishing is a sport when the fish is fighting for its life?" We had been down to the Sabie to catch tiger-fish, and from that day to this I have never caught a fish.

While we were at Modderbee we bought our first car. This was a Dodge and was known as a Seawater Dodge. A load of cars would arrive from America [by ship], stored on deck, and when the sea was very rough the Dodge factory would not guarantee them. When this particular consignment arrived it was auctioned in Johannesburg, and we bought the car

---

2   Charles Lawrence Butlin was manager of Modderbee Mine. He became Phillipa's father-in-law.

very cheaply for 100 pounds. It was a six-seater with a canvas roof, and lasted us for years and years. The running-boards which connected the mudguards were very useful. I fixed up poles on them, and for camping trips I put all our provisions there; they acted as wonderful luggage carriers. Louis taught me to drive on the stretch of road between Modderbee Mine and Modder East Mine. He showed me how to put the car in reverse, use the brake, and after I had done that a couple of times he said, "Now you can drive, how about taking the children up to the farm for the Christmas holidays?" So I packed the Dodge with all my five children, our luggage, the kitchen "boy" with his luggage and a crate of Bantam hens. When I got to Pietersburg I went to see old Pohl, the Town Clerk, and said, "Mr Pohl would you give me a driver's licence?" "Well," he said, "Can you drive? … You have just come from Johannesburg with your children? … Oh! That's all right then." That's how I got my licence!

When we came to the Sand River the water had broken its banks because they had had a heavy rainstorm above the drift. There was no bridge, no causeway, and usually you had to drive through the sand, but on this occasion the water would have run right through the car. The children slept in the car whilst I slept under one running board and the "boy" under the other. I never used to take tents – it was a waste of space. For supper I had some milk and bread for us, but Gub, who was only two years old, wanted an egg. She became quite troublesome about her "edi-ed-egg". Fortunately when M'Pateng checked on his Bantams, he discovered an egg in the crate!

My parents also owned a car by then. My grandmother Eastwood had died in June 1923, and Father and Mother bought a two-seater Chevrolet with his inheritance. The *Zoutpansberg Review* published a small story under the heading "Lucky Man", which told its readers that "Our old friend, Mr A.K. Eastwood, the Haenertsburg 'Apple King', floated into Pietersburg on Friday morning, full of smiles and enthusiasm. He told our Review representative that he and Mrs Eastwood were starting on a three thousand mile motor trip taking in Johannesburg, the towns of the Eastern Province, Knysna Forest, Pondoland, Durban, Lourenço Marques and back through the Eastern Transvaal. Mr and Mrs Eastwood are using their Chevrolet recently purchased from Zeederberg and Company, and crammed as it is with tent, cooking utensils and other camping out necessities, the car will be put to a severe test. Good luck to them both and we hope to get some good copy from Mr Eastwood."

I still have their postcards and a couple of letters from this trip, which they made in May/June 1924. With regard to the appellation "Apple King",

Father's journal shows sales, for example, of 100 trays of Ben Davis for 11 pounds 5 shillings to A. Wolpe in Pietersburg, and also the sale of dehydrated apple rings. Plums were taken to market as well and his cheese still went to Johannesburg to be sold by his brother-in-law, Gordon Bidwell, the then Market Master at Newtown. Other entries of interest in the journal were "Badenhorst Wagon repair – 1 pound; Miss L. Woodward and M. Brummer wages – 19 shillings 6d and 3 pounds respectively." In addition, there was a very extravagant 1 pound 6d for M'Pateng's birthday present. The Indian Moosa (second generation) at Veekraal and Hepworths in Johannesburg also feature. Finances had definitely improved over the past 20 years.

Whilst we were on the mine, Emily Murray and her friend, Violet Cowsmaker, looked after Otterholt's farming activities, while Mr and Mrs Capes lived in our house, helped by our maid, Eva. When they left, they gave old Eva a *pasella* of one penny! Eva was a quick-witted and humorous person – she pushed this penny into the cement under the bathroom window and said to me, "In years and years to come, when you and I and all of us are dead, somebody will pull down this house and they will know that this penny is a very valuable coin!"

The Murrays, Emily, Meg and George, lived on Weltevreden, which adjoins Wegraakbos. The original owner was an old Afrikaner who sold it to Lieutenant-Colonel J. Sholto-Douglas, who played a part in the establishment of Ofcolaco.[3] Another officer, Lieutenant-Colonel H.G.O. Bridgeman, bought the farm from him, and for a time a Mr Ivor Ray McLachlan was his manager, after which a relative of his, Major George Murray, looked after it for about six years until 1928. George was a professional soldier and had been wounded during the First World War. When he met my cousin, Joan Eastwood, Uncle William's daughter, he felt that he could not marry her before he had had a thorough medical check-up. As the doctor's report was favourable, Joan took the boat with George's sister along the east coast to England to meet his people.

They were married in 1928 from our Aunt Daisy Hand's house called The Hermitage in Seaford, Sussex – the same little town where grandmother Eastwood had owned The Manor House. They came back to live at The Downs, where they acquired a small farm from Mrs Cufflin, born Baragwanath. They had one son called John [the present Duke of Atholl, residing in Haenertsburg]. George was prepared to drop rank to be able to

---

3   A farming settlement of British ex-officers, started in 1920 in the Lowveld. Ofcolaco stands for Officer's Colonial Land Company.

Pietersburg in about 1930, looking south from the corner of Grobler and Maré Streets. The Grand Hotel, where Dr Thompson had his rooms is the double storied building second from left – today Woolworths. Across the road was Zeederberg's Garage.
(Louis Changuion collection.)

Further south in Maré Street with the National Bank (later Barclays and today First National Bank) on the corner.
(Louis Changuion collection.)

join up in 1939, but unfortunately he contracted pneumonia at Voortrekkerhoogte in Pretoria and died in June 1940. Joan is now living near her brother, William [Eastwood], north of Louis Trichardt.

Lieutenant-Colonel Orlando Bridgeman was a wealthy man, and even now the family is connected with this area. His sons have a share in the re-established Coach House [Hotel], previously Mrs Strachan's hotel at New Agatha.

It must have been in 1927 that one of the Bridgeman girls wrote a nativity play which she called *Three Roses*, and which Emily Murray produced at the Haenertsburg Hotel. Meg Murray was the Madonna, John Cunliff the babe, George a king, Mr Cunliff a shepherd and my children were the angels! Emily made them big wings and Gub had to give three roses to Mary. When she was about to present them she said, "But they are full of thorns," so quite unperturbed she walked to the side of the stage, took the thorns off and then gave them to Mary! I was really quite proud of her. Perhaps some of the old-timers will remember the occasion, and their own joyous singing of *Once in Royal David's City* at the end of the play.

That season of 1927–1928, when we lived at Modderbee Mine, we had trouble with the apple trees because woolly aphids got into their root system and would eventually have destroyed them. This happened even to the Northern Spy stocks which the Government had allowed to be imported from Australia, and which were supposed to be more resistant to aphid. Fortunately we had a visitor from the Elgin apple-growing area, a Colonel Gordon, who told us about the wasp *Aphilanis mali*. This lays eggs into aphid eggs and so destroys them. Emily, accordingly, went to the Cape and brought cuttings of apple-wood with stung aphid eggs in a tin of water back with her on the train. These twigs were tied all over the orchard. Fortunately the method worked well and our apples were saved.

The Murrays became very good friends of ours. George was adored by the children, and Emily was very close to me. She also liked walking so we went on a long hike to visit George and Joan on The Downs. Orrie Baragwanath and his sister, Mrs Cufflin, members of the big Baragwanath clan, were their neighbours.

When Orrie saw us in our walking outfits of men's long socks and shorts with a smock over them, he was disgusted with us! Mrs Cufflin was less disapproving. She was just having breakfast, which consisted of mealie porridge mixed with parsley and fried butter. She said, "This has been our main food ever since we arrived here, complete with one pig and a few sheep. Before our own mealie crop was ripe we bought the meal from the blacks."

Pietersburg in about 1930 looking South down Maré Street with
the old Empire Bioscope on the right.
(Louis Changuion collection.)

Maré Street looking North with the Pietersburg Hotel on the right.
(Louis Changuion collection.)

160

The Baragwanaths were real pioneers. When they left the Rand they hacked out the road through the bushes and this is now called Jan Smuts Drive. Mrs Cufflin was proud of their humble beginning just like old Jim Smith from Yorkshire, who would tell you about his furniture-making and that his wife cured all the goatskins for the riempies, and did all the sewing for the family. He was proud of it, but the old girl said, "I don't like to be reminded that I worked like a black." Her children knew nothing about their parents' hardships and early struggles and saw only shame in poverty. They did not realise that many great people started that way. Those women had to be tough. The Boers were really wonderful people but many of them, like old Brummer, were ashamed of having come here by ox-wagon with nothing. This is something I cannot understand – I find the way they battled, overcame hardships, and tamed the veldt so admirable.

After the year at Modderbee, Louis tried to build up a private practice in Pietersburg, but he was no good at sending out accounts, and if a person said he was poor he was treated for nothing. Nearly every Sunday we went camping on Mr Möschke's old farm just to the north [south?] of the town. There was a lovely little stream coming from Witkop shaded by big mimosa trees with many birds. Our milk cow, Buttercup, had come with us. She grazed on the commonage and could even turn on the water tap to drink!

By this time Pietersburg already held agricultural shows and I took part in a milking- and an inspan-competition. One of our cows, a half-breed between a Cape cow and an Ayrshire bull, called "Malebese" ("mother of milk") by Kleinbooi helped me to make a good impression.

The inspan-competition was a more demanding challenge. You had to bring your own oxen, not less than six. Ours walked from Wegraakbos to town for the occasion. Cinguas, a red beast with white feet and white tipped tail, and Lieutenant, a black one, were the leaders. Scotland and Witlies had their place in the middle and Rooiland and Roman were the wheelers. Before you start the oxen stand in a row facing the trekchain. You inspan the leaders first and the voorloper is holding them. Then you shout their names, whereupon they bend their backs getting the chains to hang free between them. The whole point is not speed, but to do the job well. I got first prize in that event.

Louis had [his consulting] rooms in the Grand Hotel building. There was a man named Kruger who liked him and tried to find patients for him. Kruger made a living by buying oxen from the farmers and then selling them on the market when prices were good. One day he told Louis about an old Jew who had an African trading store on the Limpopo. Kruger said,

"He is very ill and very, very rich, no wife, no children and I think you should go out there and help him." Louis fetched the old man, put him in hospital and treated his malaria until he got well. He charged him only threepence a mile to go there and get him and two guineas as his fee. Old Kruger was furious and said, "If I sell you a piece of material for 25 shillings a yard you will think that you have something good, but if an African sells the same material for 2 shillings 6 pence it must be a poor quality. That's why people think you are no good, Doctor, you do too much for nothing." Louis just had no business sense at all.

Old Mrs Bertha Mockford, Tiny's future mother-in-law, said the only thing for Louis was to get a salary and so we moved again. We left the three bigger children at boarding school in Pietersburg, and I went to live with the little ones on the farm. Louis worked for some months at the newly built Jane Furse Memorial Hospital in Sekhukhuniland. Mrs Grace Davies, who published an account of the hospital's history in 1985, mentions Louis in a few sentences:

> In the interval, between the departure of John Chitty for England and the arrival of Dr Huskisson as Medical Superintendent, assistance was given by Dr Louis C. Thompson. He was able to report the installation of the first District Nurse at Marishane on 1 January 1930. He did not mince his words when commenting on the lack of doctors and the minimal health facilities in an area as big as Sekhukhuniland when he wrote, "In the Union of South Africa far more attention is paid to the diseases of animals than the diseases of human beings, and an enormous amount of money is spent on paying the salaries and travelling expenses of an army of cattle and sheep inspectors."

I can prove his point with a story of my own. Because of the danger of foot and mouth disease, you had to apply to the Dip-Inspector for permit to move your cattle from one place to another. Our cattle at Otterholt had to be dipped at Father's farm, Clear Waters, because we had no dipping facilities of our own. I applied to Pietersburg to take them there, but they took no notice of my request. I was alone on the farm and, after consultation with Mr Roodhuizen, I thought I had better move them without a permit, rather than risk being run in for not dipping. The "boys" went over with the cattle but the police caught them. Subsequently I had to appear at the next sitting of the magistrate's court in Haenertsburg. I rode into Haenertsburg and hitched my horse onto that now historic hitching post. The magistrate fined me 5 pounds or two weeks in gaol, but I refused to pay, reasoning that I had just started farming, had no money and was on my own. I certainly would not pay a fine for something of which I was not guilty and so I opted for the two weeks in gaol. This put the magistrate into a quandary, as Pietersburg had no prison for white women. I insisted that it was no discredit to me to go to gaol, even if they had to send me to Pretoria. In the end, the magistrate let me off with a warning and they were all quite amused about me!

The Catholic school in Pietersburg attended by Clifford in the 1930's.
(Louis Changuion collection.)

Messina in about 1940.
(Louis Changuion collection.)

Awdry and her friend Lucille Kehew at Messina, about 1935.

X   At Messina Copper Mine and Camping Trips

In 1930 Louis applied successfully for the job of Resident Doctor at Messina Copper Mine, and we lived there for 11 years, from 1930 to 1941. He had a matron and two nurses helping him in the hospital, and Dr Le Helico treated the blacks assisted by Portuguese natives, mostly from the Balemba tribe, who had trained as medical orderlies. While we were looking for a house and trying to settle in, Philippa and Gub lived with my parents, and attended the Woodbush Hill School on Clear Waters. Mrs Betton and Mr Taljaard were the teachers at that time. Gub recalls that her grandfather always kept them at the house until he saw Mrs Betton arrive on horseback at the school, because he did not want them to mix more than was necessary with the other "rough" children. Nan Brummer who lived on Stampblokfontein, opposite the Magoebaskloof Hotel, also attended this little school, and she remembered how the old man used to dump apples, unsuitable for selling, into the Broederstroom, and how the children tried to retrieve and eat them. My father must have been something of a bogeyman to the school children.

We had not been in Messina for more than a few months, when I received the heartbreaking news that Mother had suddenly died from a coronary thrombosis. I never got over her loss as we had been so close. Even now, I feel tears in my eyes when I think of her, but I know that she is always near me – even now – just like Louis. She died on 11 November 1930, and the little brass plate on her grave on Wegraakbos just reads "Mother, Armistice Day 1930." When Mother died, Philippa and Gub were taken in by Mrs Betton until the end of term.

After Mother died, Father wanted to go on a big fishing trip to Lake Nyassa and Lake Victoria. He sold the farm for £3000 to Mr Arthur Stanley Furner, a Johannesburg architect, and then the two of us went in his new two-seater Chevrolet to Pretoria to buy some camping equipment and food. We stayed with Aunt Minnie and Uncle Carl Rose, who had become Chief Railway Engineer for the Transvaal. The Railways had just decided to display their old steam locomotive as an historical monument outside Pietersburg station, and Uncle Carl "misappropriated" a bit of brass from it. With this he made me a sugar bowl and spoon, and for the last 50 years this sugar bowl has been in use in my house, and is always right here on my table.

After a couple of days, having completed our purchases, we left Pretoria about 9 p.m. We were supposed to drive this new car at no more than 25 miles per hour, and Father drove right through the night to Pietersburg. There I had to see about some trouble which had arisen concerning M'Pateng's boarding with Mr Organe, the Headmaster of the Primary School. Apparently he was supposed to be "ganging up" with John Ireland against his [Organe's] son, Frank. After consultation with Mr Voss, the Inspector of Schools, I installed him at the College of the Little Flower, the Catholic school.

I was worn out by the time we set out for Louis Trichardt. At Dwarsrivier, another of Ireland's farms, I fell asleep at the wheel. Father was asleep next to me and was thrown out into a culvert. He had a big gash across his head, my lips were cut and I was spitting blood – the new car was finished. The gearbox was torn out and the wheels buckled. A Mr Minnie, who succeeded Mr Voss as School Inspector, picked us up and took us to Louis Trichardt. Fortunately the car was insured. Father stayed with us in Messina until he got a new car. He took this down to Otterholt, and had another accident at Moosa's Store at Veekraal. Father consequently never started his trip. His sternum was crushed – it was pressing on his lungs and he died of pneumonia in Messina Hospital in July 1932. He is also buried under the big blackwoods on Wegraakbos.

We lived very quietly in Messina, and, as I had complained in an earlier letter to my parents, addressed "Dear old angels", "life has no savour for me without the kids. I never dreamed it could be so dull. I simply hate it. No lunches to get, no nothing." The children were all at boarding school, either in Pietersburg or at Pretoria Girls' High, but they came home for holidays and every year in July, I took them camping in the bush. This was the cheapest way of entertaining them: they all learned a great deal about plants, animals and also about the history of the region. Our first winter holiday, in July 1931, took us to Tshipise. Many farmers arrived there by wagon to enjoy the hot springs. I came across a man who had dug a hole and he was sitting in the hot mud. He had driven four poles into the soft soil and put sack-cloth around three sides while one side was open to the bush. When he saw me he scowled and waved me off and I flew for my life.

One year the children and I were on our way to a camping place at the Nwanedzi river, when we met Mr Ely who was District Commissioner in Rhodesia. He suggested to the boys, Potty [Clifford] and Harold [Mockford who later married Tiny], that they should shoot wild dogs and get 10 shillings per tail from the police. Being a bit of a butcher myself, we asked several blacks where we could find wild dogs. An old man took us to an earth mound with entrances to underground burrows. I made Tiny creep into one of the holes with a torch and put a belt around her ankle to pull her out if she screamed. She realized that there was a drop after about two yards and shining the torch downwards she saw lots of puppies and some bitches.

We knew the dogs would come back at dusk and waited but they must have got our scent and although we spent the whole night sitting on that mound they did not appear. It was wild country and we did not dare to move around in the dark. At one stage we saw a pair of eyes and Harold let fly. In the morning his kill turned out to be a porcupine.

Louis was very interested in the archaeology of the country around Messina and across the Limpopo, where the Balemba used to work iron and copper mines. They made metal hoes and traded with the tribes in the south. Old Josiah, on David Luther's farm, said that in his grandfather's time people used wooden earth-working tools to till the soil, as only the rich could afford the metal hoes made by the Balemba. There were many ruins and old mine workings up there. Louis could not come with us because of his work and his lame leg. However, before each camping trip he would tell us what to look for, and he also made sure the car was fixed up before we left.

As a result of our travels and his talking to the blacks, he wrote an article about copper ingots, *mu-tsuku*, of the Balemba, Vhavenda and Basotho, who lived near the old copper workings on both sides of the Limpopo in Zimbabwe and in the Northern Transvaal. They have two kinds of copper ingots, the commercial and the ceremonial ones, and I have a few of these ingots on my bookshelf. The Ovambo at Tsumeb also mined copper and their women wore pure copper anklets. We saw them around the women's legs in Ovamboland during the First World War. These were thick round rings and some people say they were ingots, but they are not.

Louis also had contacts with the National Museum of Southern Rhodesia and the editor of *N.A.D.A.*,[1] Mr N.H.D. Spicer, who accepted another article from him on "The Ba-Lemba of Southern Rhodesia". The material for his article came from a trip that my husband and I did on our own. We camped at Belingwe for a couple of months, moving around by car with a tent and studying the Balembas' way of life. They made good pottery and were quite well off because they had found gold, iron and copper, which they mined.

---

1   The *Southern Rhodesia Native Affairs Department Annual.*

A picture taken as late as the 1880's, showing how the Venda was still melting iron and copper.
(Photo: H.F. Gros, Louis Changuion collection.)

Copper ingots of the Mu-Tsuku type of the Ba-Lemba from the Thompson collection.
(Photo: B. Wongtschowski.)

One year, when I went camping with the children near the Mtetengwe River, about 16 miles north of Beit Bridge, I got talking to an old African who asked us what we were looking for. He must have wondered why we were walking so far in the bush, and I might add, getting very exhausted at times. I told him that we were looking for the ruins where the old people used to live, and he then asked us if we wanted to see the *thutlwa*. I did not know what he meant but I said yes and we all took our *padkos* and started walking. Eventually we got to a large granite rock, flat with no cracks, and there on top of it was a petroglyph. It depicted a most beautiful and perfectly proportioned giraffe. Black moss and lichen had settled in the grooves, but the body markings, mane, tail and horns were perfectly outlined. It measured 9 foot from head to hoof. I took Mr van Riet Lowe to see it and he tried to preserve it from vandalism by building a little wall around it – I wonder whether it did. Rock engravings are quite rare in Zimbabwe, so my "discovery" was mentioned by Neville Jones in his book *The Pre-History of Southern Rhodesia*.

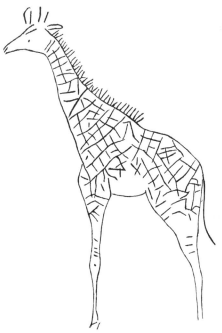

The rare giraffe rock engraving discovered by Awdry.

On an earlier trip, we had been invited by a Mr Pearl to camp near his store on the Nwanedzi Ranch which belonged to the Imperial Cold Storage Company. All these store-keepers bought their supplies in Messina and they generally stayed with us, because they also often wished to have a medical check-up. We became very fond of Mr Pearl and his wife and he took us up in his delivery truck.

He had asked the famous Major Philip Jacobus Pretorius[2] for permission to camp on his section. That evening, after we had settled in, Major Pretorius came to see whether everything was all right and when he heard that the only meat we had was bully beef, he brought us an impala and then started to reminisce with stories from his past. The children were absolutely enthralled, particularly M'Pateng and his friend, Harold Mockford. Pretorius knew the country inside out, had been an ivory hunter, and during the First World War General Smuts had used his vast knowledge of the African continent for intelligence purposes. The German cruiser, *Königsberg*, had done a great deal of damage to Allied shipping along the East Coast. An African Chief had told Pretorius about a ship anchored in the Rufiji Delta in Tanganyika so Pretorius disguised himself as a servant to the Chief and with a crate of fowls on his head, eventually found the ship. It was well camouflaged with plants all over the deck. Because it had run aground on a sandbank, it could only get out at high tide. He measured the tide and was able to direct the fire of a British gunboat that came to destroy the *Königsberg*. She was blasted from the sea.

Major Pretorius had high cheekbones, blue eyes and was very tall, but in spite of this he looked rather like a Bushman. He was unassuming, quietly spoken and had a good command of Swahili and various other African languages. Unfortunately, he [later] rather fell in our esteem when he shot some of the last Knysna elephants. Gub remembers that we were nearly washed away on the trip, when unseasonable rains came down the riverbed where we were camped. Mrs Pretorius, a mousy little woman, took us in and helped us in a most motherly way.

The other adult in our party was Mrs Harding, wife of the accountant at the Limpopo Stores in Messina. Her father, Mr Booysen, had bred ostriches at Oudtshoorn during the boom time, and he also had quite a herd of eland running with the cattle. Enid Harding told us that a travelling Russian noticing their good condition on very frugal grazing, bought three bulls and seven cows paying 80 gns a pair, and exported them to Russia. When the question of transporting the eland arose, Mr Booysen sug-

2   1876–1945.

170

gested driving the animals together with some cows [cattle] into a railway cattle truck. In Cape Town the exercise could be repeated when getting them on board ship. Years later, Louis read in *The Field*, an English sportsmen's journal, about a herd of eland thriving somewhere in Russia. We wondered at the time if these could have been bred from the original eland from Oudtshoorn. I now hear that Gerald Durrell in his latest book *Durrell in Russia* mentions eland being bred and milked in the Askaniya Nova Nature Reserve. According to him a German by the name of Fein imported them from East-Africa to the family farm north of the Black Sea. Perhaps this was an additional batch?

One of our most exciting trips was made in July 1939, when we managed to reach Sofala on the Mozambique coast. My husband had read Captain William F.W. Owen's book *Narrative of Voyages to Explore the Shores of Africa, Arabia and Madagascar*, (vol. 2; 1833) and he wanted us to follow the old trade route from the interior and hopefully, to find some artefacts. Captain Owen was in the British Navy and made a hydrographic survey of the African East Coast in the mid-1820's. He found at Sofala a mangrove-free harbour and re-discovered the old Arab settlement, which had been used as a trading post for gold and ivory from the interior.

For three years running we tried to get to Sofala [just south of today's Beira], but on two occasions we only reached Mambone [about 150 km south of Beira on the coast]. The participants in our first trip were all my children with the exception of Potty, who was at school in England, and Mr and Mrs R.A. Turner together with their children, Robert [later to marry Gub], Kenneth and Elma. Mr Turner was the head of the Primary School in Messina. This trip was Gub's first long camping trip but unfortunately she developed a severe bout of malaria. On the second trip Box's friend, Molly Macindoe, accompanied us as well as Mrs Margaret Moss[3] and her son, Arthur. Mrs Moss was a lecturer in Botany at the University of the Witwatersrand and the widow of Prof. Charles Edward Moss,[4] after whom the Moss Herbarium at Wits is named.

She was interested in collecting various seaweeds, and badly wanted to look for them on a particular peninsula which could only be reached by boat. I therefore thought that I would sound out the Portuguese *Chefe de Poste* and ask for his help. So of I went in my bedraggled khaki dress, my old shoes, my burnt Henry Heath hat, with my hair sticking out at the top. The *Chefe's* house had big white steps, and on each side of the entrance

---

3   1885–1953.
4   1870–1930.

stood an African in snow-white uniform. I asked in Fanakalo to be taken to the *Chefe*, and these smart blacks must have wondered what sort of creature this was coming out of the bush – I must say I felt awful! However, the *Chefe* was very kind and organised a boat and sailors to take us out for the day and bring us back in the evening. Finally he even went so far as to present us with a bucketful of crayfish, which were not really appreciated by my family's unsophisticated palates, but the Mosses loved them!

Somewhere along the road one of the children had found a little genet kitten which they called Pussel. We tried to get some milk for "the baby" – and even from the *Chefe de Poste* at Masangene – without success. Mrs Moss suggested to keep it going with pigeon liver. During the night we saw the lights of a car that turned out to be the *Chefe de Poste*'s who had brought some milk that he had organized from the local hospital. We got away with our lie by saying the baby was asleep and he could not see it! Pussel usually slept with Tiny in her sleeping bag. One night it must have got away to Philippa who accidentally crushed it to death with her weight. There were lots of tears that day.

The next year saw us again en route to Mambone via Pafuri, Dumela, Covane, Chefo and Jofane. The country was terribly wild, with no roads whatsoever. We did, however, find several ruins made of dry stone walls, built in the same style as the Zimbabwe Ruins. These were about 15–20 miles apart, next to dried-up watercourses, and I thought that a camel would just have been able to cover this distance in one day. The Chief at Covane presented us with some *padkos* in the shape of a goat, but we declined the gift politely. He then brought us two fowls, a yellow and a whitish one, which we called Goldie and Silvie. They used to flutter onto the car when I hooted and then take up their seats on a box whilst we drove away.

When we got to Chefo and camped there under a bucksail, an old man came along to find out whether or not we had some food for him. He had snow-white hair, looked very old to me, and I thought I might get some information from him concerning the origin of a particular bead which my husband had given me.

Beads play a very important part in the history and culture of the African people. This one had been found by Captain Guy A. Gardner at Mapungubwe, an important archaeological site on the farm Greefswald in the Messina district. It was turquoise in colour, about 12 mm long, had sharp edges, and because of its shape was called a "garden-roller-bead". Captain Gardner had already sent a couple of these beads, together with some chips, to Mr Beck at the British Museum. Mr M.C. Beck, who was an expert in this field, analysed the chips and noticed that the bubbles ran transversely and perpendicularly, but he could not, at the time, give any information as to how they had been made. Louis had given me one of Gardner's beads with which to make some enquiries along the road. As usual, Louis had done all the reading on the subject and was the brains behind my amateurish exploring.

I asked the old man at Chefo whether he knew anything about this kind of bead and how it was made. I wanted him to have a close look at it and hold it in his hand, but he would not touch it and simply assured me that he knew nothing about it. We gave him some food and the next morning he appeared again. He then reported that he had spoken to an even older man than himself, who told him the story that had come down by word of mouth, of how these old beads were made by the Old People. The beads had not come down from the whites.

First the craftsmen would make tiny moulds out of clay, with a hole at the bottom, and they would smooth the insides very well with a little stone and bake them. Two of these moulds were then cemented together with clay and put back into the fire. After this, they melted some "Beads of the Water" – *vhulugu a madi*, the sacred blue-green glass beads belonging to the Vhavenda of the Zoutpansberg, which they bought from them at a high price. The melted liquid was poured into the little moulds, and someone with an ebony stick as thin as needle would twirl it around very rapidly with an up and down movement, rolling the stick all the time between his hands. The full moulds were then left to cool, the stick was taken out of the hole, and the clay mould was broken away.

The colour of the garden-roller-beads ranged through all the shades of blue into green, just like the "Beads of the Water". Both these types of beads were very scarce. The Vhavenda must have one of them on their necklaces because they play a role in their traditional beliefs. Their witch-doctors say they are coloured with seawater. They are buried with their owners, which accounts for their rarity. Incidentally, we found one of them on the necklace of a dead Bushman when we were in South West Africa during the First World War. Bernhard H. Dicke, who had a trading store in the Lowveld, confirms in his book *The Bush Speaks* that the Vhavenda value their beads very highly. Apparently Chief Tshivhase offered Dicke 5 pounds for 100 grams of them. Mr Dicke tried to have the beads imitated by Venetian glassblowers, but when he brought them back from Italy to his shop the Africans said, "Aowa, a ya loka", no good. At any rate, we stored the old man's information in our heads and pushed on to Mambone. Here we left Goldie and Silvie with an African who had taken a fancy to them. His name was Aarone Machava and some years later, by sheer accident, he became a trusted servant in my house – but more of that later. Eventually we reached the small tumble-down settlement of Sofala and camped under some palm trees on the beach. One morning at low tide, when Potty went for a walk, he had the incredible luck to find a midden, to which he took us. We found some tiny gold beads, some pottery shards, and also some large hand-made glass beads. There were also a few copper implements, boat nails, a fine hook and two needles together with the piece of a small buckle. We noticed some ruins in the area, and what appeared very much like one of Vasco da Gama's stone crosses; one arm of it was protruding from the sand and the foundation stone was unmistakable. (I must mention here that when I returned to the site sometime in the early sixties with Box and Michael Brawn, there was nothing left and the shore-line seemed to have changed.)

When we got back to Messina, we were very excited and keen to divulge our discoveries. I was full of my new knowledge about the turquoise garden-roller-beads. But before I could explain to Louis about them he told me that the archaeologists at Mapungubwe had found a pile of shards of pottery beads with big holes in them. "How can you call them beads?" I asked, "Beads are used for ceremonial dances and for rough wear; they would have had to be strung on a thick string or riempie, so that they would not rattle or break." I then poured out my story to him and to Captain Gardner. Later, Mr Beck confirmed that he had found some glass stuck to the inside of the shards and he agreed that my explanation had thrown considerable light on the subject. It was all very exciting.

My husband gave most of my finds to Mr C. van Riet Lowe at the University of the Witwatersrand but we kept a few beads back for ourselves. The one I like best is black, white and reddish-looking, like two pyramids put together. My sight is so poor that I can't see them any more. In 1988, I gave them all to Dr Karl Schultz who lives in Boksburg, and has a kind of private museum. Van Riet Lowe thought that Dr Gertrude Caton-Thompson who had worked at the Zimbabwe Ruins in 1929 would be the right person to dig at the place where we had made our discovery. As she was not available, I went to see Vice-Consul Señor Ferreira in Johannesburg and asked him whether it would be possible for me to dig. He agreed, but wanted me to employ only Portuguese Africans and only a set number of white men. We would have to use sandbags at high tide and I became very nervous about the whole venture. I was, after all, not an archaeologist, and of no account in professional circles. However, everything was arranged, when the outbreak of war interfered with the scheme.

I mentioned before that Clifford [Potty] was with us on this trip. He had spent three years at Epsom College in Surrey, where my husband had been educated. The college was established for doctors' and parsons' sons and the fees were reduced if one could not afford them. We certainly could not have afforded to pay them except for the fact that Louis's mother had died and left him 180 pounds. Louis thought it was a good idea to use this money towards Potty's education, so in August 1934 I went with him to Durban and saw him off on the ship to England. I cried when I saw this little boy [14 years of age] all on his own, going out into the world. We thought he was very fortunate to have the chance of acquiring an English education, but he says he made no friends. Perhaps his earlier free life and independent character had made him unsuitable for a boarding school back "Home". We were grateful to Edgar and Millicent Pam, our friends from the time at Modderbee Mine, who took him to the continent for his long holidays.

After matriculating in 1937, he came back to South Africa and joined Wenela (Witwatersrand Native Labour Association) which was the recruiting company for which [his friend] Harold Mockford worked. Potty was stationed in Botswana and did not train for anything in particular, nor did he want to go to university although we had an insurance policy which would have covered the expense. My husband was sorry about this and we begged him to qualify either in Engineering or Botany but he could not face more years of study. It was a great pity. I regret it every time when he comes to see me because he is an excellent mechanic and a good botanist, though hopelessly untidy and an unsystematic collector. Like me he is somewhat aggressive. He is, however, always interesting company.

We suffered a great deal from the heat at Messina. It was so hot at night that I put my bed into a corner of our big stoep, and used a large wet bath-towel as a blanket; I found it was the only way to keep cool. Twice a week we went to the open-air bioscope and on many occasions played bridge until the early hours of the morning with our friends, the Kehews. Lucille Kehew taught me to smoke, and I have done so ever since.

We did not join in the usual dinner parties, but we had many good friends and also many visitors passing on their way through to Rhodesia. Once I was reprimanded by a woman concerning our aloofness from the social set. I replied, "My husband is a good doctor, a good man, and I am here to make it possible to educate our children. I am not here to waste money on dinner parties on the mines." Neither Louis nor I were social climbers and all our children got a good education. Box studied Botany at the University of the Witwatersrand, Tiny took a secretarial course after she finished her schooling at the Convent in Pietersburg, and Philippa completed a medical B.Sc. degree. Gub became a teacher in Physical Education. Stellenbosch [University] had been the only place that offered this course, and she found it hard doing all the subjects in Afrikaans.

In Messina I spent a great deal of my time horse riding. Mr Franklin who looked after the mules of the mine and some horses that were owned by its employees had asked me to help with exercising them. He would send a horse around to our house everyday about 9 o'clock in the morning when Louis had gone off to work.

When war broke out, in 1939, a gymkhana was organised to raise funds for the Red Cross. A race meeting was also planned which was supposed to bring in money for the owners as well. Hans van der Merwe who had a farm on the Limpopo, owned two thorough-bred horses which he wanted to enter. He had a rider for one of them. For the other, a small mare called St. Kilda, he expected a professional jockey to be sent from Johannesburg. When he went to meet him at the regular train he did not find his man. However, by phoning down the line, they discovered him blind drunk at the Grand Hotel in Pietersburg.

Hans implored Mr Franklin to find him another rider, and I started – and ended – my career as a jockey on that momentous Saturday! I wore Van der Merwe's colours which were green and beige, and although Mrs Harding said that green was unlucky, quite a number of my friends put 10 shillings on me. Mr von Breda, who had often seen me on horseback, ventured 25 pounds.

Hans gave me the following advice, "Don't hassle her. The whole distance is eight furlongs, that is twice around the track. When it comes towards the straight, tap her on the neck with this little mopani switch, give her her head and you will see that she will not let any other horse pass her." It worked like magic. Towards the end there were four horses in front of me. I flicked my switch and we passed them one by one; then I got onto the rails and St. Kilda could not have gone faster if she had had wings. When the spectators saw I was leading they went wild with excitement, shouting, "Mrs Thompson, Mrs Thompson."

As I reached the winning post several of them leapt over the barriers on to the track and were all for lifting me from the horse onto their shoulders. This was the proudest moment of my eleven years in Messina. Kenny Turner [years later to marry Gem Lee of Haenertsburg] had bet half a crown on me and our cookboy, Jim Manege, 7/6. While I seemed to lag behind he kept on covering his head moaning, "Tšhelete ya ka", "My money, my money." Mr von Breda made quite a tidy sum out of my win, I think. To

176

crown it all, I also came first in the race of the winners from all the other events.

I remember two incidents which occured in Messina, both quite amusing. When we moved to Messina I had a tame *kiewietjie* [plover] and an old crow, which was also very tame. In nature they are deadly enemies, but these two were the greatest of friends, and the minute the crow called "Waw-waw" the little plover came running to see what was the matter. It was a crowned plover with long red legs and white markings on the back of its head – I called her Lucy Longlegs. She used to come with us when we played golf, and pick up many of those little worms that live in the holes in the ground covered with sand, like a lid. One day when we got back from playing golf and the crow welcomed us, it was quite obvious that it was really looking for the little plover, but she was not with us. I rushed back to the golf course, but failed to find her. Louis suspected Mrs Osborn's son of having caught Lucy to give to his mother who kept many pets and lived at the bottom of the village.

Early next morning I took the cook and we each went down different streets calling "Lucy" in front of every house. When I got to Mrs Osborn's house (I did not know it was hers) Lucy answered me from inside with the typical plover call "Kwe-kwe". I knocked on the door and said, "I think you have my little lapwing in the house." Without any sign of guilt, she answered, "I have no birds of yours", and banged the door in my face. I was very angry because I knew that Lucy was there. I rushed back to my husband, asked him to get out of bed right away, take a basket and find my little bird. Mrs Osborn, on seeing Louis, exclaimed, "Hullo Doctor, why are you up so early?" He was asked to come inside and sure enough there was Lucy! In fact, Mrs Osborn kept a number of animals: a kudu which walked all over the village, a jackal, hornbills, three squirrels – all very special pets. In addition, she also had a python some nine feet long, which was kept locked up in a store-room with bags of mealies, together with white mice and rats. The python used to catch its own food. After this incident, and because of our mutual love of animals, Mrs Osborn and I became great friends.

The day finally came when she had to dispose of her pets as Mr Osborn had accepted a better job in Johannesburg. She sent them all to the zoo, but the python was rejected. She put it into a bag and took it to the Sand River, about ten miles from Messina, and then set it free in the koppies, where she had originally found it when it was very young.

However, that was not the end of the snake's town life. Mrs Osborn was giving a farewell tea party for her friends, including Mrs John, the Compound Manager's wife, Lucille Kehew and me in a rather dark room, when suddenly I heard a funny swishing noise at my feet and on looking down, saw something moving. "Oh my God! It's the python," I thought, but on enquiry I learned that it had been taken to the Sand River a few days previously, in the hope that it would be able to fend for itself. I said, "I think it's come back again", and as I said this, the python slid past me and was starting to crawl up Mrs Osborn's leg and around her neck! All the other guests at the tea party either climbed on to their chairs screaming, or dashed out of the room! I thought the whole incident was hilarious – there was the python all the way up Mrs Osborn's body, with its tongue in her face! She stroked it, all nine feet of it. Later she put it in a sack and took it to the Nzhelele Valley, near Tshipise, some 25 miles away. Some people say that pythons are very intelligent. This one obviously knew where her mice had come from!

My other humorous Messina story has to do with the only evening dress I ever owned in my life. This had been given to me by Cousin Ethel and was made of gold lamé lace. Quite obviously I had no real use for it, but thought that I might possibly wear it one day at one of the mine dances. Not that I ever danced, but I thought that I would look very glamorous for a change. I hung up the dress in our spare room in a wardrobe which had only a curtain in front of it.

Sometime later, Major John, the compound manager, sent a boy with a sack and a note which read, "Dear Mrs Thompson, I think the contents of this sack will interest you – I don't want any harm to come to it, so I am sending it to you for refuge." There, inside the sack, was a scaly anteater; it is the only one that I have ever seen. The creature rolls itself into a ball when it is frightened, so I put it into the spare room. Louis suggested that we wait until sundown, then take it down to the Limpopo and set it free in the bush, where the Africans would not be able to find it, because they love to eat them. When the time came to catch it, I could not see it anywhere, but then, suddenly, there it was at the bottom of the wardrobe, all mixed up with my beautiful gold lamé dress. I had to get a pair of scissors and cut around each of the scales, and so ended the story of my glamorous social ambitions!

People make too much fuss about clothes. I myself had taken to always wearing khaki dresses, and was called *Magolowa*, "woman in khaki" by the Africans. For decades I made and wore these khaki dresses, cut like a shirt with short sleeves and big pockets. The blacks don't approve of women wearing shorts, and I don't like them either. I used to make all the girls' dresses and also all their school dresses. Fitting them out for boarding school at the High School for Girls in Pretoria was always a great expense. They had to have six pairs of white drawers, six pairs of black satin bloomers, six pairs of stockings, six vests, two gym dresses, six long-sleeved white shirts, one white Sunday dress, a raincoat, an umbrella, three pairs of shoes and a blazer. If they could have gone to school at home, these garments could have been washed and there would not have been the need for so many. However, Louis and I felt that the heat in Messina would not have been good for them. I missed them badly while they were away.

I regularly went to the farm to check up on the work that was being done. One misty and rainy day, while wiping off the top shelves in the kitchen, I knocked down a tin of caustic soda and some grains fell between my big toe and the next toe on my right foot. Instead of putting on some acid like lime or lemon juice, I treated this with oil, which was apparently the worst thing I could have done. Back in Messina, Louis sent me to see Dr Le Helico, but unfortunately my foot went septic. Dr Brebner, at the Kensington Nursing Home in Johannesburg wanted to amputate the whole leg below the knee. I wouldn't have it and said to him, "I want to die with my two legs – I am not living with one. I want to walk with two legs, or die." However, Dr Mudd put the leg from below the knee into wads of flannel soaked in cod-liver oil for two whole weeks. It was a very smelly business. Fortunately I got away with the amputation of the second toe, but it took me six months to recover fully.

By 1935 our apple trees were starting to bear well. My husband always took his leave during the month of January, when it was unbearably hot in Messina, and I stayed with him on Otterholt, getting the boxes ready. The slats for the boxes were imported from Sweden, shipped to Lourenço Marques and transported by the firm of Mitchell Cotts to Tzaneen where I picked them up. They were sixpence cheaper than those produced by the local sawmill. After he left, the job of packing the apples started and went right through to April.

My helpers with the packing were, for years, Johanna Badenhorst, Lena Woodward, and for a couple of seasons, Miss Wienand, the hotel-keeper's niece. The bus which collected our apples came twice a week, and we had to load five tons at a time. I did the cooking early in the morning, and also supplied the girls with sandwiches for their 7 and 11 o'clock tea breaks. When the Empire Show was organised in England, in 1936, I sent a commercial consignment of 50 boxes to the market of Covent Garden. Out of these 50 boxes, five were chosen by Dr John Haddon to be exhibited. We called these apples "Black" or "Striped" and "Ben Davis", but Dr Haddon and four of his colleagues, all members of the Royal Horticultural Society, identified them as "Barnack Beauty", when they visited this country. The label on our apple boxes also claimed "free from codling moth". One of the horticulturalists came to the farm and said to me, "There can't be an apple free from codling moth!" He banded the trees and went to look in the morning whether the little pupating larvae had crept up the stem. But there really were none. All the varieties of apples, which had been brought out by Thomas Southon, were later attacked by a virus and their fruit deteriorated.

The big game hunter P.J. ("Jungle man") Pretorius.
(Louis Changuion collection.)

XI Packing Oranges and Prospecting for Tungsten

Miss Wienand, our help during the apple season, went regularly every winter to the Zebediela Estates [near Potgietersrus] to make some money by packing oranges. She advised me to watch how the packing of fruit was done on a big scale, and how it was best organised. I thought this was a very good idea, and as Box had just finished her degree, both of us signed on as packers [late 1930's].

In all there were some 570 white women from the surrounding area and most of them were desperately poor. We had to sign a form agreeing to pay 2/– a day for board and lodging, and we had to work 8 hours a day in two shifts of four hours each. The first shift started at 5 a.m. We had a cup of black coffee and nothing at all to eat. It was really hard work and one had to be proficient. At 9 a.m. we used to go back to the hostel, have some breakfast, and rest for four hours. Lunch consisted of a soup made with meat, but it was all mashed up with cabbage and dried beans, or cabbage and potatoes. Supper was at 5.30 p.m., when again the soup was served together with bread and jam with black tea. We were not allowed to eat any oranges – not a single one, and I felt so sorry for these poor girls from the Limpopo Valley. The one who slept next to me was covered in sores and had lice as well. I was terrified that I would catch these and would wash my hair every day with carbolic soap. One day when she was working next to me, I could see she was dying to eat an orange. I said to her, "Sit down next to my legs and eat one now – I will warn you if the floor lady comes." The poor little girl was so thin and starved!

We were paid one and a quarter pence per 100 oranges. Box was so slow that she could not even pay her board and lodging, and I did not do much better although I managed to make 2 pounds 10 shillings for the whole season. There was one woman with us who was really a champion packer. She moved like lightning. Her time was so precious that she hardly found the time, or so I thought, to blow her nose! To my horror, I watched her one day at mealtime, wolfing down her food, quickly wiping her nose on her sleeve and at the same time pointing out a dish to someone as she called out, "Gee my die sous aan." (Pass me the gravy.)

We were not allowed to go out in the evening, but some girls just climbed out of the window and went to meet some of the men. When we asked for permission to visit our Jewish friends, Mr and Mrs Lesous, who had started an African trading store in Zebediela, we were flatly turned down. We had known them from Messina days. Their children went to school in Pretoria, and as the road up north was so bad, they had moved to Zebediela. To get to the packing shed we had to cross a sort of paddock, with some bushes and a water tap in the middle. Next to it was a small wood and iron building in which the so-called doctor sat with his feet up on the table reading the paper. On this piece of ground the sick Africans lay, and if they were too weak to get to the tap, a friend would bring them water in an empty jam tin. This was the kind of hospitalisation deemed adequate for the blacks employed by Schlesinger [owner of Zebediela Estates]. If they had a sheet of corrugated iron over them we knew they were dead. In the morning the lorry which brought our meat, picked up the corpses and took them away. Most of them died of malaria and many had come from as far afield as Nyassaland, Kenya and Central Africa. For 600 blacks and 570 white women the Estate did not employ a single trained doctor – it was really shocking.

The Canadian nurse that they tried to put in charge of the little hospital for the whites, did not stay for more than a week. She remonstrated with Dr J.P. Quin, Director of the Estates, asking what she should do if there were an epidemic of some kind adding that there was no equipment, no blankets, no pillows and no sheets. "Oh," said Dr Quin, "The girls can bring their own bedding from the hostel." The nurse had no desire to be struck off the Nursing Register and left shortly after her encounter with Zebedielan hygiene. The day after her hasty departure, the Matron of the hostel announced that any two girls could take on the job of looking after the hospital and be paid 7 shillings and 6 pence a day – this for dishing out aspirin tablets!

Our experiences in Zebediela remained in our minds for a long time and had an aftermath, which could have been unpleasant for me. I had told Mr Chamberlain, who had a farm just outside Louis Trichardt and who did some recruiting for the mines, of our experiences and the kind of health services available to over 1 000 people. All these farmers in the Zoutpansberg area grew oranges, bananas and avocados, but as there was little or no profit in this, they made some money by recruiting Africans.

Some months afterwards a large car arrived at our gate, a gentleman got out and introduced himself as a District Commissioner from Nyassaland. He wanted to talk to me about my allegations concerning the treatment of blacks at the Zebediela Estates. I insisted that he send his driver away because I did not want any witnesses to be present. I said to him, "What I am going to tell you is the truth, but I have not the money for a lawsuit against Mr Schlesinger." Over a cup of tea I told him about our experiences and he thought that it was "a very serious thing" that I was "spreading around". He had been sent by the Nyassaland Government to investigate my story, because their Africans were dying like flies in Zebediela.

He came back a few weeks later, when my husband was at home, and again over a cup of tea he said to me, "You never saw half of what is going on there – I am horrified and my Government will have to take steps to improve our men's living conditions. After this visit, Mr Schlesinger was forced to employ two resident doctors and a qualified nurse. In addition, eventually a proper hospital, Groothoek Hospital, was built. I know that Mr [Dr] Quin had a great deal of trouble over my report, because his daughter told Box with high indignation about "two masquerading women" at the packing sheds, and that "the whole of Africa" was writing to her father about their Africans. Box had happened to be having lunch with her friend, Molly Macindoe, and her uncle, Mr Parr, when they were joined by young Parr and his wife who was Dr Quin's daughter. Naturally Box did not "let on" that she was one of the so-called masquerading women as she would not have been able to cope with the situation.

Box and I had another exciting experience on one of our last joint trips before the War, but this was of a quite different nature. We were camped on the Rhodesian Sabi River, at Morrumbene, at the bottom of Spraggon's Koppie, where Mark Spraggon (later owner of the Punch Bowl Hotel north of Louis Trichardt) had a shop and a transport business taking parties of Africans to the Rand mines. He told us of the good luck that Mr Osborne, one of the old prospectors, had had when he found tungsten near Fort Victoria and was able to sell it to a Mr Cowan for 75 000 pounds.

Osborne knew of another deposit somewhere down the Sabi River. He described where it was situated to Mr Spraggon, because he himself did not feel like going into this wild country again as he was getting old and was quite happy with the money that he had already made. Old Spraggon also got cold feet, and when I happened to ask him whether there was anything worth investigating during the last few days of our holiday, he mentioned Osborne's find. He offered to let us use his prospector's licence and a bundle of linen prospector-strips which were issued by the Mining Commissioner, together with the licence. All he could tell us was that the deposit of tungsten (wolframite and scheelite) was somewhere downriver at the foot of an island in the river-bed.

We decided to leave early in the morning [by car] and try to follow the Sabi River but as there was no road, and as it was very much wild bush country in which elephant, zebra, and kudu were roaming, we did not get very far. On the second day we managed to reach the river and resolved to stop, have a bath, wash our clothes and cook some food. When I looked across the Sabi I saw the reflection of the sun on a car a long distance off and wondered who was in it. We hurriedly ate our food, rolled up our clothes, put them on our heads and walked across the river. The water came up to our chests, but we did not need actually to swim. On the other side we dressed and went on through the bush until we reached a car and its occupant. He was an old man looking rather the worse for wear. We greeted each other, and he said, "Would you like a drink of whisky or brandy?"

"No," I said, "we don't drink brandy but we would love some tea."

"Well," he replied, "you won't live long in this country if you don't drink something stronger than tea." He called his "boy" to make some tea, and while we were talking I asked him what he was doing there. "Ah," he said, "you shouldn't ask questions like that – I'm looking for tungsten. What are you doing here?" I told him that my husband was a very keen archae-ologist, and that he was trying to find old ruins. He advised us to go to the Belingwe district, which I naturally knew about, but was not going to let on that I did. He offered to show us his map and I chatted to Mr McNeilage, which was his name, while Box got her bearings on the map. She found an island, which could possibly have been the one we were looking for, about 25 miles downstream.

When we got back to our car we marked the speedometer, and when we had done 25 miles we stopped. It was then quite dark so we decided to sleep there. About 4 o'clock in the morning an African passed, greeting us with the Shangaan *Aushene*, while walking on. I thought this rather ex-traordinary as there were no people living in the area, and I wondered where he had come from. After we had had breakfast, we made straight for the river and reached the island as if we had known exactly where it was. There was an enormous outcrop of rock which had a whole band of some other rock formation, which we thought must be tungsten. I got out my prospector's pick and chipped out 12 pieces from various places. I then took off the sleeves of my dress and tied them up in little pockets and put in the samples. I also had to use my socks for this purpose.

We then drove back to Messina and I went to see Mr Weber, a German geologist. He was a very pleasant and clever old man and I told him our story. He was about to go off to Johannesburg but he promised to have our samples analysed and let us have the report in about 2 weeks' time. About a fortnight later I saw him at the bioscope, and he assured me that the samples contained tungsten. He said that one band was rich and the other rocks less so, but that if there was a good supply of water it would be profitable to extract the metal. He advised me to peg my claims and get them registered at once. Unfortunately, when we had first pegged our claim, I did not know that one had to use the Rhodesian way of pegging a claim, with the writing on the claim strips on the outside. The way I knew, was with the writing on the inside, the Transvaal way, which was invalid. This was on a Wednesday, and quick thinking and acting were of the utmost importance. I said to my husband, "I am going to the garage now to fill up with petrol and I am leaving at once. I'll be at Beit Bridge when they open the border post, and by the day after tomorrow I'll be at the site." Because of the wild country, Louis made me promise to be back by Sunday. So I filled up, took my sleeping-bag, "scoffbox", kettle, knife, spoon, pan and tea and accompanied by Tiny, set off to stake our claim. When we got there I found that my claim had been misappropriated by someone who had pegged over it the correct way, We then realised that the African who had passed us in the night must have been Mr McNeilage's servant who had been asked by the old drunkard to follow us – he must have guessed that we were after the tungsten.

In those days the mining company would often give these old prospectors 5 pounds a month to go and take themselves off into the veldt looking for minerals. I think that many of them simply bought a case of brandy, enjoyed themselves and then came back for more. However, as bad luck would have it, McNeilage was really prospecting when Box and I stumbled upon him. Tiny and I should have stayed there, waiting to see if McNeilage would come to cut his lines, because only then could he have registered his claim with the Government, but I had promised to be back on the Sunday night. Our next best strategy was to drive back to Spraggon's Camp, where Harold Mockford was stationed with Wenela. He offered to go and sit there for seven days, and if McNeilage did not come back he would re-peg our claim and have the lines cut by his "boys". "Cutting the lines" means that the distance from peg to peg must be a certain number of yards and that the bush from peg to peg must be cleared.

Tiny and I got back to Messina about 2 a.m. on the Monday morning, and as we were having breakfast the door opened and in walked Harold Mockford. I said, "What are you doing here? You should be sitting on our mine!" His reply was crushing. "Mr Wilson must have been listening to you all the time while we were making our arrangements. You know Spraggon left him in charge and as soon as you had left he told me that I had to go to Beit Bridge to fetch a truckload of petrol and said that I was not working for Mrs Thompson!" Harold said that he would drive through the night and see what was happening. When he got back to Spraggon's Camp he was told that Mr Wilson had gone to Fort Victoria. Harold immediately picked up a light delivery van, and went straight to our island. There he found old Wilson with two men from Fort Victoria and a man from Johannesburg and they had pegged their claims.

This, today, is the Hippo Mine which employs hundreds of Africans, and old Wilson did me out of it. Meanwhile Mr Cowan had offered me 29 000 pounds if I would show him where the mine was. However, we would have lost it anyway because we personally did not have a licence to peg – it belonged to Mr Spraggon. That was the nearest I ever got to being rich, and this is my hard-luck story, but at least we had some fun and excitement. We had another good laugh when Roy Stevenson sent us a newspaper clipping jokingly egging us on to sue Mr McNeilage for libel because for some, to me, obscure reason the old prospector had related how he met us in the bush and referred to us as "two amateur archaeologists, real amazons, Mrs Thompson and daughter from Messina".

Aarone Machava.

XII Wartime, Limpopo and Fundudzi Trips

When the Second World War broke out in 1939, four members of our family joined up in various units of the Forces. Clifford went to Southern Rhodesia and trained as a pilot in the Royal Air Force. Box joined, in 1942, the Corps of Signals, Louis served from 1941 to 1945 as a Medical Officer at Sonderwater and I myself went to the recruiting office in Pretoria, where I lied about my date of birth, and was enlisted as a driver. I undertook transport driving at Roberts Heights, and I thought it would be rather fun, but the routine was boring. There was only one interesting assignment: a Harvard aeroplane had crashed near Gwanda [in southern Rhodesia] and Mrs Violet Myrtle Syme, who was in my unit and later lived on Kopje Alleen [near Haenertsburg], and I had to take Major van Reenen and 21 men up to the wreckage.

My truck had a long trailer on which we would be able to put the plane and bring it back to Pretoria. Syme and I had to cook for the men, but there were no suitable pots in which to do this, so on our way North we stopped at a garage in Messina, bought a number of paraffin tins, cut the tops off, and used them as pots. We brought the plane back to Pretoria, and really enjoyed the trip. Later on I was supposed to go to Egypt and do clerical work, but this was not for me and I left. I was in the Army for only a year and then I bought myself out for 10 pounds. My job as a driver could easily be done by anyone, and as Louis had given up his post in Messina it was important that I should look after our apple-trees and improve our home.

When I came out of the army in 1941 I lived alone at Otterholt. Apart from the usual farming activities, I supervised the making of terraces below the apple orchard, because Box wanted to start a nursery. She had taken a B.Sc. in Botany and Zoology at the University of the Witwatersrand and her first job had been to act as Technical Assistant to Prof. Cornelius Jan van der Horst,[1] Professor of Zoology at the University. He was working on the elephant shrews of this country. In search of them they travelled all over Sekhukhuniland, the Louis Trichardt area and, with a group of students, even to Inhaca Island in Mozambique. The Portuguese had estab-

---

1   1889–1951.

lished a research station for the Professor there, and he duly published his findings on *Elephantulus myuris jamesoni*.

At that time Box earned 10 pounds a month. After she had saved some money, she ordered some lily bulbs from England and when they arrived I put them into prepared beds next to the ones she had imported from Holland in 1938. To be precise, she received *Lilium sargentii*, *Lilium sulphurium*, *Lilium henryi* and *Lilium maxwill* from England. The Dutch lilies were *Lilium speciosum*, *Lilium regale* and *Lilium tigrinum*. The idea was to sell the lilies as cut flowers in Johannesburg. Later Louis got interested in her project and ordered *Lilium formosanum* from a Constable catalogue (nursery in Tunbridge Wells, Kent). They are the lilies that went wild and can be seen on all roads around Haenertsburg in January.

I have already mentioned that Box joined the Special Signal Services, the S.S.S. There was a radar screen put up all around the South African coast and the Signal girls were stationed at places such as Durban North, Port Shepstone, Knysna, Ysterfontein, and Mouille Point in Cape Town. They were often transferred from place to place, and this gave Box a wonderful opportunity to follow her collector's passion for indigenous bulbs and other plants. On her off-duty days she also helped in the Bloem Erf nurseries of Miss K.C. Stanford (in Banhoek, near Stellenbosch), who was very knowledgeable on the Cape flora and undertook a number of lecture tours in the USA on this topic. Box had a good time while she was in the Signals. When she came home on leave her kitbag was always full of bulbs and seeds.

In July 1942, Potty was reported missing over the Mediterranean, and for a few weeks we lived in suspense and sorrow until we heard that he had been picked up by an Italian boat. He and his navigator and two gunners were shot down on 29 July, but as they had as standard equipment an emergency dinghy they were able to keep afloat. Their rescue was closely linked with an incident in which Lieutenant Ted Strever of the R.A.F. and his crew of three had hijacked an Italian seaplane which was taking them as prisoners of war from the small Italian Air Force Base on the Greek Island of Levkas to the huge Italian Naval Base at Taranto. Ted made a dramatic forced landing in the sea off Malta, and when the Italians went to look for their seaplane, a Cant, they found Clifford and the three other men. Ted Strever now lives only 5 km from Wegraakbos on Stanford Farm, and in a way Potty owes his life to Ted and his daring crew. [Ted died on the 18th of February 1997.] When a prisoner of war, Potty made a couple of unsuccessful attempts at escaping, but the third time he managed to get away and crossed the American frontline near Monte Cassino in October 1943.

After the end of the war, in July 1945, I went up to Messina to say goodbye to all my friends. Actually, my main purpose was to have a rest from farm and family obligations and go on a long walk, all on my own, along the Limpopo to Pafuri. Tiny had married Harold Mockford in 1942, and was living with him and her little daughter, Donella, in a house provided by Harold's employers, the Witwatersrand Native Labour Association [WENELA], right on the Portuguese border, in the north-eastern corner of the Kruger National Park. When Box heard of my plan, she did not mince her words. She called me a "silly old fool" and assured me that I would die of fright on the very first night of my trip! My frustrated response to this warning was: "I want to get away from *everybody*. I want to do as *I* want to do; I want to walk when *I* want to walk; sleep and eat when *I* want to sleep and eat, and I *don't* want to talk to anybody."

In Messina I stayed with the Turners who became Gub's parents-in-law when she married Robert in 1946. I could have started walking at Main Drift, where we used to go for picnics, but below Beit Bridge there are some old copper workings which I wanted to see, and these were only ten miles further. Before Mr Turner took me to Beit Bridge I went to see Mr Evans, who was the Chief of Police in Messina. I told him about my plan, because, just after the war, all sorts of strange people were going through Beit Bridge to Rhodesia, and the authorities had to know that I was going into that wild country all on my own. His warning was couched in somewhat more polite terms than Box's. I thought if I kept to the river, I could not die of thirst or get lost. My provisions consisted of two packets of raisins, a little bag of Tiger Oats, a packet of tea, some saccharin, and I had a chunk of bread given to me by Mrs Turner. For additional food I depended on the blacks, who would, I hoped, like some money for a bit of meat. I made a little billycan out of a jam tin, and I also took a big bath-towel with me. All of this went into my rucksack.

On the first day I got to about 5 miles below Main Drift, where I spent the night. I had passed no African kraals, no human habitation, and when I found a big dead log of a leadwood tree I made a fire under it and cooked myself some Tiger Oats. As I was busying myself, I heard a stick break, and on looking back saw what I thought was a mongrel dog. I had not seen any people so far so I took another look and found that it was a hyena standing there! This made me think of Sir Robert Coryndon, who had once mentioned in conversation with my husband, that a hyena will start eating your face when it finds you asleep! This was definitely not a reassuring thought when a little later I wrapped myself in my bath-towel, putting my head on my rucksack. I was drifting off to sleep when I felt something touch my hair.

"The hyena," I thought. "It's going to eat my face!" I jumped up quickly and discovered that it was an enormous toad, which must have come out from under the log. I had a jolly good laugh and put the thought of the hyena right out of my mind.

The next day I reached the Messina Company's ranch Doreen. I was very tired and exhausted because I had walked a long way in the heat. I decided to have some tea and was just beginning to make a fire when two men came up to me, Afrikaners, armed with rifles. Our conversation went something like this:

"What are you doing here?"

"I am camping for the night."

"Where are you going to?"

"I am going to the Portuguese border to visit my daughter at Pafuri."

"You can't sleep here. It's not safe. You must come up to the house. Are you armed?"

"I have no arms or ammunition, I am quite safe and I am not moving from here tonight."

"We don't trust you – empty your rucksack." At this command I emptied out my rucksack, produced my food, a little pocket knife with two blades and an attached tin-opener plus corkscrew, and to my utter embarrassment there were also some sanitary towels. After my assurance that I would come up to the house in the morning, they left me alone.

The third day, a Sunday, saw me climbing up a little steepish hill to the Steenkamp's house. My reception was quite different from our encounter of the previous evening. Mr Steenkamp had contacted the police and found out that I was Dr Thompson's wife and quite harmless, though I wondered what Mr Evans's actual words had been when he described my eccentric behaviour! The Steenkamps were having a little service, in which I joined, and in our devotions they also prayed for my safety. I had a very good lunch with them, roast chicken and potatoes

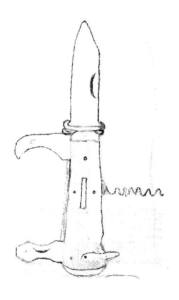

A sketch Awdry made of her pocket knife.

and many other good things to eat. For siesta, they took me to a big bedroom which seemed to be full of beds. Mr and Mrs Steenkamp settled on one of the double beds and invited me to sit at the foot of it whilst a whole pocket of oranges was served as refreshment. The three of us sucked oranges all afternoon, chatting, and to top it all, we had a wonderful supper of pap with thick milk and hardboiled eggs. Meanwhile, some friends had arrived in a cart [car?], so I went back to my camp and spent another night there.

At dawn, early next morning, I set off again. There were stretches along my route which were not easily negotiated. For instance, at one spot the Limpopo runs under rocks, and I had to jump from rock to rock for about two miles – that was the hardest part of my trip. It is this gorge that posed such difficulties for Mr Wilfried Southey Ramke-Meyer and his friend Robertson in 1925. Because "Brownie Ramke" became such a well-known character in Haenertsburg, I would like to mention a few facts about his Limpopo trip. He and Robbie Robertson had set off from Main Drift at 4.30 p.m. on 30 April 1925 in their light, self-built boat, Louie. The whole journey to Delagoa Bay [probably Xai-Xai where the Limpopo enters the sea, 150 km north-east of Delagoa Bay] lasted six weeks, but unfortunately Robbie was bitten by a spider and left for Lourenço Marques in a hurry, where one of his fingers had to be amputated. They parted company at Xinavane, 336 miles from Messina. The new crew member was an African nicknamed "Mr Chaai Chaai" and the trip was duly completed. We met Mr Ramke when he became an engineer on the Copper Mine in Messina. He lived with his young family in the house next to ours from 1933–1936, and my husband was their family doctor. In 1941 he bought Pippin Hill farm opposite the Magoebaskloof Hotel [his daughter Joan Provis is still on the mountain].

Coming back to my own walk, I had ample time for observing and enjoying the plant and animal life. One day I saw two Verreaux's eagles [commonly known as Black Eagles] chasing baboons which had ventured too near to their nest on the krantzes. On another day, when I got to the confluence of the Bubye River, I followed it to our old camp site and explored the graphite seam. The blacks used to extract this graphite and with it their women made the diamond shaped black patterns on their pots, for which they are well-known; they bartered these for mealies.

Eventually, towards the end of my walk, I came across people again. They were a crowd of blacks bunched together, who scattered when they caught a glimpse of me. I wondered why they had done that and went to see what they had been doing and came upon a newly killed sable antelope. They must have thought I was a policeman, because I was wearing my usual outfit of a loose khaki dress, felt hat, and my hair was short like a man's. The sable antelope proved to be a welcome stroke of luck. A few nice steaks cut off with my pocket-knife provided a good meal that evening, and when I arrived a couple of days later at Harold and Tiny's house, I was not even hungry. It had taken me about ten days to cover the 135 km as the crow flies, and nothing more terrifying had happened to me than the incident with those two Afrikaners who came after me with their rifles.

After the success I had had with my Limpopo trip, I thought I would go on another extended walk, starting at Lake Fundudzi following the Mutale River up to its confluence with the Levuvhu and on to Pafuri. The whole distance is about 110 km as the crow flies. My husband, Emily Murray and I, some years before, had camped near the lake which is sacred to the Venda people. They used to bury their chiefs in it, and a crocodile is supposed to be the re-incarnation of these chiefs, which makes the crocodile, *Kwena*, their totem animal. Louis, at that time, was doing a locum for Dr Peter Parnell who was the Medical Officer for Wenela from 1940/52. He had to vaccinate the new labourers against smallpox and yellow fever, and to sort out the men that were underweight. I have already mentioned Aarone Machava, whom we had met at Mambone near Sofala; he was just one of these "rejects". When Tiny asked me to look after little Donella at the farm because the child could not take the heat at Pafuri, she arranged for a reliable man to work in the kitchen, and thus Aarone entered my employment and has been with me ever since, for the last 40 years.

At the time of my intended trip, the Vhavenda were suffering from a famine, and the Government was sending mealie meal by lorry for distribution amongst them. One of these lorries picked me up at Louis Trichardt, and dropped me somewhere between Sibasa and the Siloam Mission Hospital. It was already October when I started my walk, at the west end of the lake, a season really too hot for this kind of undertaking. I should never have attempted it, but if you never try you never get anywhere. In addition, the going was very rough and I had to jump from rock to rock for long stretches over the many little streams that entered the lake. When I came to the eastern end I found what must have been a landslide centuries ago which had dammed up the course of the Mutale and thus created the 5 km-long lake. The water was bubbly, fresh and beautiful, and I could see across an enormous tract of flat land covered with big stumps of trees. An old man told me that a fire had destroyed a forest of umzimbeet (also called kaffir ironwood – *Millettia grandis* = *Millettia caffra* – and that no planting of crops was allowed there. The land belonged to the spirits of their ancestors.

I found all this very interesting, and after I had some tea, I lay down to sleep. It was very hot, I was very tired, and about half way through the night I developed a splitting headache. I took some aspirin, but this did not help. The next day I walked a little way, but not very far. I felt very sick, so I lay down under a bush and when darkness came I was still lying there. My head was bursting and I was aching all over. Round about 8 or 9 o'clock some blacks passed and said, "You can't sleep here, the hyenas will eat you. We will take you to Chief Mphephu's kraal." However, I would not move because I just could not face getting up. The Africans did not argue and went off. About 1 o'clock in the morning they returned with a donkey. The Chief had sent them to fetch me and they were not to come back without me. On the way they had apparently come across a young baboon which they killed and meant to eat. They hoisted me onto the donkey, the baboon lying in front of me. With one man on each side of me they manage to hold me upright.

Oh, I felt so ill and it seemed as though we were travelling for about a month. Eventually we reached the kraal, and the Chief's first wife wrapped me up in her blanket and made a big fire in her hut. She then boiled some tea and looked after me for three days and two nights.

During this time I did have some lucid moments and found some of their ways and customs most interesting. For instance, the Chief's second wife prepared porridge for the whole kraal. She scooped the cooked pap out of the pot and made flat cakes out of this and then placed them in a *sešego* – a shallow basket which they used to separate the bran from the mealies. She filled the basket with these cakes, and in between them she put masonga worms, rolled inside out and roasted. The cakes were eaten cold and were delicious. The men ate first, then the young women, after them the children, and lastly the old women, like me, and the babies. Nobody encroached on anybody else's portion. The women also told me that at every initiation school a sheep or goat would be boiled and put into a hollowed-out trough shaped like a crocodile; the boys had to eat this meat kneeling down and without using their hands. When the trough was not in use the hollow was not noticeable as it was turned around to lie on its belly. The same rite is observed by the Baphuti, the People of the Duiker, and the Baphukubjê, the Jackal People. (The name Mapungubwe given to the archaeological sites near Messina is a distorted form of the word Baphukubjê.)

In this context it may be of interest to quote some lines written by H. Rider Haggard in a foreword to one of his books, *The People of the Silver Mist* widely read at the turn of the century [19th to 20th century]:

The People of the Silver Mist of my adventure-story worship a sacred crocodile, to which they make sacrifices, but in the original draft of the book this crocodile was a snake. A friend suggested that a snake was altogether unprecedented and impossible. Accordingly the change was effected, when Mr R.T. Coryndon, the slayer of almost the last white rhinoceros, published in the "African Review" of 19 February 1894, an account of a huge and terrific serpent said to exist in the Dichwi district of Mashonaland. Still, the tale being in type, the alteration was suffered to stand. But now, if the "Zoutpansberg Review" may be believed, the author can take credit for his crocodile also, since the paper states, that in the course of the recent campaign against Malaboch, a chief living in the north of the Transvaal, this fetish god was captured, and to this god, a crocodile fashioned in wood, offerings were made. Further, this journal says that among these people the worship of the crocodile is a recognised cult. Also it congratulates the present writer on his intimate acquaintance with the more secret manifestations of African folklore and beast worship. He must disclaim the compliment in this instance as, when engaged in inventing the "People of the Mist", he was totally ignorant that any of the Bantu tribes reverenced either snake or crocodile divinities. But the coincidence is strange.

To continue with my own story, Chief Mphephu sent a message requesting the driver of the lorry who used to bring the mealie meal, to come to his kraal and pick me up. I was taken to Sibasa, the Native Commissioner's residence. Johnny Butlin, Philippa's husband, then a doctor at Elim Hospital, came to fetch me. He diagnosed that I was suffering from heat stroke, and I had to spend some time in the hospital before I was well again.

XIII The 1950's and 1960's in Haenertsburg

Back at home, on Wegraakbos, I became more and more involved with Box's nursery. At first, most of the activity took place there, but then we gave Box the 48 morgen portion Ongeluk of Goedvertrouwen, which Louis had bought from Brummer in the 1930's. The name Ongeluk was given to it by Koos Brummer because, when he did transport driving from Pietersburg to Haenertsburg, his wagon once collapsed above our little dam wall.

Already during the war I had thought about my children's inheritance, when my husband's health began to decline and I grew tired of farming. I decided to divide the farm between Tiny, Philippa and Clifford, keeping the portion with the house on it for the latter. For Gub we wanted to buy a portion of Nooyensboom or Good Hope, but the land was too expensive. In the end 11 morgen of Ongeluk were registered in her name and she retained the name Goedvertrouwen for her home. In the meantime, Box built a house for herself, using the 250 pounds that she got as a gratuity at the end of the war. It is this house that we are living in now. It was built by Guiseppe Pent, an Italian who had established himself near Haenertsburg as a shop-keeper and builder. He had been a prisoner of war at Sonderwater near Pretoria, and was recommended to Louis by a colleague, Dr Robert Patrick McNeil.[1] Dr McNeil had a practice in Benoni, but he acquired part of Waterval from Constant Fauconnier and built himself a holiday house there, which he called Merrick. As a matter of interest, Guiseppe Pent did not have any training or experience as a builder then, but his father was a master builder in Italy. Whilst he was erecting Box's house, his father came to visit him and he did not approve of his son's work. However, it is still standing and we are very happy here.

Before the house was built, Louis, Box, Potty and I lived together at Otterholt [Wegraakbos]. Potty spent two years on the farm, and then went beekeeping with a friend, Peggy O'Neil, in the Cape for about a year. He also took a course in pruning and fruit-tree grafting at Pickstone's Nursery. He then returned to us, acquired two sections of Waterval, and ran a little sawmill on his own, which we used to call the Bottleneck Sawmill. Machinery used to break down frequently, but he mastered these technical prob-

---

1   1879–1968.

A scene in the Wolkberg.
(Louis Changuion collection.)

A drawing of the Haenertsburg Hotel.
(Louis Changuion collection.)

lems with great skill; his partner in this venture was John Wilson. The sale of some of his timber was organised by a Mr Hans Wongtschowski [years later to marry the compiler of this book] from Johannesburg, whom he had met whilst walking with his dog on Table Mountain. The two of them became good friends. Both were members of the Mountain Club of South Africa and our home always provided sleeping facilities for young people passing through on their way to the Wolkberg. Potty was instrumental in building the hut belonging to the club whereas Hans and Mr Latham organised the buying of the two morgen of land from Mr Greathead (1951).

At times I got a bit annoyed with these "birds of passage"; they did not seem to take any interest in botany or zoology and had only their rock climbing at heart. I should not be so harsh on them though, at least not on Hans and Else Wongtschowski [Hans' first wife], because they took Box and me on a wonderful holiday to the Drakensberg. We travelled together through the Free State and Oliviershoek Pass to Cathedral Peak Forest Station, then up Mike's Pass to the top of the Little Berg, and at the contour path we parked the car. From here we climbed along the ridge to the Organ Pipes. Under the Indumeni Dome the Transvaal Section of the Mountain Club had a lovely little hut, just inside Lesotho. While the other members of the party went rock climbing, Box and I walked great distances for the ten days of our stay, botanizing and enjoying ourselves. One day we also carried a slaughtered and skinned sheep back to the hut; we had bought it from some blacks. Most welcome grub it was!

On the 1 September 1954, Potty got married to Eva Horstmeier, one of a group of German nurses who came out in the late forties, and then my husband and I went to live permanently with Box. I put my bed on the stoep in a convenient corner and have slept in the open air ever since.

My husband retired in 1945, and went to see patients in the vicinity only when the need arose. He did a couple of locums like the one at Pafuri, and another one, in 1948, on the tin mine Rooiberg near Rustenburg. Unfortunately, he had lost an old congenial friend in Mr H.D.M. Stanford when the previous Native Commissioner was accidentally drowned on 8 January 1941, in the lake which he had created on his farm Good Hope and which to this day is such an attraction in our area [Stanford's descendants still stay on this farm].

Time did not lie heavy on Louis's hands. He kept up a lively correspondence with various friends and institutions, mostly on archaeological or ornithological matters. However, his main love was fishing. His best old-time friend was Roy Stevenson, then Compound Manager at the Selukwe Asbestos Mine. All his life Roy had been a keen collector of about everything except money! In particular he had an outstanding collection of wasps and moths. His knowledge of birds was also exceptional and his long letters to Louis were packed with information on the bird-life of the Rhodesian Midlands, together with requests for specific bird skins, which he felt were missing from the National Museum in Bulawayo. After his wife died, Roy always spent his one month's annual holiday with us. On one occasion he got a bit tired of my breakfasts and presented me with a book entitled *Three Hundred Ways of Cooking an Egg*.

Roy Stevenson had a special bookplate which showed all the plants and animals which had been named after him, for instance a monkey, a butterfly, a bird and a wasp. When Louis died in 1955, Roy wrote to me in his letter of condolence, "I shall miss him more than most of his friends as we had so much in common." Louis had been interested in so many things and he kept the active mind of a young man. When he became interested in a specific subject he was determined to know all about it. For instance, he became acquainted with D.A. [David, also known as Swanie] Swanepoel, who was a barman at the Great North Hotel in Pietersburg, and who was to become a well-known specialist on the butterflies of South Africa. Louis read several books on the subject and decided to start collecting himself. He bought a special cabinet and then tried to teach his first grandchild, Donella, how to go about organising a butterfly collection. He said to her, "Donella, this cabinet is for our butterfly collection. I'll show you how to use the killing bottle and the setting-boards. Look how clearly most of them are marked." Donella was not very enthusiastic, replying, "Oh, Oupa, I couldn't kill any of them – they are all fairies, you know." That was the end of that little project, and thereafter the cabinet was used for storing beads.

Only a couple of years ago, in September 1983, Mr Swanepoel visited me and told me how he was living in a caravan and following the sun. He must have had a pretty steady income from his book *Butterflies of South Africa: where, when and how they fly*.[2] He found a Little Blue on top of Witkopje near Pietersburg, now most probably extinct because the hill is being worked by the Silicon Smelters. His beautiful tall tamboti wood cabinet with his valuable collection is housed in the Transvaal Museum in Pretoria. He had it made to his own design by Mr Elsden from Pietersburg, who had been trained by the royal cabinet-makers Blundel-Maple in London. Mr Swanepoel is the most affable man you could wish to meet, and although I could not recognise him, because of my near blindness, I was so pleased to see him! (sic)

---

2   Cape Town: Maskew Miller, 1954. *SESA*, 2, 630b and 636b.

In 2001 this plaque was erected at the hut on the Wolkberg.
(Louis Changuion collection.)

Harley Stanford at the falls (now halfway covered by the waters
of the Ebenezer Dam) below the lake, which he had created.
(André Strever collection.)

199

Another enthusiastic butterfly collector we met was George von Son. He was an entomologist at the Transvaal Museum and published *The Butterflies of Southern Africa*. He stayed with us and said that the Woodbush near Haenertsburg was one of his favourite hunting grounds. While Louis was lying in hospital in Pretoria, the Von Sons put me up, and I was very intrigued by an ancient green parrot which they had and which they called "Babushka" after his Russian grandmother from whom they had inherited it.

There is another story in a lighter vein relating to Louis and Mr Frederick Wartenweiler, a Swiss engineer, who had made good in this country. He had bought our neighbour Bridgeman's farm, Weltevreden. I had gone to The Downs to fetch Potty and I think also Robbie Turner [Gub's husband], who had been on a long walk together. When I got back on the Sunday night, the lights of my car showed up two heads in the window. On going in I saw that they belonged to old Wartenweiler and Louis who had given him supper. I was rather baffled as to what meat had been dished up by the piccanin in the kitchen, and was horrified to find that he had given them the minced lungs which were meant for the dogs! The next time I saw Mr Wartenweiler in the village, I enquired, with tongue in cheek, how he had enjoyed his supper. He replied, "We had quite a good supper, but I don't know what kind of meat that was." He left a large amount of money to the University of the Witwatersrand, to which his wife, Jean, added a sum when she made her last will. The Wartenweiler Library on the campus was finished in 1972 and is a monument to both of them.

By 1950, Louis had become very ill with emphysema. A lifelong habit of heavy smoking had made itself felt. He spent two months with an old friend at Bandelierkop, because he thought that the dry air would do him good. He then had to have a prostate gland operation in Louis Trichardt, which was not a success. Louis was ailing for about four years and went from one hospital to another. On one occasion, Potty's friend, Hans Wongtschowski asked him, "Doctor – what exactly is your complaint?" He replied with his typical Irish sense of humour, "Senile decay, my boy, senile decay!" Louis died on 2 March 1955 in the Pietersburg Hospital. We buried him on Wegraakbos, where my parents and Eva's brother lie. The Messina Copper Mines had a small copper plaque engraved in his memory and Mr Richard Cunliff attached it to his gravestone. Doc Thompson, as he was generally known in Haenertsburg, or "Ranobi", Father of Otters, had been well-liked for his gentle, kind and considerate nature. For me, my children and my grandchildren, Oupa's loss meant that a certain quality in our respective lives had disappeared forever, and with him died the last of the old guard of

English Gentlemen in Haenertsburg.

Shortly before Louis passed away we received the news that his elder brother, George Clifford, had died at the age of 81, in an asylum where he had lived for many years. He had had an accident in the early 1920's at the Blue Jacket Mine near Leydsdorp. Apparently he had been busy setting up a stamp battery, and his 14lb stone hammer got caught in the stamps. He sent his "boss-boy" to turn off the electricity, and George somehow managed to lever out the stone hammer when the stamp suddenly started up again. Obviously the man had not yet turned off the current. The hammer flew straight at his head and broke his skull. Louis, who was District Surgeon at the time, together with his brother-in-law, Dr Val Watts from Barberton, operated on George and removed bits of bone from his brain. George recovered, but thereafter was somewhat mentally affected. He was given a very simple job on the tin mine Zaaiplaats near Potgietersrus. Although he was quite harmless, he had to be put in a home for which we had to pay 8 pounds a month. When the question of George's funeral arose, I did not want Louis to be troubled with it, so their sister, Winnie Watts, arranged it all.

Apart from Louis's brother George and his sister, Winifred, his younger brother, Edward, had also come out to this country and worked as a shift-boss at the mines in Johannesburg. I never met Louis's family in England, but we supported his mother and his sister, Vera, who looked after the old lady. They lived in a cottage bought by Louis in a village near Bristol, Somerset.

I derived a great deal of joy out of my grandchildren when they either came to stay with us, or when I took them on camping trips, mostly to Rhodesia, just as I had taken my own children. Fortunately they did not live far away. Tiny and Harold Mockford's children, Donella, Dorrit and Harold junior, called Buddy, grew up in Pafuri. Clifford with Eva and [their children] Louis and Julie, stayed in the old house on Wegraakbos. Gub and Robbie Turner, with their children, Erilyn, young Robert, called Oki, and Jane, lived just down the road, as it were, on Goedvertrouwen.

Robbie taught at the local school from 1948 to 1966, where Mr Piet Seegers, a very fine man, was the headmaster of the old school and later also of the new school. The old school, opened in 1889, stood alongside the Haenertsburg Hotel [in the village]. It was a wood and iron building consisting by now of six rooms. This was replaced in 1954 by new and extensive buildings, with hostel accommodation, on a rise to the south of the centre of the village. Early in 1969 the road from the village to the school was tarred. Gub also taught there, on and off, until Robbie was seconded to Capricorn High School in Pietersburg.

The Turners were entitled to use the Old Residency, the home of previous Native Commissioners [in Haenertsburg], as their living quarters, but they preferred to stay on the farm. Robbie sublet the building for 8 pounds a month to Medardo Ruggeri who lived in it for a few years, from 1952 to 1955. He was followed by other tenants, like Mr Smit, the Cattle Inspector, but eventually in 1966, the solid building put up in the same style, with the same kind of stone as the old Police Station opposite the Post Office, was demolished. One could say that the ways of the Provincial Administration in general, and the Public Works Department in particular, are tortuous and incomprehensible. Dan Symonds maintains that the old house had just been painted and renovated at the cost of 400 pounds.

Lastly, Philippa with her husband, Dr J.L. [Johnny] Butlin, and their children, lived on a little farm near Louis Trichardt, where he had a private practice. There were times when they wished to take a holiday, and I used to go and look after Diana, Carol, Lawrence and Shelley, together with the Jersey cows that Johnny kept.

When my grandchildren came visiting I kept them occupied by giving each of them a bit of garden, and we built a house for the fairies. The children worked there like little beavers, growing flowers and making a little path for the fairies, who often left them presents. These consisted mainly of sweets, but sometimes I bought small china objects from Mrs Iris Lee [mother to Gem Turner and therefore James Turner's grandmother] who had a small shop adjoining what was then the new and impressive Tank Trap Store in Rissik Street, the main street of the village. I had to take these presents to the Fairy House, whilst it was still dark, because at crack of dawn the children would dash up there, still in their pyjamas, to search for the gifts.

All my grandchildren started to call me "Googoo", the anglicised version of the Sesotho word *Koko* for grandmother and my husband Louis became "Oupa". It was very interesting to observe the development of the children's characters and rather sad to watch Dorrit, who could not compete with them. She was a Mongoloid child and a great heartache to the family. The Swiss nurses at Elim Hospital, where she was born, called her Chouchou (a French term of endearment). When she was eight years old, I took her to Johannesburg in order to get regular lessons for her from a speech therapist. For three months we stayed with Miss Kathleen Brabazon, the sister of Mrs Stella Latham from Glenshiel farm. Kathleen taught English at Jeppe High School for Boys and whilst I was living there I did her housekeeping.

Recalling the villagers of that time, various characters come to mind. Mrs Christabel Everitt was now living on her own at Homewood where she entertained the Anglican congregation with cucumber sandwiches after church on Sundays. She died in 1964, and rests in the local cemetery together with her husband, who passed away in 1946, and with the baby daughter they lost in 1905. The grave is marked by a monument of a beacon with a cross on top. You may remember that Mr Maurice Everitt had been the local Beacon Inspector in the olden days, and the inscription on the beacon reads: "Known to all – Loved by all." This well illustrates their standing in the community.

Joe and Flo Greenwood had moved from their farm, Wellstead, into the village, and had bought the house [in Rissik street] built by the Israelsohns. Joe took over the Goods Delivery Depot of the S.A. Road Motor Services, the R.M.S., from Cecil Wienand and he used the old shop as a storage room [today used by a local church]. Another part of the old shop where the Barclays Bank Agency now functions [lately Lin's Hair Salon], housed the first library, started during the war and moved to the Agricultural Hall when that was built in 1952. It was run by members of the T.A.U. and Mrs Emily Zeederberg acted as librarian for many years.

The R.M.S. bus provided the only public transport available. It ran from Pietersburg to the Magoebaskloof Hotel, and after the road was tarred, it continued on to the Rest Camp, now called Magoebaskloof Holiday Resort. On occasions the driver did not dare attempt the slippery road into the village, and he would stop at Mr Walter Lee's farm, Stylbult [now known as Gemfarm]. Mrs Lee would then take the mail in her jeep to the post office. Villagers who wanted to do shopping in Pietersburg had to take the return bus which got them to the town only at 4 p.m., and thus they had to stay overnight and come back the next morning.

The Haenertsburg Hotel [corner of Kantoor and Church street], which had been owned since 1916 by Bill Wienand, was now inhabited by his son, Cecil, although it did not function any more and the liquor licence must have expired in the late forties. Dances were still regularly held there. In 1964 Mr Andries Grundlingh,[3] who used to cut the schoolchildren's hair, bought the empty shell that it had become, and demolished it.

Next to the hotel [in Church street] was the house of Mrs Long[4] who had run a private school there. It was later sold to Mrs Edith Symonds who, in turn, let it to her newly married son, Dan, who lived in it from 1948 to 1952. He, his two brothers and his sister, Eva, now Mrs Fanie Human, grew up on

---

3 Andries Machiel Grundlingh, 1895–1978.
4 Her husband William Jeremiah Long, 1868–1946, had managed Koningskroon for Harvey and Storey for a time.

their father's (Owen Symonds) farm, known as Annie's Fortune. Dan Symonds had, as a young man during the depression joined the Special Services Battalion, the S.S.B., and fought in the armoured cars section in North Africa. Later the armoured cars were replaced by Sherman tanks.

When Dan returned after the war, he hired Joe Greenwood's shed [in Rissik street] and opened a general dealer's shop in opposition to no less than four Indian traders. One was Mr Adam on Cooyong farm and another Mr Suleiman, on a site above the present cafe. Dan employed Calabash, the redundant hotel cook, a very efficient man who had married Julia's daughter, the same Julia who had been my childhood companion. For six months Dan rode on horseback to and from work, until one day his horse died on him while he was in the village. Herman [Mac] McComb, the garage proprietor [corner of Rissik and Rush Street – now the home of Paul and Joey van Wyk], took him home in his car, but charged fifteen shillings for the fare, which took nearly all Dan's earnings for the whole week! Dr Parnell then lent him an even older horse until Dan could eventually afford to buy a second-hand truck from Mr Rankin, who had built the Magoebaskloof Hotel in the late 1930's, and at the time still owned it. Unfortunately the truck had a broken axle, but the local smith, wagonbuilder and jack-of-all-trades, Simon Barkhuizen, repaired it on his anvil. In 1956, Dan Symonds moved into his new shop [corner of Rissik and Rush Street], aptly calling it Tank Trap Store, where he and his wife, Thora, became fixtures for the next 25 years [today owned by the Strangs].

Dan also had an interest in Mrs Violet Fridjhon's New Look Store, which she kept from about 1955–1960. The name of her shop calls to mind the revolutionary drop in women's hemlines in the 1940's, dubbed "the new look" in the fashion world. Her shop was in the house [corner of Rissik and Gold Street] opposite the Greenwoods, now [till recently] owned by Mrs Ann Stott, and had previously been used by Harry Zeederberg, and later by Simon Barkhuizen as a butchery. The present butcher shop [now Blackburn Agency] was taken over by Mr Wiggil from Percy Wienand in 1957. Mrs Fridjhon, as I have mentioned before, had been governess to John and Bo Ireland, and now lived in her house built by Isak Beukes. It is situated opposite the charming little Catholic Church[5] erected in 1961, and she called it "Rondalong" after her dog of the same name – an animal which

---

5   There had also been a small stone-built N.G. Kerk in Kerk Street which functioned from about 1925–1935. Services were conducted by Ds Swart and Mr Andries (Makka) Bekker was the church warden.

6   Violet R. Fridjhon, b. 1891 Manchester d. 26.4.1964.

always "ran around and along". I liked Mrs Fridjhon[6] very much. She was a go-ahead, vivacious and resourceful woman, who scratched a precarious living for herself and her daughter, Ruth. Amongst other things, she bought and sold old and sometimes antique furniture and had small pieces of furniture made to order – like Mrs Lee's sewing box – and in her spare time she acted as an agent for the Century Insurance Company. In addition, she took in boarders like Mrs Amy Garthorne had done, who had kept a guest-house for a short while in the old Residency, way back from 1934 to 1936.

One of Mrs Fridjhon's regular visitors was the painter Bernie Hesselbarth, who became a firm friend, and whose paintings hang in many of the homes in the district. Another visitor was young Ian Yates, who spent weeks at a time in one of her rondavels. He also painted and sketched in the Woodbush, and gave her a very fine pastel of Rondalong, signed and dated 1959. To my knowledge it is the only painting in existence of one of the older houses in the village. She took it with her when she sold her "establishment" and went to live in a small cottage built by the two Italian builders Medardo Ruggeri[7] (whose books she kept) and Guiseppe Pent. Actually both her houses were successively bought by Mr Ian Harding, and it was at the house in Bok Street that Mrs Harding, who had to dispose of Mrs Fridjhon's effects after her death, found an interesting old photograph album. Mrs Fridjhon loved walking, knew the area well, and the album contains many good snapshots of Haenertsburg and its surroundings. Her daughter, Ruth,[8] became English mistress at St. Mary's Convent in Johannesburg and married Wolfe Miller, author of the novel *Man in the Background*. Ruth herself wrote poetry and was awarded the Ingrid Jonker Memorial Prize in 1966 for her first volume of poems, *Floating Island*, published in 1965.

Mrs Fridjhon together with Herman McComb [father of Graham McComb of Bali Wil Wil], conceived the idea of beautifying the village. They planted chestnut seedlings, obtained from Gub, down Rissik Street, some ash trees past Joe Greenwood's, a few Chinese elms next to the garage, and one cork oak at Tank Trap Stores. I believe there is no headstone on her grave, but she came to be buried next to Colonel and Mrs Wolff under the Keurboom tree next to the Garthornes' resting place. As in any other small community, a cemetery is a veritable "Who's Who" or rather, in this case, "Who was Who" in Haenertsburg. The graveyard had to be extended after Mr Ernest Stubbs, whose station-wagon was used to act as a hearse in the not-too-distant past, came across old bones, when he wanted to bury his mother-

---

7   1.6.1913 – 25.6.1987.

8   13.2.1919 – 31.5.1969.

in-law next to her husband, Bob Cooper. Perhaps the annual veldt fires destroyed many of the wooden crosses, and in any case the section containing African graves did not have headstones. As a matter of interest, the oldest gravestone reads: "Heinrich Karl Kremling, born Dassel, Germany – 10 May 1857 – 25 June 1894". I wonder whether he was one of the old gold prospectors. According to *Jeppe's Transvaal Almanac and Directory for 1889*, out of the fifteen white male inhabitants of Haenertsburg eight are listed as gold diggers.

With my family living near me, and working day in and day out in Box's nursery, there was not much time for socializing. We were, however, on friendly terms with most of the local farmers, and I saw most of the women fairly regularly after the Haenertsburg Horticultural Society was founded in 1955. A meeting was called with a view to starting the Society and was held at Scilla Hill Lily farm, Stewart and Josephine Gilkison's nursery, at 3 p.m. on Saturday 13 August. Robert Turner was elected Chairman, Box, Hon. Treasurer and S.V. Gilkison, Hon. Secretary. The first general meeting took place in the hall on 30 September 1955. The list of members reads rather like another "Who's Who" and "Who was Who" in Haenertsburg. For instance Dr G. Crewe-Brown was with us then and held regular clinics in the little building with the Dutch gable built by Dan Symonds, next to his Tank Trap Stores.

Although the honour of organising the first "Flower Show at Haenertsburg", according to the *Zoutpansberg Review* of Friday 24 December 1954, goes to the local branch of the T.W.A.U. [Transvaal Women's Agricultural Union] and was opened by Mr Owen Symonds Snr. in his capacity as Chairman of the Horticultural Society, from the very next year onward the Agricultural Society took over. The names of the exhibitors and prize-winners repeat themselves throughout the following annual flower shows. An article appeared in the *Transvaal Horticultural Society's Journal* dated February 1956 that gave credit to several of our old friends like Mrs Helen O'Connor for her "outstanding exhibits – a vase of arums of many colours". No doubt the apricot-coloured arum lily named after her by Sima Eliovson was amongst them. A rather less praiseworthy feat of hers was the introduction of blackberries into the area. Her idea was to supplement her income after the death of her husband, Alexander J. O'Connor, the Woodbush forester, by selling blackberry jam. However, the brambles ran riot as they so often do.

Originally there were six silver cups awarded as prizes for the various sections. These were acquired from "A.E. Lock's Art Emporium", Market Street, Pietersburg, for the proud sum of 7/6d each, making an outlay of 2 pounds 5 shillings. For later shows more cups were donated by Messrs Betton, Carst and Iuel, Turner, Gilkison, MacIntosh, MacKenzie, Schonland, George Smith, Symonds, Stubbs, Werndle and Zeederberg. The Dr L.C. Thompson Cup, a floating trophy, was awarded to the most outstanding indigenous flower grown by an exhibitor. We all thoroughly enjoyed the bustle and the activities connected with the show. In February 1972 the Haenertsburg Garden Club was founded as the successor to the Haenertsburg Horticultural Society.

Sheilah (Box) Thompson.

Aloe Thompsoniae.
(From Barbara Jeppe: *South African Aloes.* Purnell, C.T., 1969.)

XIV Development of the Nursery and Road Case

Since my husband's death, my life has been even more closely linked with Box and the development of her nursery, which is nowadays a very special attraction for lovers of plants and beautiful gardens. Every year up until 1974, we sent out a Summer and a Winter Bulb List to nurserymen in South Africa and overseas. Some of our contacts stretched as far as the USA, Holland, Switzerland and New Zealand. However, owing to the planting of pines over vast areas of the Woodbush, the quality of the light changed, and influenced the growth of the exotic bulbs, which were used to a Mediterranean climate.

The idea of growing azaleas on a large scale, instead of cut flowers, came from J.C. van Balen, the then Director of Parks and Estates for the City Council of Johannesburg. He thought that they would do well in our acid soil, and would not involve us in so much work. We met Mr van Balen at the home of a friend of ours, Stewart Gilkison, who lived on part of the farm Glenshiel near the Stanford Lake. The first cuttings were given to us by Potty, who saw them on the Phillips's place and on our neighbour, Colonel Bridgeman's farm, Weltevreden, where he was helping with the pruning of apple-trees. Others came from Mr Reinecke's nursery in Duiwelskloof, and a few thousand rooted cuttings were imported from America. Amongst these were Kurume azaleas which have a smaller flower and do not grow so tall. Box taught herself about their propagation by reading relevant literature and talking to other growers. Mrs May van Eeden, who had a nursery in Magoebaskloof, had taken a trip to Carter's nursery in Pietermaritzburg and noted that they stuck their cuttings close together, using old oil drums filled with sandy soil, and as soon as they were rooted they planted them further apart. Box realised that the cuttings did well when taken in December, when bushes did not have any buds.

Later on Dr McNeil gave Box one of his two deciduous azaleas, a mollis hybrid. This first yellow mollis must be about 30 years old by now – mollis azaleas are propagated from seed and take seven years to flower. As a present, I ordered some Exbury[1] hybrid azalea seed from the English firm of

---

1   Sir Lionel Rothschild developed on his estate Exbury a vast and wonderful collection of orchids, azaleas and rhododendrons.

Thompson & Morgan. I paid 25 shillings for as much as you can put on a fingernail, but one year after another we seemed to have bad luck. Box put the first mollis seed into a little tray in a cool area under a tree, but our tame hadeda birds came and ate them. Potty had given us these bothersome hadeda fledglings, and I fed them on nothing less than fillet! I had a standing order with the butcher, Percy Wienand, for 1 lb a week and in addition, I dug out earthworms for them from the compost. The next year Box protected the newly-bought seed with a sheet of glass, but they died when the sun got too hot; however, with the third lot we were lucky. Their colours range from bright yellow to varying shades of orange, and they are now a very special attraction at the Annual Flower Show, often called the Cherry Blossom Show. This is run each year in our nursery by members of the Haenertsburg Garden Club and its indomitable Chairlady, Mrs Helen (Jackie) Jackson.

Box got the idea of planting ornamental cherry trees from Collingwood Ingram's book called *Ornamental Cherries*.[2] Collingwood Ingram had travelled all over the Himalayas and Japan and had brought budwood of these cherries to England by sticking them into big potatoes so that they would not dry out. Box wrote to him asking how she could obtain them, and he answered with a charming letter in which he referred her to Lady Bourne, who lived in Elgin. He himself had taken her, sometime before, 19 scions of his collection and he suggested that Box ask Lady Bourne for cuttings. They arrived in due course in July, which is the right time for grafting.

We now had to look for stocks. We first tried the little dwarf cherries from the Phillips's old farm on the Broederstroom, but they were incompatible and they all died. Then one day we visited our old friend, Dr McNeil, who was busy digging out an old cherry tree that had a mass of fat suckers, and he gave them to us. Box cut them up, planted them and they all took. Most kindly, Lady Bourne sent more scions, a little bundle of each variety that she had, and that is how our trees started. There were so many of them all on the Turners' part of the farm, before Box gave that portion to Gub, that her husband, Robert, wanted to throw them out. Box therefore took them away and planted them out and that is why they are much too close together. At that time we could not sell them as nobody knew about ornamental cherries. Their botanical name is *Prunus serulata* and some of the varieties we have are *Prunus serulata kanzan*, *shirofugen* and *ukon*. We also have the Japanese hill-cherry, *Prunus subhirtella*. Box grew these herself. Dr Rikujie of Tokyo sent her five pips and all of them germinated.

---

2   London: *Country Life* (Ltd.), 1948.

I learned much from our experiences in the nursery and met many of the well-known botanists and zoologists of the country. Some wanted information from Box about certain plants and animals of the region, but I can only mention a few of them. There were, for instance, Dr Leslie E.W. Codd and Miss Eileen A. Bruce from the National Herbarium in Pretoria who came to look for a special poker lily, a *Kniphofia*, that was first described by Dr Anton Rehmann.[3] It is of historical interest that Dr Rehmann made the first substantial collection of plants of the Zoutpansberg region of the Northern Transvaal. Before, only Canon William Greenstock and William Nelson had collected a few plants in August 1875 and February/March 1878 respectively in this area. Dr Rehmann was German-speaking, though born in Cracow, Poland, then part of the Austro-Hungarian Empire. Sometime between 1879 and 1880 he stayed with the Knothes on Mphome, the home of the missionary in the Woodbush. The pink arum lily, *Zantedeschia rehmanni*, was first reported and collected by him. At any rate, Dr Codd and Miss Bruce asked for our assistance in their search for that particular *Kniphofia*, but we could not help them. After all, the magisterial district of Zoutpansberg stretched right down to Pietersburg and Rehmann had not given a precise location.

Whenever work in the nursery was slack, Box and I used to go camping and botanizing in Rhodesia, Mozambique, or nearer home. I remember a trip in 1950 to the Chimanimani National Park in Rhodesia, as it was then. It rained so hard that Box kept the flower press and I the sugar on our chests during the night. The crows ate our soup and the contents of an open tin of beans, so that by the time we carried the tins with *Streptocarpus* on our heads down the hill we were so hungry our knees were shaking.

On another occasion we took time off to meet Dr Neil Reitz Smuts in Mbabane. He was a medical doctor practising in Johannesburg and he used to order indigenous bulbs from us. We had not met him before, but he wanted to show Box some *Watsonia flavida*, which have a small delicate flower, and which grew near Pigg' Peak in Swaziland. We arranged to join him in Mbabane and set off in our little Willys Jeep. When we got to the top of the hill overlooking the town we decided to camp there. The next morning I got up, made porridge and tea for ourselves, and then went to look for a pool to have a wash. I gathered up my towel, my soap and a clean dress, yet when I got back, Box had not made a move. We were supposed to meet Dr Smuts at 10 o'clock that morning, but Box told me that there were no buttons on her fresh dress, and she would not go in her dirty one. So there

---

3   1840–1917.

we sat, taking the buttons off her old dress and sewing them onto the new one. Whenever I say to Box "get ready", this is the sort of thing that happens; she says it makes life more exciting!

Eventually we drove down the hill into Mbabane and then slowly along the street past the hotel. As we passed it I saw this man sitting under a tree out on the pavement looking at his watch. I said, "That must be Dr Smuts," and he appeared to be very put out because we were late. He was a very prim and precise person, but we soon got over our initial embarrassment and he showed us the *Watsonia flavida*.

Dr Smuts[4] was also very knowledgeable about aloes. He had been with Gilbert Westacott Reynolds,[5] the writer of the standard work *The Aloes of South Africa*[6] on botanizing trips to Malawi, Tanzania and Zambia in 1958 and to Angola and Zambia in 1959. Reynolds's book was dedicated to Dr N.R. Smuts and Dr R.A. Dyer and we have two copies of it. One was bought by my husband as a subscription copy and the other one was Dr Smuts's private copy, which has all his own loose photographs in it. His sister, Mrs Margot Mackay, gave this to Box as a present after his death. She also gave Box two albums containing beautiful photographs of plants he had collected, meticulously captioned. The aloe which is named after me and described by B.H. Groenewald also appears in Reynolds. I found it growing amongst some rocks on the Wolkberg when I, with my husband and Harry Whipp, a farmer from the Lowveld, rode on horseback to the flat area below the peak to inspect Harry's cattle, which were grazing there. A beautiful colour drawing of *Aloe thompsoniae* is included in Barbara Jeppe's book *South African Aloes*.[7]

Dr Smuts lived at 180 Hay Street in Turffontein and once, while visiting there, I mentioned that my favourite jam was watermelon *konfyt*. "Well," he said, "here is a big bowl for you." I tasted it, thought it was not watermelon, but found it was delicious. He told me it was made of the leaves of *Aloe marlothii* – that certainly was a surprise!

Dr Smuts told us an interesting story about his maternal grandfather, Mr James Reitz, and the South African painter Jan Ernst Abraham Volschenk.[8] Reitz, a Government Surveyor in the Cape, was working in the veldt near Riversdale when he noticed some shale on the ground which was covered

---

4   1895–1963.

5   1895–1967.

6   Johannesburg: Trustees of the Aloes of S.A. Book Fund, 1950.

7   Purnell, 1969.

8   1853–1936.

with drawings of little buck, sheep and houses. A young herd-boy, a white farmer's son, came up to him and when asked about the drawings, admitted, "Ek het hulle gemaak. Dis so vervelig om skape op te pas." [I did them. It is so boring to herd sheep.] Dr Reitz spoke to the boy's father about his talent and suggested that he should take him on his surveying trips and train him as a draughtsman. Old Volschenk said, "Meneer kan hom maar vat. Hy is niks werd as 'n wagter nie." [You can take him, sir. He is a useless shepherd.] Volschenk's animal drawings were absolutely life-like. One day old Reitz came home with a *kiewietjie* and a dove, which he hung up in the pantry and Volschenk drew a picture of them. He substituted the paintings for the birds, and when the cook came in to pluck them he was completely taken in! Dr Smuts had this painting in his house and it was incredibly realistic.

Whilst writing of animal paintings, I must mention Charles T. Astley-Maberly, born in Bristol in 1905, who came to South Africa in 1924 under the 1820 Settlers Memorial Scheme and who became a great friend of ours. He lived on a farm near Duiwelskloof. He illustrated several books on the animals of the Kruger Park (1951), Rhodesia (1959), East Africa (1960) and Harry Wolhuter's *Memoirs of a Game Ranger* (1950). The picture of a lizard buzzard over our fire-place is by him. His wife, Annette, a daughter of Dr Burman, had to wage a continuous battle to keep at least the inside of the house free from "invading wild-life". Spiders' webs and tarantulas were welcome on the stoep, and he used to feed the shy bush pig with mealies because he wanted to draw them. The garden smelled like a beer garden because of these fermenting mealies. His indulgence of monkeys was absolutely silly. Every morning he made his cook prepare a big pot of pap, and at 12 o'clock he banged on a piece of iron whereupon the monkeys converged on the house. The situation got so intolerable that they could not even keep the windows open and a whole pile of his books was pulled out of the bookcases and left in shreds. It must have been at this time that the long-suffering Annette decided that she and Charles must live in separate houses, he on the farm with his bush pigs and monkeys and she in Duiwelskloof.

Old Charles started a lawsuit against a black who laid bush pig snares on his place. After the judge had sentenced the man to six months in gaol, the prisoner, on walking past Astley-Maberly, said to him, "You'll be sorry for this." Charles felt very unhappy about the threat. Years later in 1972, he was murdered in his house and a black was found guilty and hanged, but I do not know whether it was the same man who had threatened him. Astley-Maberly was more acutely attuned to the bush than anybody I knew. One evening we were having dinner with him at Dr de Souza's house when he said to Box, "Listen to that bird, it has seen a snake." Sure enough, when Box doubted this and they went to have a look, there was a snake trying to get at the bird's nest.

There were a few zoologists whom we tried to help when they were collecting specimens, either while we were on camping trips or in our own back garden, as it were. One such effort had to do with *blaasops*, or to give them their scientific name, *Breviceps sylvestris sylvestris*. Vincent Wager, who wrote the book *Frogs of South Africa* (1965) had, as a youngster of about seventeen, stayed with some friends in the Lowveld. Here he found a tree frog, *Chiromantis xerampelina*, right at the bottom of the Debegeni Falls, but his holiday was interrupted when he contracted what I think was a mild dose of malaria. Dr Austin Roberts brought him to my husband, and I looked after him until he recovered. The acquaintanceship continued, and when he became Chief Mycologist at the Botanical Station in Durban he asked Box to go out during the night to look for *blaasops* between the stones in her terraces: They would appear after the first rain in the spring and could be found under the soil.

Another find that we made was accidental and gave us no trouble at all. Our friend Mrs Pam from Modderbee days, way back in 1926, came to see us from England in 1956. Whilst we were visiting Gordon McNeil on his farm, Cyprus, near Ofcolaco, and walking up his kloof we came across a batch of dragonflies [Gordon, the son of Dr Robert McNeil died in 1986 but his wife Margot is still on the farm]. Box caught some of them in her hat with no particular purpose in mind, then put them into a folded oblong piece of paper made into a triangle and left them in her chest of drawers. A little later on, on a misty rainy day, a man turned up at the house where I was on my own, and asked rather brusquely whether there were any dragonflies around. I did not know the man, and put him in his place by informing him that if he knew anything about dragonflies he should know that they did not fly in the mist. At that moment, Roy Stevenson appeared with Box and introduced the gentleman as Dr Elliot Pinhey, the author of *The Dragonflies of Southern Africa* (1951) and the Keeper of Entomology at the Bulawayo National Museum. Apparently they had been passing through Pietersburg and Roy had implored Pinhey to make a detour to see us, hoping against hope that Box would have some dragonflies for him. When Box went to look for the ones caught at Cyprus, Pinhey would not let her out of his sight. Eventually, with vests, bras and panties flying out of the drawer, they were unearthed and turned out to be *Chlorolestes elegans*, a genus for which Pinhey had been looking for.

By the end of the 1950's Box had become well-known amongst nurserymen as a grower of indigenous wild flowers of the summer rainfall area. Eve Palmer wrote about her achievements in an article entitled "A Transvaal Garden" for the *Journal of the Royal Horticultural Society*. A pleasant outcome of this was a letter which arrived one day from her godfather, Charles E. Legat, that old friend of mine and my parents more than fifty years before. His letter was written from Farnham in England and recalled, "Awdry's deep regard for a rather scraggy dog of doubtful parentage afflicted with *verkeerde* fever," and he went on to say, "For some reason or other our friendship was not sustained and I had hoped to meet your mother again at Magoebaskloof when I was there with Mr Lane-Poole after the Empire Forestry Conference of 1935 in Pretoria, but she did not appear. Your brother then came here one afternoon, when he was staying with Mr Pam to get information about forestry training, but I heard nothing further about or from him. However, I often think of my visits to those lovely Woodbush mountains, and of the kind hospitality your Grandfather and Grandmother extended to me there."

A similar "once-upon-a-time" story happened at about the same time. Dr McNeil's son, Gordon,[9] who was a well-known horticulturalist in the Lowveld and who, by hybridization, developed a big but not stringy mango, brought two eminent botanists to see us. They were Sir George Taylor, curator of Kew Gardens, and the Hon. Lewis Palmer, also of Kew Gardens. Gordon was taking them to Pietersburg to catch the train and Palmer said, "I simply must see Pietersburg again." Box asked, "What on earth do you want to see Pietersburg for?" He replied, "Pietersburg has a very special place in my heart. When my father, Lord Selborne, opened the branch line from Lydenburg to Steelpoort in 1910, he left me with the station-master in Pietersburg. I was spotted by a kindly engine-driver, who invited me to drive the train, and I spent many exciting hours with him in the heat and grime of the engine. It was the fulfilment of a boy's dream, one of the highlights of my life."(16)

Times and our immediate surroundings have certainly changed over the past 75 years. The scenery and ecology of the "Woodbush" had been altering from the 1940's onwards. The Forestry Department had started planting pines and gums as early as 1910 when Alexander James O'Connor became Forest Officer at the Woodbush Forest Station. Soon the farmers saw that money could be made from timber and planting started in earnest. Mr D.E. Hutchins in his *Transvaal Forest Report* of 1903 had suggested the importation of these exotics, but he could not have visualised the extent to which they took over the open grasslands. Charles Lane-Poole had more foresight of what might happen to our water catchment area during a drought, and twice he gave up a promising career when he had orders to eradicate the giants of indigenous forests. In his obituary which appeared in the *Commonwealth Forestry Review*, after his death in Sydney on 22 November 1970, it is stated that:

> In 1921 Lane-Poole found himself at odds with the Government of the day [in Australia] over its decision, taken against his advice, to extend concessions and a leasehold by large private timber concerns in the Karri Forests. He was not prepared to implement what he considered to be an incorrect policy and resigned. This action stands out as a highlight of the steadfastness and the courage that he displayed through a long and meritorious career. He was later re-employed and worked for many years with the New South Wales Forestry Department.

The subject of pine- and gum-growing is a very sore point with me because I loved the veldt with its multitude of diverse plant life. Nothing grows under pines and gums. The wattles are not so bad because they do not have tap roots and do not absorb so much water. Even where no replanting takes place, it is no good thinking that the indigenous forests will come back to the "purple veldt" on their own. Where you find St. John's wort (*hypericum*) you could plant some yellowwood, bitter almond, or vaalbos, and they have a fair chance of growing because these are found in the indigenous bush. Incidentally, Dr Hamish Boyd Gilliland[10] who was a lecturer in Botany at the University of the Witwatersrand, once asked me to give him a morgen of land on Wegraakbos because he wanted to fence it in and see how long it would take for the indigenous forests to return. The war intervened and Gilliland later left South Africa for a job in Singapore.

On the other hand I pride myself on the fact that I was instrumental in preserving a portion of bush which was not even situated on our own farm. Old Mr Charles Kingsley Latham, who owned Glenshiel, was a very concerned conservationist who went as far as to fence off his piece of indigenous forest to keep his cattle out. In 1953 he sold out to Mr Pierre Carst on whose initiative the Bruply Sawmills were established. He wanted to make the farm pay by growing pines like everybody else. One day his neighbour, Stewart Gilkison, approached Box and me with the rather unusual request that we should do something about Mr Carst destroying the bush and that

---

9   3.12.1908 – 20.8.1986

he was relying on our help. Box and I got into our little jeep, and Stewart showed us where the workers were busy chopping down an enormous cabbage tree, a cussonia, and yellowwoods that were about 7 to 10 feet in diameter. We walked up to Mr Carst's house, and were welcomed with the words, "This is a pleasant surprise – you are just in time for drinks!" I said, "Mr Carst, I wouldn't set foot in your house! You are cutting down indigenous forest to plant pines and I think you are a wicked old man!" His argument was that the land had to pay dividends and that he was acting on advice from the Forestry Department. I continued giving him a piece of my mind saying, "You are an old devil. You just think of nothing but money and you will suffer! These forests are full of spirits and if you go on felling you will have bad luck. Just look how Harry Klein, the author of *Land of the Silver Mist*, has gone bankrupt on The Downs because he felled the bush."

The next morning Box and I set out in the pouring rain visiting every house in the district and asking every farmer to sign a petition addressed to the Extension Officer in Pietersburg, demanding that nobody should do away with the few remaining small areas of indigenous forest in the Haenertsburg region. Everybody signed it. We also went to see Mr O'Connor, the Woodbush forester, who was very glad that somebody was taking a stand. He told us that General Smuts and he himself had managed to have patches of indigenous forests protected for the period of the war, but after that, unfortunately, the restriction had been lifted. "Felling really shouldn't be allowed and I will willingly sign your petition," he said.

The outcome was a meeting of the farmers in the area. Mr O'Colmor and Stewart Gilkison addressed the gathering and appealed to all of them to preserve the indigenous bush on their land. Our fight did some good because Mr Carst fell in with the generally strong sentiment expressed, and I know that his daughter, Karen Iuel, the present owner of Glenshiel, is very pleased about it. (It is also gratifying to note that the bush on Good Hope, portion Woodmore, is being proudly preserved by Steve Schoeman, a local sawmill owner.) [Steve died when his helicopter crashed on 6 July 1992.] Because of the incident concerning the petition, Box and I earned the onerous appellation of "The Two Witches".

Towards the end of the 1950's we had some trouble concerning our access road through that part of Goedvertrouwen which we had sold to Mr and Mrs Wolff. After their death the 25 morgen portion was auctioned on behalf of Mrs Wolff's brother, Mr Witton from England, and it fetched 8000

---

10 1911–1965.

pounds (1947). For a few years it belonged to Mr Crighton-Slight, and then Cheerio Halt [the new name for that portion of Goedvertrouwen] had come into the hands of an elderly man, Mr Douglas Harold Green who did not want us to use "his" road. He asked Piet van der Merwe to fell some gum trees across it but Piet refused, so he did it himself. In fact this road is an old public road which was already being used in Kruger's time, by wood-cutters traversing Goedvertrouwen (now Cheerio Halt, Ongeluk and Peasant's Perch) on their way to the Outspan on Kopje Alleen, and so on to Pietersburg.

The Magistrate advised us to remove the gums, but the quarrel led to a court case, "Green versus Turner and Thompson". Douglas Davidson, later the owner of Peasant's Perch, was an advocate and offered to take on the case without remuneration. All that Box had to do was to get an attorney, Julian Meyer, to brief him.

The case dragged on for over three years from 1959 to 1961. It took place originally in Pietersburg and the magistrate, Mr Viljoen, from Potgietersrus presided because he was very *au fait* with the law concerning public roads and water rights. Later, the court was moved to Haenertsburg, to the Agricultural Hall, as it would have been too expensive to pay for the many witnesses to go to Pietersburg. There were Messrs Collins, Symonds, Betton and Brummer and Mrs O'Connor supporting our claim and Mr Badenhorst and Mr Oosthuizen trying to help Douglas Green's case. Part of Mr Davidson's write-up of the case reads:

"George Badenhorst (1861–1935) was described as a virtuous old man who would always respect people's rights to an outspan and the two witnesses, son and son-in-law, should have had a better knowledge of the locality than the one they pretended to have. The defendants' witnesses all describe how the Feeskop Road was so steep and rocky that for choice people took the Goedvertrouwen Road which was grassy, although also moderately steep. The Feeskop Road only came into some sort of general use as preferable to the other road at the time that Cunliff and later Betton made the new road with a bulldozer."

Our best witness was an old servant, Alphius, living on Good Hope, who had been the *touleier* of the oxen that had brought the Long Tom cannon through the mountains at Boyne during the Boer War and deposited it at Feeskop on the farm Rondebult. He testified as to the route that the old road had taken, and when the Magistrate asked him, "Who told you all this?" Alphius replied, "Told me? Nobody told me; I'm telling you!"

I mentioned this cannon earlier, when describing my childhood, and it is interesting to record a little piece of local history, namely that the Boers, when celebrating Dingaan's Day, did so on Feeskop – *Fees* meaning feast. The English however called it "Cannon Hill".

Mr Douglas Green's advocate was a Mr William Schreiner, who incidentally visited me very recently in September 1985. He tried to trip me up with silly questions when I told the Court that when I went with my father to collect sheep at Louis Fouché's farm, Bergplaats, we had to use this road to get to Clear Waters [Googoo meant Jan Fouché, Louis' father]. He interrogated me as to how we crossed the Ebenezer Dam but this was obviously irrelevant, because there was no dam at this time [the dam was only built in the 1950's]. Eventually we won the case.

Awdry (Googoo) Thompson in 1987 at the age of 92.
(Photo: Struan Robertson.)

XV A Journey to Persia

Despite working very hard in the nursery, I kept on going on extensive camping trips. There was, for instance, the trip to Angola together with Potty's family. Our neighbour, Lyn Davidson, who was in charge of the Moss Herbarium, lent me a press for the collection of botanical specimens. I kept these plants in an apple box, together with a pile of *Farmer's Weekly* for blotting paper and I sat on it throughout the journey.

On another occasion we teamed up with Michael Brawn, my cousin Grace's son, who since 1962 has lived on his farm Boscobel on the Houtbosdorp road. His friend Dr Richard Liversidge, curator of the McGregor Museum Kimberley, joined us on this trip to the Okavango swamps and further north into Rhodesia.

Mike was also with us in 1961 when Box and I set out to re-visit Sofala. We did not find our old midden again, but enjoyed the countryside, eventually returning home via Pafuri. For part of the way Paul Methuen, now Lord Methuen, was with us. I had originally offered to take him to the Makgadikgadi Pan in Botswana, to give him a chance to paint the famous group of baobab trees, first drawn by John Thomas Baines. However, I think he found our way of travelling a bit too rough. He preferred to spend some time with the eminent botanist, Illtyd Buller Pole Evans,[1] who had retired in Umtali (now Mutare). There Paul found ample time to discuss his main topic of interest – crinums. He joined up with us at Umtali and came along to the Province of Gorongoza, all the time talking mainly of crinums, with the result that Mike called him Lord crinum! According to a newspaper cutting from the *Chronicle and Herald* for the year [1961], he also exhibited a painting of a Transvaal crinum at the Royal Academy of which he was a member.

Dr Pole Evans, the meeting with whom I have described above, was very impressed with a letter that Box had written to him,[2] after our Kalahari trip – mainly about botanical matters. He submitted her name to the Royal Horticultural Society and offered to institute everything necessary to have her accepted as a member.[3] It was typical of her not to take up this offer, or

---

1   1879–1968.
2   Letter Box to Pole Evans 26.5.1963.
3   Letter Pole Evans to Box 12.7.1963.

perhaps she was just too busy that particular year. The Haenertsburg Horticultural Society was organising a flower show down on Limberlost, the outspan area near the Helpmekaar Drift on the farm Grobblersrust, which was then still owned by Mrs A.D. Cunliff.[4] It was in springtime when the lilies and azaleas were all in bloom, and Gordon McNeil brought up a large number of clivias from the Lowveld. Box put cut irises all over the grass, and Potty's son, called "The Nipper", and his friend, Norman Jeffes, built little bridges over the river [Nipper/Louis with his wife Sylvia and their children today owns part of Wegraakbos]. It was the most beautiful show we ever had. Mr Bruins-Leich, Head of the Parks Department, came to judge it and was most impressed.

Alec Benjamin, who owns Boscobel Nurseries, was the chairman of the Haenertsburg Horticultural Society at the time. This was the first occasion that the annual flower show was held in the open, and he recalls that doubt was expressed by some members as to whether or not "wild animals would eat the exhibits". This proved to be unfounded. People were enchanted. Alec overheard only one dissident voice, that of a gentleman who had obviously been dragged along by his good wife. When he saw the stark splash of colour created by the azaleas he exclaimed, "My God, this looks like a Chicago gangster's funeral!" The Limberlost used to be a beautiful forest and proof of this exists in the black and white postcard in Mrs Fridjhon's old photo album, in the possession of Mrs Iris Lee which shows the giants of "The Bridal Path – Limberlost".

My longest and most exciting journey, the fulfilment of a long dream, "happened" to me when I was 71 years old, in 1966. Box and I had gone to Pietersburg and were having lunch at a steakhouse, when we met Mike Brawn who mentioned that he was planning a trip to Persia. I told him there and then that I was going with him and I can never be grateful enough that he accepted me as a travelling companion. As a young girl I had read Gertrude Bell's book *The Desert and the Sown* (1907) and Freya Stark's *Riding to the Tigris* and ever since I had wanted to see the Near East and Persia before I die. I had to borrow 500 pounds from Box, and Alec Benjamin took us down to Durban by car. Because of a delay of a couple of days, I stayed with the family of my cousin, Wilmot Rose. Eventually we sailed on the Dutch ship *Van Riebeeck* on 16 February. We were supposed to get to Dar es Salaam on the 23rd, but the vessel sprang a leak and we were sent to the dry dock at Diégo Suarez on the northern tip of Madagascar. I did not mind the delay in the least. Even the cockroaches could not dampen my

4   1891–1972.

enthusiasm. The voyage is well documented in my letters to the family, and I would like to quote just a few passages:

> On Friday the 25th we reached Diégo Suarez at dawn. What a lovely place it is. The bay looks as if it has been an old crater. There are miles and miles of smooth water, huge cliffs, lush mountain tops and the ruins of a very old fort. I am dying to go ashore and see what grows in the bush, but it's mighty hot. How very lucky we are for this leak to have developed, it's marvellous. Mike says Hitler wanted to put the Jews here. What a pity they didn't come here instead of where they are. It would have been so much nicer for them and they would have made it so beautiful. What a beautiful end to my life and old Mike is a wonderful companion to me! You see, if one has an aim in view and it does not hurt anyone, it does come by in time. Your dream, Box, of a beautiful valley will come to you soon because it is such a selfless, philanthropic dream. Mine was very selfish. Still, I did not hurt anyone by it, I hope.

For the next week we travelled around Madagascar by car. The country-side and the faluccas were very pretty to see, however the filth in the villages was terrible and the soil erosion ghastly.

Exactly a month after we embarked at Durban we finally reached Mombasa. Here a herd of dairy cows was loaded and housed in beautiful air-conditioned stables. "I believe that two old hags had raised hell in Kenya through the S.P.C.A. and since then the animals have had first-class accommodation. Some people are really wonderful and so civilized." I used to go down and see the cattle every day until they were offloaded in Kuwait – doesn't this show what a farmer I am at heart?

Here is a further entry from one of my letters:

> *21st March:* I was up at 4.30 a.m., had my bath and rushed up to the deck to see if I could see Cape Guardafui [also known as the horn of Africa]. I could hardly believe my eyes because what I had been imagining was a bank of clouds suddenly became, with the dawn, a huge mountain. This was stark-naked, rising sheer out of the ocean with not a blade of herbage on it and so unlike anything I had ever seen before. I gazed and gazed and, with each second, as the light came, the colours changed. To make the scene more beautiful there were all the Arabs on the deck below on their prayer mats. It was so impressive that I could have cried and I thought how much better off

we would all be if we took time off three times a day just to give ourselves up to meditation. There are some perfectly beautiful old men and one can pick out the sincere ones. One particularly lovely old man was being watched by a little boy and when the old thing had finished he took the little boy's face in his hands, pointed to the huge mountain and kissed him – and it was a moving scene. These Arabs are so completely unconscious of themselves when they pray and I can't believe that they are such crooks.

When the Chief Officer saw me alone on the deck, he invited me to the bridge and showed me, through the Captain's binoculars, tiny villages on this stark coast. He also pointed out to me a ship on the radar screen which, believe it or not, was a sailing ship with full sails – presumably an English or German training ship. What a sight, but so beautiful, you have no idea. I thought, gosh, what a lucky old woman I am. I am sure that if this dream of my whole life could have been fulfilled when I was younger, I would never have gone back so perhaps that is why God kept me waiting for so long. I am loving every moment, but the other passengers are fed up because of the food, which is awful, even by my standards. I told them that I did not come to eat, saying that I was putting on weight like a slug. Mike says that it is because I am having food that I am used to – dried bread and black tea – but I am glad that my skirts are so wide as I have only one safety-pin! Oh, we have great fun and the crew is so nice to us. The Chief Engineer hinted to me that he himself does not eat the cooked food – but gets curry and rice from the Arabs. I am doing the same now.

At the port of Mukalla we went on land and walked through a street with shops that were really just holes in a wall. I don't remember any specific incident there but Mike says he watched me looking at a big open basket with dried arabic gum, a grey and gold substance. I felt it, I sniffed if and then started to chew a little bit, while the shopkeeper was slowly getting cross with me. It didn't take much chewing and the viscous stuff got stuck in both my dentures and the men looked on with glee when I had to take them out and pop them into my purse. Further down the street were some camels and when I stroked a baby camel the mother pursed her lips and spit a load of green stinking sputum at me. The last straw was when some schoolboys started hurling stones at us foreigners.

The high-light of our time on the *Van Riebeeck* came with the arrival of two very special passengers. At first two bearded Arabs, retainers of the Sultan of Muscat, boarded the ship. They wore their long white jellabia girded with a wide red sash and sabres whose handles were covered with jewels. They checked on the accommodation in the hold below the waterline where the cattle were kept. When they decided this would not be good enough for two Arab horses which were being sent as presents to the Sheik of Bahrain, two separate boxes made from planks, with a manger and trough for water, were erected on the deck. As there was no roadstead at Muscat harbour the animals arrived in a lighter, were put into a sling and then hoisted on board. They were two outstandingly beautiful stallions, one white and one dark bay – the most splendid horses I had ever seen. They were fed on dates and green lucerne and not once during their journey were they left alone. There was always one of the attendants with them.

In addition there was a servant whose whole duty was to look after the two hunting falcons of the Sultan's emissary. These passengers, being strict Muslims, were allocated a roped-off section of the boat – deck covered by a canvas awning for the entire trip to Bahrain.

Letter 21 March continued:
At the bazaar at Bahrain I saw a basket full of rosebuds with just the pink showing. The Arab merchant told me that they came from Persia and grow on the mountains. They are expensive and they use them for cakes, chopped up, and for salads. I imagine it's the same rose that grows at the bridge at Stanford Lake. We must try them one day. The officers on the ship shrieked with laughter when I told them how much I had paid for a Chinese lock. One of my little grandsons will adore it though. I must get a couple of their beautifully embroidered caps. How lovely my granddaughters will look in them. The mosques and minarets in Bahrain are very beautiful. The harbour is bristling with warships. An American destroyer came in on Saturday. They all patrol the coast to prevent the carrying of arms and oil to poor Rhodesia. However, the dhows that transport gold and slaves across the Gulf they let go, I have been told!

5 April: We arrived here in Kuwait last night. All our deck passengers are waiting to be offloaded, poor things, they are short of food but so patient. All their clothes are washed and clean and looking so colourful. Mike really got the hell in today and is furious with me because we came by this boat and did not fly. Anyway, I don't care. We have decided to fly back because we lost so much time. It will cost an additional 180 pounds – I hope you do not mind, my poor Box, with an old mother stiffing it on you.

After the ship had first gone up to Basrah to load dates, we eventually got to Khorramshahr on 13 April. We left here in a crowded bus at 2 p.m., driving non-stop for the 450 miles through the desert, packed like flies, and arriving at Shiraz at 9 a.m. the following morning. I looked with wonder and amazement at everything around me, including the Firdusi Shrine. On the way to Persepolis about 30 miles from Shiraz, I observed the unfamiliar vegetation and bird life.

14 April: Persepolis is at first indescribable, with all the carving on the stairs. I simply can't write about it. Mike is very cross with me because I started picking the seeds off the loveliest little mauve salvia. He said, "Do you realise that you have travelled 6000 miles to see this ruin?" "Well, I can't carry the ruins away in my bewitched little bag," says I, "but if I can grow these lovely flowers how much more can I remember of Persepolis." Tops of high mountains enclosed this seemingly lifeless place. Their world-famous gardens round the tombs are all in earthenware pots – millions of them – all up the steps to the tombs, long pools in the lawns, all round, and they, in turn, surrounded by pots of plants. Petunias, stocks, pansies, larkspurs, all tightly wedged into pots. Residences and hotels enclose a courtyard and we have our breakfast under a gigantic apple-tree and little whispy, cherry trees simply packed with blossom – a botanist's dream!

After we crossed the Zagros Mountains to Isfahan, we travelled by bus to Tabriz and along the Caspian Sea to Mashhad near the Persian border with the USSR. From Teheran we took a taxi to the foot of the Elburz Mountains, still snow-clad, and I remember how we climbed up, meeting small children coming down with their hands full of small yellow tulips. There is just too much to tell, and I must restrict myself to mentioning only one more rather bad experience that we had when we got into a sand-storm in the desert near Tabas, and the bus was buried up to its runningboard. At Yazd a Zoroastrian taxi-driver took us to the Tower of Silence, where this particular sect takes its dead to be devoured by vultures.

Altogether, we travelled 14 000 miles over the length and breadth of Persia, all by local transport. The local inhabitants must have been just as amazed at us as we were at them. People used to pluck my hat off my head, which made me rather angry, but we did not experience any dishonesty or theft. Even my handbag, which I left somewhere in a toilet, was returned to me intact with both money and passport. Although my letter writing became rather sporadic, all along the route we were able to keep in contact with the family. I learned that Robbie did not get the principalship at Haenertsburg School – a great loss to the district, I thought, and that Eva had broken her leg. I think she works too hard and one gets no joy out of life if it is a grind. Work should be a joy and not a grind if it is to be a success.

Haenertsburg in about 1930.
(Louis Changuion collection.)

XVI The Past Twenty Years (1967–1987)

My own and Box's way of life changed completely when I could not drive any more, as this was the end of our camping trips. Already in the 1950's my eyes had given trouble and I used to get dreadful headaches. My husband sent me to Dr Meyer, the eye specialist in Johannesburg, who first gave me bi-focal lenses, but later diagnosed that I had a detached retina, that it would get worse, and nothing could be done about it. By 1970, I felt when driving that I was leaving the road. One day a policeman came to the house and told me that there had been complaints about my driving and that my licence was being withdrawn. He said I could have a new driving test in Tzaneen, but I declined, because I knew I was becoming a danger on the road – this happened about 1975 [Googoo was now 80 years old]. I also slowly gave up reading, and neither was weeding in the garden any good. I got lonely with nothing for me to do in the nursery.

Life improved when I got to hear about the Grahamstown Library for the Blind and the services of Tape Aids for the Blind[1] in Greyville, Durban. Tiny and Gub had gone to a specialist in Pietersburg to get more information about my condition, and apparently a woman overheard them questioning the doctor. She suggested that they should go to the librarian of the Pietersburg Library, who would know all about the services for the blind. They were lent a tape-recording machine which happened to be available, and from then on I have never looked back. I get such worthwhile books to read, and I find that I still learn so much. I also told my cousin, Bill Eastwood, who lived on his farm north of Louis Trichardt about these tapes and they have been a godsend to both of us, particularly now that my hearing has also deteriorated. I tried hearing aids, but they go wobbly in my head till I could scream. Being blind is not as bad as not being able to hear. When you are deaf you are thoroughly left out. Some people I can understand better than others. Box is difficult, and Tiny in her lifetime was almost impossible because of her high-pitched voice. However, you have to get philosophical about all your ailments otherwise you would go crazy. On the other hand we have such wonderful and helpful friends.

---

1   They have put this book on tape now.

I am a very happy old woman. I had an extremely happy childhood and my husband and I were very congenial company for each other. I also have the incredibly good fortune to live with a devoted daughter. I have been living with Box now for thirty years – she never felt like having a family, but just wanted her own home, garden and plenty of friends. She says there is nothing in life like being an old maid – you do just as you like!

Obviously, if you live with somebody you have to be considerate in order to get on. I think that if you have a grudge you should have it out, and that is how Box and I get on so well together. You must be able to convey your feelings. If you keep them to yourself you also keep in all the good that you might have given out. I must be open and if people do not like an open discussion it is just too bad. Sometimes Box and I shout at each other, but you can only do that if you basically understand each other. Box was always a happy child and she is a bit soft and perhaps not firm enough with her labour force, but her philosophy is wonderful. When she was at school she never once asked for a sixpence, she made her pocket money do and never asked for extras because she knew that we were hard up and could not afford very much. Jackie Jackson, who keeps her books, complains that she has no business sense. If Box has a little money in the bank, she spends it. I cannot bear people who hoard it and sit on it – I like generosity.

Politics do not interest me at all. I have never been able to understand them, so I do not worry about them, and I do not think I have lost anything. I realise, however, that South Africa's future depends mainly on our attitudes towards the blacks, and there I have definite opinions, as I have a life-long experience of close contact with them. I was brought up with them and I have real friends amongst them. The older blacks have perfect manners. They are like my own relatives; colour does not mean a thing to me. Look at Moses Kgatle, Box's driver – he is a thoroughly well-bred charming, Christian man, and as much of a gentleman, or more, than most of the white people that I have known – loyal, honest, gentle and compassionate. I know they have their own shortcomings. For instance, if you ask them a question they have a very cute idea of what you would like to hear, and so they tell you that.

Take our old servants, like Aarone, Sam and Kleinbooi; they took care of the farm when we lived in Messina and were absolutely reliable and trustworthy. All they ask for is justice. When we reaped the apple crop we gave them a good bonus and made it worth their while. Isn't that only fair? When we first took over Wegraakbos, blacks squatting on farms still had to work for 90 days without remuneration and their women for two days a week. A paper with squares was used to tick off the number of days they had worked. If it rained they were sent home. It's a wicked system because they could not accept work elsewhere. In a way they worked for their tenancy and some land for their private use. Louis and I always paid our blacks for their labour. These people are worth everything to me and I cannot hate them. I can quite understand that educated youngsters desire more than being good servants, and it grieves me that they seem to have absorbed many of our vices, like the greed for money and possessions, but I could never hate any of them, not even the ugly ones.

I used to be very good at hating. I hope that I have overcome this to a great degree and that Norah Devenish would no longer have to call me "Mrs Flint!"

Hatred between the Rooineks and the Boers was mutual. The Boers never did forgive the English for confiscating their country and the English were very sore that after the establishment of the Union many of them were pushed out of their government jobs. Both were hurt and the feeling was passed on to the next generation. I too had that feeling, but, as I said to my husband years ago, every time I have been in trouble on the old road from Messina to Haenertsburg, which used to wind in and out through the bushes, it has always been an Afrikaner who has helped me. I am very fond of the Afrikaners and I think their own life was very picturesque. They should have stuck to their old values instead of chasing after money and possessions. You cannot put your faith in money. I am a firm believer in God. You do not even have to call it "God", but there must be some power that runs this wonderful organisation of our world, with summer and winter, with its infinite variety of plants and animals. I believe that everyone is responsible for his own life and if anything goes wrong it is his own fault, whether his life be happy or unhappy.

Look at the Jews. They have been persecuted throughout the centuries and yet they have survived by faith and by love and by helping one another. I am very sorry that I never went to the Holy Land. I would have loved to have gone to see what they have made of it.

Some people say there is no God, but I think God is very angry with us. Who would not be? Supposing you had a farm, a big farm, and your manager did to it all that we do to God's World, his beautiful world. We are going to wipe ourselves out with all these bombs, but I do not think God intends us to do all these horrible things.

God is my best friend and I think of him every day, all day and every time that I have a minute to spare. He is permanently in my life and as near to me as Box, and I could not do without Him. We have had many problems in our family. You keep on caring and looking after your children but when you do not see any way out, you can only say, "God, they are Your children, now You must take over and look after them."

It does not enter my mind to think about an after-life. I do not know what is going to happen and I do not believe that I shall go and sit on the clouds! Now is the only time and God tells us through our conscience what is right and what is wrong. We must listen to it.

Now, in my 93rd year, I feel at times that I am only using up air, particularly after Tiny's death last April. Perhaps I still have not learned enough and will never become wise? I am not afraid of death. How can people be afraid of death? If you are afraid of death you might as well be afraid of going to bed at night.

I love life and I am sorry mine is coming to an end. [This book was first published in 1987. In 1990 Brigitte Wongtschowski decided to republish Googoo's story. She then spoke to her for the last time and, apart from a few alterations here and there, she also added one more paragraph]:

When I die I don't want a funeral. I want to be wrapped into a blanket and put into a hole – that's how I buried all my dogs. Otherwise my family should bury me next to Mother and Louis in a simple coffin. The bearers could be Mapolowa, a heathen, Moses, who belongs to the Zion City Morija sect, Hans, a Jew and my son Clifford, a catholic. I would like him to say, "Dear God, I now give into your hands the spirit of your faithful servant, my mother. Thank you, God." [Googoo died a year later – age 96.]

NOTES

1. The school was founded under Charter of Edward VI as a charity school, mainly for the sons of the clergy. The boys wear long dark-blue belted gowns or cassocks and yellow stockings. There was a sequel to this story. During the Boer War when I was six years old, Mother and I were staying with Grandmother in her modest house in Uitenhage. Grandfather had died in 1899 and Granny had to be careful with money. To my amazement she suddenly seemed to indulge in a spending spree and inexplicably, household linen, crockery and even dress materials were purchased. It was only in later years that Mother explained this turn of events to me. Grandfather's benefactor, Professor Frison, from the London days had left him a small legacy, the value of which roughly equalled the amount that the young Henry had refunded in payment for his boarding school fees. It seemed that only from the grave was his old friend able to derive the satisfaction of giving Grandfather "something for nothing". It is often said in the family that, while working for *The Times*, Henry Bidwell first met the great novelist, Charles Dickens, who listened to his boyhood experiences and then used them in *David Copperfield*.

2. Extracts from *The Uitenhage Times*, edited, printed and published by Henry William Bidwell, Caledon Street, Uitenhage. **18.8.1865** New Books, &c. The undersigned has received ex *Hero of the Nile*, 500 of the latest and most popular Novels and other works, H.W. Bidwell, Uitenhage *Times* Office, 11 August 1865.
3.8.1865 *The road to Health and Long Life* assured by Holloway's Pills. Weakness and Debility. Despondency, Low Spirits. All Disorders affecting the Liver, Stomach and Bowels. Impurities of the Blood. Influenza, Diphtheria, Bronchitis, Coughs and Colds, Diseases of the Blood and Heart.
The Great Remedy of the Age. Holloway's Ointment. The effect of the Ointment on the System. Bad Legs, Bad Breasts, Sores and Ulcers. Piles, Fistulas, Strictures. Imprudences of Youth, Sores and Ulcers. Agent for Uitenhage H.W. Bidwell.
11.8.1865 Birth – At Uitenhage, on Friday, 28 July, Mrs H.W. Bidwell of a Daughter.
It cannot have been easy to provide for a big family!

3. William Heugh, "Big Uncle Bill", was a railway engineer at Zwartkops near Port Elizabeth. He and Aunt Flora had five daughters: Mary, Rosie, Edith, Doris and Lucy. Rosie later married Harry Sellick, the son of grandfather's successor on the *Uitenhage Times*. I well remember playing with all these girls at their home adjacent to the Smith Brothers' Flower Nursery. Big Uncle Bill's house was built on a fairly large plot of land, which enabled him to produce oats, vegetables and grow fruit trees and to rear pigs. His brother, Peter, after he became Secretary of the Provincial Council, lived on a farm near Uitenhage called Kamaëhs. Uncle Peter bought this property from his brother-in-law, Mannie Solomon, whose wife, Emily Bidwell, did not like living in the country. He kept cattle on the farm, grew lucerne and also had an orchard. He and his wife, Cecilia, had three children, Robert, Hugh and Grace. Later Robert built a dam on the farm before he in turn sold it to his brother-in-law, Dr Harry Brawn, who had married his sister, Grace. Their son, Michael, subsequently sold Kamaëhs to the town which was in need of water.

4. A similar adventure, rather amusing in retrospect, occurred to my mother's brother, Gordon Bidwell. He was neither by nature nor in appearance a soldier, but had felt in duty bound to join the British Forces. He soon fell into enemy hands and his captors were not particularly impressed by this *Rooinek*. They stripped him stark naked and, frightened out of his wits, he made an ignominious retreat with the Boers shouting after him, "We'll give you five minutes to get over that rise and then we'll shoot." At that time Uncle Gordon must have been about 24 years of age. According to the 1936 *South African Who's Who* he was born in 1876 and became Municipal Market Master in Newlands, Johannesburg. He held this post for many years.

5. The Morant incident has many contradictory variations. Compare books by Witton, Denton, Zöllner/Heese and Changuion as listed in bibliography. I believe new sources have come to light and the 1988 volume of the Van Riebeeck Society is summing up the subject. See bibliography under Davey.

6. As a matter of interest there are other Eastwood Roads named after members of the family. Eastwood Road in Dunkeld, Johannesburg, is named after my uncle William Edward, quote from Anna H. Smith, *Johannesburg Street Names*:

"... who was on the staff of the Consolidated Goldfields of South Africa, the company which laid out the township. Another Eastwood Street in Turffontein may also be called after Philip Bailey Eastwood, who, according to the Transvaal Civil Service List 1904, page 155, was the Organising Secretary to the

Transvaal Land Board from 14 June 1902 and the Chief Inspector to the Land Board from 1 July 1903. It is possible, however, that this street was named after E.C. Eastwood, who was the Township Manager of Turffontein."
The latter was not a relation of ours.

7. It might be of interest to Lowvelders and Haenertsburgers to read Dora's abridged handwritten memo lent to me by Esmé Shackleton, née Zeederberg, which reads as follows:

"Frank Eland had come to settle in the Duiwelskloof District with his mother and cousin, Mrs Heckford, a well-known traveller and trader in the Transvaal, who rented part of the farm Platland on the Brandboontjies River. In November 1893 they bought Ravenshill, partly because it was free from malaria, but also because they thought it a good site for trade as it adjoined Modjadji's location. In 1894 the war with Magoeba broke out and all non-combatants were ordered into laager at Agatha or Houtbosdorp. However, my family were on very good terms with Magoeba and chose to remain at Ravenshill. Prior to the outbreak of the Boer War, my father left the Transvaal and joined the British forces in Natal. My mother, Dora Scrimgeour, returned to England, where I was born in 1900. My grandmother remained at the farm during the whole conflict and was joined after the war by my mother and myself. We had a happy life at Ravenshill and in 1938 I married Captain Hugh Merton Graham, who had come to the Transvaal under the 1820 Settlers Memorial Association Scheme. He was one of the pioneers of carnation growing in this district, together with C.T. Astley Maberly, the animal painter. In 1948, owing to failing health he had to give up active farming and began to devote his days to landscape painting and the collection of indigenous aloes and succulents. He died in 1961."

8. The hotel was bought from Heinrich Schulte-Altenroxel who had emigrated in August 1889 to South Africa at the age of 22. He first joined the firm of Natorp and Tamsen in Tweefontein near Warmbaths as a shop assistant. In 1890 he made an exploratory trip to the Lowveld via Pietersburg and Houtboschdorp, a village with about ten homesteads. At the Thabena he met a German, Richard Kietz, a gold prospector whose quartz outcrop was not up to expectations. He joined Altenroxel in his venture to open a shop and hotel on New Agatha and supervised the actual building while Altenroxel carted provisions from Pretoria. The opening of the hotel took place in September 1891. It consisted of a main house which had a bedroom for Altenroxel and Kietz, the bar and a shop for whites. A rondavel served as dining-room, three more rondavels as guest rooms, each with two canvas stretchers plus two horse blankets and a pillow.

The open-air washing arrangement for the guests was a hollowed out tree trunk. All buildings were made of daub and wattle with thatch and the floor was stamped clay smeared regularly with a cow dung mixture. There was a further rondavel serving as a shop for Blacks and another one was a storeroom.

Kietz died in 1893 of malaria. Altenroxel asked Konrad Plange, another employee of Natorp and Tamsen, to throw his lot in with him. During a visit to his home-town, Münster in Westfalia, Germany, he raised enough money to found the Thabena Farming Association on 15.12.1893. The two partners then slowly divested themselves of their hotels and the old shops, both at New Agatha and the Thabena Drift, and started farming on a big scale.

Mrs Margaret Douglas Strachan and her daughter Millicent are buried in the Haenertsburg cemetery. Millicent first married Percy Dickenson, owner of a hotel at the Thabena, and after his death, Michael Doogan, who worked for the Pietersburg telegraph office. A daughter of this marriage, Margaret Douglas Doogan, (b. 25.12.1906 – d. 1984) married Col. Richard (Dickie) Dagge (b. 1898 – d. 9.10.1987) later owner of the Magoebaskloof Hotel. Mrs Dagge's ashes were also put to rest in Mrs Strachan's grave. The faded inscription on the tombstone reads: "Sacred to the Memory of Margaret Douglas Strachan who died 6 October 1914 aged 75 years. Erected by her loving children and grandchildren. Her duty done. R.I.P."

9. According to Louis Changuion, *Pietersburg 1886–1986*, the last Long Tom cannon used during the Boer War was stationed near the present day beacon on the farm Rondebult, at one time owned by the late Mrs J. Ellis, with a good view onto the road from Houtbosdorp. The cannon was blown up on 30 April 1901. Perhaps Mr Neethling salvaged part of it and disposed of it as described. Louis has, however, in the meantime established that what Neethling presumably threw into the river, today under the waters of the Ebenezer Dam, must have been the remains of the Long Tom destroyed at Letaba Drift and not of the last one.

10. Another school existed for a while at Houtboschdorp shortly after the Boer War. It was a government school consisting of big tents which all children had to attend whether English or Afrikaans-speaking. Mariechen Herbst (b. 12.6.1891), daughter of missionary A. Herbst at Mphome, recalled how she and her sister Frieda (19.7.1894 – 1973) had to walk down the mountain every day; not easy for the younger girl. She also enthused about Tante Knothe's garden where the Herbst children admired the many kinds of lilies, hydrangeas, fuchsias, white and blue violets, as well as the orchard. This information was

recorded by Erdmuth Knothe-Kuckenburg, daughter of Gerhard Knothe, the youngest son of missionary Knothe, who interviewed M. Herbst in Berlin/Germany in 1978.

11. "My dear Mrs Eastwood, we have had bad news of Sir Lionel. Here is the actual wording of the telegram sent by Lady Phillips. 'Send messenger instantly and quickly as possible to H. Phillips to come immediately **stop** operation performed successfully – and bullet in lung very dangerous and severe'

"We think she wrote it in excitement as it sounds so contradictory saying 'operation successful' and yet very dangerous. The word 'stop' must be a telegraphic mistake [could also mean fullstop]. Harold intends to motor to Joh'burg tonight with Thrupp the motor mechanic from Pietersburg. Would it inconvenience you to let our arrangements for Christmas day stand as they are and if impossible for Harold to get back, I will let you know on Wednesday by a boy. With love Hilda."

The attacker was J.L. Misnum, a trader on the mines.

12. Sir Robert Coryndon, 2.4.1870 – 10.2.1925, Resident Commissioner in Swaziland from 1907–1916, later in Basutoland, and Governor of Kenya. see *SESA* 3, 446 b.

13. The Hawkers camped at the top of Bob Collins's farm. It will be appreciated that Mrs Eastwood, who did not drive a donkey cart herself, could not easily get there, particularly in bad weather. Mr Hawker's foreman was Jack Lawless who married Mabel, sister of Flo Greenwood. It was Jack Lawless who gave the post office of Boyne its name. He happened to visit the Allisons on Kleinfontein where Mrs Allison ran the post office. All her suggestions for a name had been turned down as too unoriginal. The Boyne River is in Ireland.

14. The botanical name of this deciduous tree is *Taxodium distichum*. It is indigenous in eastern North America and Mexico. The wood is weak and soft, but long-lasting and is used for vats and water pipes. It contains a fragrant oil which repels white ants and can therefore be used for house building (quoted from Patrick Synge, *Dictionary of Gardening*; 2nd ed. Oxford U.P., 1965).

15. Princess Alice, Countess of Athlone, wife of the Earl of Athlone who was High Commissioner and Governor-General from 1924–1930. The reception for the local farmers was held on the outspan of the Limberlost. Gen. Smuts invited the couple to re-visit S.A. in 1948. Princess Alice writes in her reminis-

cences: "Smuts then arranged for us to stay with Dr Merensky at Westfalia, Duiwelskloof. He was a charming personality and a scientist interested in soil preservation, water conservation and forestry. He took me to see the piece of land Sir Lionel Phillips had given me on a high and delightful spot where a little stream bordered with gladioli and agapanthus ran through the bush. I had promised never to cut the bush, so as to preserve the water from the hillside which fed the trout streams below. Now, alas, I have sold the land to a Mr Naudé, who is very attached to it and has preserved it so that it will ever remain, as was intended, a beautiful holiday camping site. He named it Princess Alice Camp." D.J. (Dap) Naudé was a member of the Pietersburg Town Council and seven times mayor [and a brother of parliamentarian Tom Naudé]. The Dap Naudé Dam in the Broederstroom, built in 1956–1958, is named after him. Princess Alice Camp has now been incorporated into the Woodbush Forest Reserve.

16. William Waldegrave Palmer, Lord Selborne, High Commissioner after Lord Milner from 1905–1910.

Family Trees

EASTWOOD, John William (1832– ±1891) Bank manager Bradford/
Yorkshire m. Emily Anne Bailey (d. 26.6.1923)

1. Emily, single, lived with mother, brought up Harold Eastwood, 3b.

2. Philip Bailey (1861 – Nov. 1917) Fought in Basutoland Rebellion of 1880–
    1881 before he drifted to the Transvaal goldfields. Acting Commis-
    sioner of Lands under Milner m. Blanche Eedes.
    (a) John Helperus Ritzema (b. 3.5.1907)
    (b) Joyce Wilhelmina (2.11.1910 – 20.6.1989) m. Jim E. Kelly: Tom.

3. William Edward (7.9.1862 – ±1944) Uncle Bill, Accountant and farmer m.
    Caroline Edith Bidwell (1870–1963)
    (a) Phyllis (1896 – 28.2.1923) died of malaria
    (b) Harold (1898–1917) died in East Africa campaign
    (c) Marjorie (b. 1899) m. Geoffrey Eastwood (1.1.1895 – 1982): Rosemary,
         David, farmer near Selukwe, Zimbabwe
    (d) Joan (b. 23.6.1902–?) m. 1928 George Murray (1884–1940): John
    (e) William Bailey (4.12.1903 – 12.5.1989) m. 1934 Doreen Language:
         William, Edward, Mary
    (f) Ruth (d. ±1965) m. Andrew Dredge: Andrew, Ann; Ruth divorced,
         m. Monty Green

4. Alfred (b. 1865) m. Mabel Carey, Australian girl
    (a) Geoffrey (1.1.1895 – 1982) m. Marjorie Eastwood (b.1899)

5. Ethel m. Dr William Morgan
    (a) Oswald Gayer (eye specialist, see cuttings from WWI)
    (b) Dermot, Col. and Brigadier in India, painter
    (c) Dorothy (single, musician)
    (d) Eileen

6. Arthur Keble (8.4.1867 – July 1932) m. 5.2.1894 Jane Mary
    Emma Bidwell (15.11.1863 – 11.11.1930)

(a) **Edith Awdry** (b. 2.1.1895) m. 25.1.1916 Dr Louis Clifford Thompson
(24.6.1877 – 2.3.1955)

7. Margaret (Daisy) m. Cecil Hand, teacher at Wakkerstroom &
Krugersdorp

BIDWELL, Henry William (27.12.1830 Norwich – Jan. 1899 Uitenhage)
Journalist and founder of *Uitenhage Times* in 1864 m. at St. John Church,
Hoxton, London in 1859 Mary Elizabeth White (4.5.1836 London – 1909
Uitenhage) They sailed to South Africa on 1.3.1862 and arrived 9.6.1862

1. Flora White (b. 29.1.1860) m. 17.2.1886 Frederick William Alexander
Heugh (Big Uncle Bill)
   (a) Mary (b. 3.12.1886) m. Charles Brereton-Stiles: 1 son
   (b) Rose (b. 14.12.1888) m. Harry Sellick, lawyer
   (c) Edith (b. 23.3.1892) m. Tom Hoek
   (d) Doris (Polly) (b. 18.2.1894) m. Clifford Cawood: Margaret m. John
Kettlewell
   (e) Lucy (b. 17.7.1900) m. Cecil Watts

2. Cecilia Maria (b. 6.1.1862) m. 20.4.1880 at St. Katherine's Church,
Uitenhage Peter Robert Heugh
   (a) Mary Rosa Granger (5.8.1881 – 10.4.1886, scarlet fever)
   (b) Robert Hamilton (b. 16.7.1883) m. Rhoda Hudson: Jack, Grace
   (c) Hugh William (9.1.1886 – 1932) m. Enid Hurndall (1888 –1963): Peter,
Joan, Granger, Anthony
   (d) Grace Cecilia (22.11.1887 – 1957) m. Dr Harry Brawn (d. 1954): Molly,
James, Helen, Elizabeth, Michael

3. Jane Mary Emma (b. 15.11.1863 Grahamstown – 11.11.1930 Haenertsburg)
m. 5.2.1894 Arthur Keble Eastwood (b. 8.4.1867 Bradford/England –
July 1932 Messina)
   (a) Edith Awdry (b. 2.1.1895 Johannesburg) see Thompson 3

4. Emily Mary (Tootsie) (b. 28.7.1865) m. 23.4.1889 Mannie Solomon, lawyer
   (a) Maude (20.5.1890 – 3.6.1904)
   (b) Bertha (b. 11.12.1893) m. Eric Bell
   (c) Ethel Phyllis (b. 17.2.1895) m. 1921 Glenham Davis: (Suzanne,
Denise)

5. Minnie Grace (b. 13.4.1867) m. Carl Rose
   (a) Wilmot James (b. 20.8.1909) m. Joyce Geffin

6. Henry William (4.7.1868 – 8.5.1869)

7. Edith Caroline(Aunt Edie) (b.25.3.1870 – 1963) m.12.7.1895 William Edward Eastwood see Eastwood 3

8. Maude Alice (8.8.1871 – 14.8.1937) m. 29.8.1900 Dr George William Freer (d. 21.3.1935)
   (a) Gordon William (5.9.1901 – 1919)
   (b) Cecil Bertram (b. 16.4.1905)

9. William Porter (Little Uncle Bill) (1.7.1874 – 1960) m. 17.12.1910 Bessie Fraser Grant (1885–1950)
   (a) Henry William Grant (b. 29.9.1911) m. 1945 Catherine Edith Thomson (1915–1968)
   (b) John Gordon (8.5.1913 – 1978) m. Catherine Shorn: Elizabeth, Diana
   (c) Mary Elma (b. 7.11.1916) m. James Dyke Robertson: Andrew Grant, Joan Bidwell

10. Gordon Sprigg (b. 31.8.1876) m. Gladys Hirsch

THOMPSON, George Medical doctor at Bristol and superintendent of asylums m. Mary Anne Egan (15.7.1848 – ±1932) daughter of surgeon John and Phoebe Egan

1. Clifford Clifford (20.2.1876) m.

2. George Clifford (20.2.1876–1955) twin to above, mental after accident.

3. Louis Clifford (24.6.1877 – 2.3.1955) m. 25.1.1916 **Edith Awdry Eastwood** (2.1.1895 – 2.8.1991)
   (a) Sheila (Box) Clifford (23.4.1917 – 23.12.1998)
   (b) Diana (Tiny) Clifford (6.12.1918 – 25.4.1986) m. Harold Mockford (25.8.1917 – 10.7.1985): Donella b. 7.8.1943, Dorit b. 1946, Harold b. (1947 – 19.11.1997)
   (c) Louis (Potty) Clifford (29.2.1920 – 19.11.1997) m. 1.9.1953 Eva, Luise Horstmeier (26.1.1923 – 27.6.1998): Louis William, Julie

(d) Philippa Awdry Clifford (15.2.1922) m. Dr John Lawrence Butlin: Diana, Carol, Lawrence, Shelley

(e) Elizabeth (Gub) Jane Clifford (b. 3.3.1924) m. Robert Carver Turner (b. 30.10.1920 – 27.02.1992)): Erilyn b. 1948, Robert (Oki) Clifford b. 1950, Jane b. 1953

4. Winifred Clifford m. Dr Val Watts: 3 children.

5. Edward (Ted) Clifford m. Bessie Juhre

6. Dorothy Clifford m. Dr Philip Davy (Henrietta Egan, their great aunt, their grandfather Bishop Egan's sister, lived and died at their house)

7. May, became an Anglican nun.

8. James Clifford m. a Brazilian girl: Norah Ruth.

9. Kathleen Clifford m. Hubert Arnold, a brewer: 2 children.

10. Vera Clifford, not married, lived with mother.

BIBLIOGRAPHY

Alice, Princess
For my grandchildren: some reminiscences of Her Royal Highness Princess Alice, Countess of Athlone. 1966. London: Evans Brothers.

Allen, Vivien
Lady Trader: a biography of Mrs Sarah Heckford. 1979. London: Collins.

Buchan, John
The African Colony: Studies in the Reconstruction. 1903. Edinburgh & London: William Blackwood & Sons.

Cartwright, A.P.
By the Waters of the Letaba: a history of the Transvaal Lowveld – Land of Adventure. 1974. Cape Town: Purnell.

Cartwright, A.P.
Golden Age: … Corner House Group of Companies, 1910 – 1967. 1968. Cape Town: Purnell.

Changuion, Louis (comp.)
Haenertsburg 100. 1887–1987. 1987. Pietersburg: Review Pr.

Changuion, Louis
Pietersburg: die eerste eeu, 1886–1986. 1986. Pretoria: V&R Drukkery.

Clothier, Norman
Black valour: the South African Native Labour Contingent, 1916–1918, and the sinking of the Mendi. 1987. Pietermaritzburg: Natal University Press.

Davey, Arthur M. (ed.)
Breaker Morant and the Bushveldt Carbineers. 1987. Cape Town: Van Riebeeck Society (Second Series, no. 18).

Davies, Grace
An Account of Jane Furse Memorial Hospital, Sekhukhuniland. 1984. Pietermaritzburg: The Natal Witness.

Denton, Kit
Closed File: the true story behind the execution of Breaker Morant and Peter Handcock. 1983. Durban: Bok Books International.

Dicke, Bernhard Heinrich
The Bush speaks: border life in old Transvaal. 1936. Pietermaritzburg: Shuter & Shooter.

Du Toit, Jacob Daniël (Totius),
Trekkersweë; met tekeninge van J.H. Pierneef. 1972. Kaapstad: Tafelberg.

Eastwood, William Edward
Reminiscences. 1934. Written at Farm Buffelspoort, Mara. Unpublished.

Gunn, Mary and Leslie Edward Wostall Codd
Botanical Exploration of Southern Africa. 1981. Cape Town: Balkema.

Gutsche, Thelma
No ordinary woman: the life and times of Florence Phillips. 1966. Cape Town: Timmins.

Haggard, Henry Rider
The days of my Life. 1926. London: Longmans. 2 vols.

Heckford, Sarah
A Lady Trader in the Transvaal. 1882. London: Sampson, Low, Marston, Searle & Rivington.

Hutchins, Sir David Ernest
Transvaal Forest Report. 1903. Pretoria: Government Press.

Ingram, Collingwood
Ornamental Cherries. 1948. London: Country Life

Jones, Neville
The Prehistory of Southern Rhodesia: an account of the progress of research from 1900 to 1946. 1949. Cambridge: U.P. National Museum of Southern Rhodesia, Memoir No.2.

Klapwijk, Menno
The Story of Tzaneen's Origin. 1974. No publisher.

Klein, Harry
Land of the Silver Mist. 1952. Cape Town: Timmins.

Klein, Harry
Valley of the Mists. 1972. Cape Town: Timmins.

Leakey, Mary
Disclosing the past: an autobiography. 1984. London: Weidenfeld and Nicolson.

Lowveld 1820 Settlers Society
Some Lowveld pioneers. ±1965. Pretoria: Minerva Press.

McKechnie, Andrew Edward
A man to remember: the life of Andrew McKechnie. 1994. Balhambra Grove.

Munnik, George Glaeser
Memoirs: covering eighty years of thrilling South African History, Politics and War. 1934. Cape Town: Maskew Miller.

Palmer, Eve
"A Transvaal Garden." (*The Journal of the Royal Horticultural Society*, vol. 83, pt. 6. June 1958).

Pauling, George
The Chronicles of a contractor: being the autobiography of the late G.P. Bulawayo: 1969. Books of Rhodesia. (Rhodesia Reprint Society, vol. 4. Facs. reprod. of 1st ed.).

Phillips, Lionel
Some Reminiscences. 1924. London: Hutchinson.

Poultney, Dora Ortlepp
Dawn to Dusk. 1936. London: Cassell.

Pretorius, Philip Jacobus
Jungle man: the autobiography of Major Pretorius; with foreword by Field-Marshal J.C. Smuts. 1947. London: Harrap.

Rosenthal, Eric
Heinrich Egersdörfer: an Old-Time sketch book. 1960. Cape Town: Nasionale Boekhandel.

Rothschild, Miriam
Dear Lord Rothschild: birds, butterflies and history. 1983. London: Hutchinson.

Schulte-Altenroxel, Heinrich
Ich suchte Land in Afrika: Erinnerungen eines Kolonialpioniers im nördlichen Transvaal. 1942. Leipzig: Seeman.

Smith, Anna H.
Johannesburg street names: a dictionary of street, suburb and other place names compiled to the end of 1968. 1971. Johannesburg: Juta.

Smith, Janet Adam
John Buchan: a biography. 1965. London: Hart-Davis.

Standard Encyclopaedia of Southern Africa (SESA) Vol. 1–12. 1970. Cape Town: NASOU.

Thompson, Louis Clifford
"The Balemba of Southern Rhodesia." 1942. *NADA: the Southern Rhodesia Native Affairs Department Annual* no. 19.

Thompson, Louis Clifford
"The Mu-Tsuku." *South African Journal of Science,* vol. 35, December 1938.

Transvaal Department of Agriculture
Annual reports of the Division of Forestry, 1903/04–1908/09.

Von Reiche, Franz
Die plaas Zaagkuil op Houtbosdorp. Unpublished manuscript.

Witton, Lieut. George Ransdale
Scapegoats of the Empire: the true story of Breaker Morant's Bushveldt Carbineers. 1982. London: Angus & Robertson (first published 1907).

Zöllner, Linda & J.A. Heese
The Berlin Missionaries in South Africa and their descendants. 1984. Pretoria: Human Sciences Research Council. (Genealogy Publication, no. 19).

INDEX